A GENERAL OF THE REVOLUTION

JOHN SULLIVAN OF NEW HAMPSHIRE

MAJ. GEN. JOHN SULLIVAN
From a picture in possession of his family.

Jnᵒ. Sullivan

A GENERAL
OF THE REVOLUTION

John Sullivan
of New Hampshire

BY

CHARLES P. WHITTEMORE

COLUMBIA UNIVERSITY PRESS

NEW YORK AND LONDON 1961

For My Mother and Father

FOREWORD

Many were on hand to offer their services at the time of the American Revolution—to voice the grievances, to lead in battle, and to help mold the new government that replaced the colonial organization. We know much about the important figures of the revolutionary period—men like Washington, Greene, Knox, and Hamilton. But we do not know so much about some of the other active men of the times, although they too made their contribution. John Sullivan of New Hampshire was an early advocate of the patriot position, fought as a general officer in the war, served in the Continental Congress, took an active role in the politics of his state, and helped fight for the ratification of the United States Constitution. Sullivan led a full life and left his mark. I have chosen to tell his story, in this revision of my doctoral dissertation, so that more may be known of one man's contribution during those exciting and troublesome times. Since the appearance of Thomas C. Amory's biography of Sullivan, *The Military Services and Public Life of Major-General John Sullivan of the American Revolutionary Army* (Boston, 1868), there has been no other biography of the man.

I have met courtesy wherever I have gone in search of materials, but I owe special thanks to Miss Charlotte D. Conover, former librarian of the New Hampshire Historical Society. No bibliographical query dismayed her. Dartmouth College and Yale University kindly allowed me study space and the use of their libraries. Mr. Philip Guyol generously gave me access to notes he had taken on Sullivan's career. Dr. Richard B. Morris and Colonel John Bakeless had a number of valuable suggestions to make. Mrs. Kathryn W. Sewny has been most helpful in handling the editorial details for Columbia University Press. Above all, I owe thanks to Mr. Samuel S. Bartlett, headmaster emeritus, and the Board of Trustees of South Kent School, Connecticut, for a leave of absence during the academic year 1954–55, to Dr. Dumas Malone for so patiently and kindly guiding the work of the dissertation, and to my parents for financial assistance.

Any errors in fact or in interpretation are mine and mine alone.

CHARLES P. WHITTEMORE

South Kent School, Connecticut
January, 1961

CONTENTS

MAPS

I: EMERGENCE OF A PATRIOT

FEBRUARY, 1740–JUNE, 1775

Colonial New England, still a virgin land, offered vast oppor-
tunities to those who had ambition and talent. Although many
contented themselves with coaxing the forbidding soil into
yielding produce, others determined to advance both economi-
cally and socially. Among the latter was John Sullivan, a man of
humble origin, who rapidly improved his status and found himself on the eve of the War of Independence as the articulate
leader of revolutionary New Hampshire. Lawyer, soldier, statesman, politician, Sullivan was to have a colorful career, for the
man craved action. With every fiber of his being he strained for
success, sought the plaudits of the crowd, and strove to advance
his own welfare. He never lost the cocksureness of youth. With
confidence in himself, he entered the national scene as the revolt
against the empire began to unfold, and fought bravely but at
times foolishly. After he put aside the weapons of war, he ac-
tively participated in the politics of the young nation and the
state which he loved. But his story begins in a small New
Hampshire hamlet on the Salmon Falls, sixteen miles from the
mouth of the Piscataqua River where it flows into the Atlantic.
Then the hamlet was known as the Parish of Summersworth;
today it is called Rollinsford, part of the township of modern
Somersworth.[1]

On February 17, 1740, Margery Sullivan, wife of Master
John Sullivan, a schoolmaster, gave birth to a son and called him
John.[2] Both parents, people of simple tastes, had emigrated to
America from Ireland, probably as redemptioners in 1731.

Family tradition has handed down many stories about John's parents, and the truth is elusive. Master Sullivan's father was Major Philip O'Sullivan of Ardea, who, after the loss of Limerick in 1691 to William of Orange, became an exile in France under General Patrick Sarsfield, and there he died soon after from a wound inflicted by a French officer. Master Sullivan's mother was Joane McCarthy, who resided in Ireland after she had become a widow. Born in Limerick in 1690, Master Sullivan apparently was christened Owen, retaining that name until after he came to America. Evidently he benefitted from a good education, perhaps received on the continent, for he spoke French and reportedly was a linquist of some talent. Why he came to America remains somewhat obscure, although there is reason to believe that he argued with his mother, who opposed his marrying beneath his station.[3]

Master Sullivan, though loath to work with his hands, soon fulfilled his obligations as a redemptioner; tradition says he persuaded a clergyman to buy his freedom for him. He soon married Margery Brown (Browne), who had been born in Cork in 1714.[4] They settled in Summersworth, most likely by January, 1737, and that parish hired him as schoolmaster in 1738.[5] There were many children in the Sullivan family, a common occurrence in early America. Benjamin and Daniel were born before John in the latter part of the 1730s. James, later Governor of Massachusetts, was born in 1744; Mary, the only daughter, in 1752, and Ebenezer in 1753.[6] In 1747 or 1748 Master Sullivan moved his family across the river to Berwick, Maine. There, in that rustic community, the tall schoolmaster became a patriarchal figure. Somewhat of a scholar, possibly even an idler, Master Sullivan supervised the upbringing and education of his children, two of whom, John and James, were to go far. His wife was noted for her beauty, vanity, and violent temper. Indeed she must have been a termagant, for earlier, in 1743, her husband sought asylum in Boston or its environs and returned home only after his wife had apologized for her "rash and un-advised Speech and Behaviour." [7]

Young John received a fair education from his father, a far better education than most boys enjoyed in a frontier agricultural community. Of his religious training nothing is known. Master Sullivan undoubtedly had been raised as a Roman Catholic, but his connection with that church was short-lived. Irish immigrants to New England had lost touch with Catholicism, and Master John may have also. Two of his sons owned pews in the North Parish Church of Berwick, and his son John may have also held a pew.[8] Certainly as the years went by John became violently antagonistic toward Roman Catholicism.

The three eldest sons, when they approached manhood, sought action and careers. Benjamin served in the royal navy and was drowned at sea before the outbreak of the Revolution. Daniel, after his marriage, moved to New Bristol in the latter part of the 1750s. John took one trip to the West Indies, then settled down to read law with the energetic Samuel Livermore, probably in early 1758.[9]

In 1760, after he had completed his term with Livermore, Sullivan married Lydia Remick Worster of Kittery, almost two years his senior, whose family had been in Maine for a number of generations. Little is known of Lydia Sullivan.[10] Her husband rarely made reference to her in his letters, and his existing vast correspondence does not contain a letter between them, indicating that she most likely was illiterate. She probably devoted her life to her family. William Plumer described her as "a woman of decent talents, but little acquainted with the world, and still less with books." [11] Shortly after his marriage Sullivan evidently began practicing law in Berwick before moving to Durham, New Hampshire, around 1763. Late in 1764 he bought from the widow of a Durham physician, Samuel Adams, a house and three acres with buildings. This was to be his home for the rest of his life, and today the stately house still stands. Elegant in its simplicity, the building is situated in a slight hollow bounded on the northeast by the Oyster River, one of the arms of the Piscataqua.[12] It is a mere two or three stones' throw across the river at that point.

John Sullivan was the first lawyer in the town of Durham, which then numbered slightly more than 1,200 persons. In addition to carrying on his practice he assumed watch over his two younger brothers and his sister. In return for this his father permitted him use of his farm in Berwick and one half of the produce. Sullivan agreed to see that James undertook law and that Ebenezer studied medicine; he further promised that he would support Mary, although she was still living with her parents, until she married. James studied under his brother, and Mary married Theophilus Hardy and settled in Durham. As for Ebenezer, his "Inclinations and Genius" led him in other directions, and in 1773 John was released from having to meet that part of the agreement.[13]

Ambition pushed John Sullivan. A young, vigorous man, he wanted to get ahead. His physical appearance lent dignity to the man. He stood erect, but not tall, had black hair, and dark piercing eyes with a dark complexion offset by ruddy cheeks. His dignified manners easily could allow him to become a leader of men.[14] But Sullivan's inordinate ambition soon led to trouble; he was so eager to obtain property that he seldom hesitated to sue, and as a result many of his less fortunate neighbors complained. Evidently they considered him a nuisance and the source of their financial troubles. Nor would they remain docile, for on February 23, 1766, over fifteen men with assorted weapons attacked Joseph Cilley's house in Nottingham with every intention of wounding or killing Sullivan, his brother James, and three other men. At least such was the finding of the jury.[15]

This was merely the beginning of a war of nerves between the youthful lawyer and the people of Durham and neighboring towns. On the night of June 2, 1766, a small mob fired into his house and, according to Sullivan, threatened to burn it down and perhaps even kill him. Although these men were irate and had been plotting since May 20, there is little reason to believe that they wished to do more than "rob him of many Writs & Notes of hand which he then had in his possession." [16] Such bellicose ways tired Sullivan's antagonists, and next they resorted to the pen when on June 26, 1766, they presented a petition to the General Court. Using such language as "Oppressive Extortive Behaviour of one Mr. John Sullivan," they continued by saying, "he with a View of making his Fortune, out of the Ruin of the poor harmless People, taking of them Unreasonable Fees from such as were not able to Command Cash enough to pay their publick Tax, or to provide Bread for their Families, he under pretence of having such Knowledge in the Law, set himself up to the highest bidder, for to plead a Case before a Justice." [17] The 133 signatures on the petition which sought an end to the lawyer's suits show that the man was at that early time loathed in his community. Yet some rallied to his defense when the matter came before the Superior Court in September, 1766. Depositions on his behalf described him as a man often trying to avoid suing, and at times as a benefactor who helped the poor meet their taxes. The Court dismissed the petition, and Sullivan sued unsuccessfully for libel. There the matter rested.[18]

The records show that Sullivan constantly pressed for debts owed him, and between September, 1764, and May, 1772, he won about thirty-five actions totaling more than £3,000.[19] These fragmentary figures do not present the complete story, but they appear to show that John Sullivan had an active practice. His reputation must have been growing, particularly after the ill feeling between him and his townsmen had abated, for Wyseman Clagett, one-time Attorney General of the Province, left his affairs in Sullivan's hands when Clagett visited England for an extended period.[20] The Masonian Proprietors in 1771 retained Sullivan, Samuel Livermore, and John Pickering as their lawyers, and in the same year the town of Peterborough had Sullivan present the petition to the Governor and Council in their controversy with their minister, the Rev. John Morrison, charging him with "profane Swearing Drunkenness & other Lew^d wicked & Disorderly practices."[21]

Thanks to his successful law practice, Sullivan found the means to acquire property, and year by year he added to his holdings. He did not limit himself to buying in Durham only, but gathered land in surrounding areas. His purchases included mill sites, the first one probably on the south side of the Lamprey River in Durham, bought in 1770. A later mill site was on the lower Piscassick Falls.[22] His ambition was finding satisfaction, and extensive mill operations added to his income. A grist mill, a bolting mill, a fulling mill, and a mill for grinding scythes—all were in operation by the eve of the Revolution.[23]

Sullivan was a gregarious man and, like so many of his fellow colonists, found that service in the militia afforded chance to swap gossip and relieve some of the tedium of rural life. In November, 1772, Governor John Wentworth traveled to Dover, a town near Durham, and reviewed the 2d Regiment of Foot. At this time the Governor awarded Sullivan a major's commission. Jeremy Belknap preached a sermon "well adapted to the Occasion," and "the several Officers being dressed in their Uniforms, made a very good Appearance."[24] All of this had natural appeal to John Sullivan who, in a humorless fashion, gobbled up pomp and parade.

By now Sullivan was a success. He had security, and his affluence enabled him to obtain some Negro slaves, for it is recorded that they used to row him to Portsmouth and that there were quarters for them to the rear of his house.[25] With material success he gained the respect of his neighbors, in spite of his early troubles with them, and he developed as a leader in the community. In the meantime his family was growing. Lydia Sullivan's first child, Margery, died in infancy. Between 1763 and 1771 she gave birth to another daughter and three sons, Lydia, John, James, and George. Their last child, born in 1775 and likewise named Margery, lived only two years.[26] With a

growing family and an active practice the young lawyer realized
that the first thirty years or so of his life had been kind to him.
John Adams, who rode circuit in York County, commented in
June, 1774, that Sullivan was worth £10,000 (probably a high
estimate), that he had six mills ("his delight and his profit"),
that Governor Wentworth looked upon Sullivan favorably, and
that he was "treated with great respect." [27]

John Sullivan now found himself prepared for the duties of
leadership, duties that would take him beyond Durham, beyond
New Hampshire. In the relative calm and peace of his native
province he was ready to cope with the problems brought on
by colonial status. Unfortunately his views on the imperial
crisis in the years of his youth and early manhood must remain
unknown, in the main, for lack of adequate information, but
surely any Irishman would not have nurtured fond feelings toward England. For a time he was friendly toward Governor
Wentworth, and, when Wentworth had to meet the attack and
charges of one of his own Council, Peter Livius, Sullivan, along
with many others, came to the Governor's defense. Livius had
challenged the decision of the Council which allowed the Governor to regrant land which former Governor Benning Wentworth had reserved for himself in each town that he in turn
had granted. Livius, a troublemaker, went to England and continued his attack from there. Sullivan offered a deposition in
the Governor's behalf.[28]

With the charges repudiated by the Privy Council, Wentworth enjoyed more popularity than ever, but he was not going
to be able to stem the tide of revolutionary feeling that was
gradually rising in New Hampshire. Although he had had the
support of men like Sullivan during his darkest hour, he was
soon to see that their paths were parting as troubles between
the mother country and her colonies increased. The Boston
Massacre in 1770 marked the turning point, and the monopoly
granted the East India Tea Company was further aggravation.
Sullivan soon became convinced that the colonial position was

right, and in March, 1774, just before the storm broke over the
Intolerable Acts, he warned about the rumored choice of Peter
Livius as Chief Justice. Because the salary of the Chief Justice
would be controlled by the Crown, and because he would hold
a commission "during the King's pleasure to Lord it over us so
long as an Arbitrary Ministry shall be pleased with his arbitrary
conduct," Sullivan was furious.[29] A "Kings Government" is entitled to the same rights as a Charter Government, he argued,
and the latter's rights are "only a confirmation of those Liberties which the God of nature had given them before." [30] Such
arbitrary appointments could result only in the perversion of
justice, and Sullivan urged an address to the King.

Livius, however, received the highest judiciary post in Quebec, and Sullivan's fears abated. Then the news of the Intolerable Acts, Lord North's reprisal for the Boston Tea Party,
burst upon the colonies. The New Hampshire House of Representatives appointed a Committee of Correspondence. Wentworth, hoping not only to stifle the committee in its infancy
but also to prevent his fellow colonists from sending delegates
to the proposed Congress in Philadelphia, dissolved the Assembly on June 8, 1774.[31] All his actions were fruitless. The various towns soon decided to send delegates to a Provincial Congress, to meet on July 21 at Exeter, a town that was more
sympathetic toward Boston's plight than was Portsmouth. John
Sullivan attended, representing Durham, along with Ebenezer
Thompson.[32] The delegates at this First Provincial Congress
refused to name a Portsmouth man to attend the Philadelphia
Congress, but instead chose Sullivan and Nathaniel Folsom, an
Exeter militia veteran who had been on the Crown Point expedition of 1755.[33] Portsmouth had not given wholehearted support to the nonimportation schemes, and Wentworth still enjoyed some prestige in that town; thus the choice for delegates
to go to Philadelphia fell to men from other towns. Sullivan by
now was well known in seaboard New Hampshire, he was an
articulate lawyer, and thus a logical choice. Not only was

Sullivan suited to represent New Hampshire's point of view, but also he was prepared to voice the opinion of all the colonies in their attempt to perpetuate their rights, liberties, and privileges. On August 10, 1774, the two delegates left New Hampshire for Philadelphia with about 150 gentlemen escorting them to the province line. From there, accompanied only by their servants, the men proceeded alone, but in "high Spirits." [34]

Sullivan had an air of importance about him; filled with self-esteem and often opinionated, he had full confidence, as he rode to Philadelphia, both in himself and in the wisdom of New Hampshire in having selected him as a delegate. He was excited about his appointment to the Continental Congress, and could only have been thrilled to realize that he, at the age of thirty-four, was to be part of such an august gathering. In New York City the two delegates called on John Adams at the radical Alexander McDougall's, then hastened "over the ferry for fear of the smallpox." [35] Through New Jersey the men rode on toward their destination. Once in Philadelphia John Sullivan readied himself for the important meetings to come, undoubtedly met the incoming men from the other colonies, explored the fascinating city, and joined in the social gaieties. But beneath the social excitement of Philadelphia ran the current of political turmoil. How far would this group of men, representing the colonies from New Hampshire to South Carolina, be willing to go? How many men would approach the ardor of Sam Adams? Would the fiery Massachusetts delegation, abetted by some of the Southerners, pull the more conservative men of the middle colonies along with them?

Sullivan went to the edge of the city to meet the men from the Bay colony.[36] From the beginning Sullivan seemed to be moving in the direction of the radical camp. Before Congress assembled, the early arrivals talked politics incessantly, and those with definite ideas tried to win over the more hesitant men. The conservative Joseph Galloway from Pennsylvania wasted no time in sounding out the New Hampshire delegates. He hoped they might be more amenable than the Massachusetts firebrands, although he suspected from the beginning that they would support nonimportation. Galloway sized Sullivan up as being "rather more warm" than Nathaniel Folsom. But he had his hopes and wrote: "I think neither of them intends to attach himself more to the particular Cause of Boston than will be for the general Good." [37] Although Galloway concluded by saying that all his observations apparently had "full Weight with them," he was to be sadly mistaken. The New Hampshire men took their stand and held that the times called for strenuous defense of the rights involved in the Boston dispute.

Right from the opening session Sullivan threw himself vigorously into the work of Congress. The first day found him debating with Patrick Henry over voting procedure. Coming to the defense of the small colonies, Sullivan insisted that vote should be by colony and not by population. Henry's comments, "Government is dissolved. . . . We are in a state of nature. . . . The distinctions between Virginians, Pennsylvanians, New Yorkers, and New Englanders, are no more. I am not a Virginian, but an American," failed to convince John Sullivan when it came to a matter of voting.[38] Although Sullivan won this round, the Congress agreed that voting by colony did not necessarily set a precedent.[39] Sullivan immediately went to work on the committee appointed to state the colonial rights and the instances of violation of those rights. He found himself on the subcommittee to list the infringements, and wrote the first draft of its report. Immediately the men had to determine the base upon which the colonial rights stood. Sullivan surely agreed with John Adams that the rights must be based not just upon the English constitution and the charters, but also upon the law of nature, for Sullivan was zealous of "Liberties which God and Nature have given to us." [40] On October 14 Congress finally adopted, after tedious debate, a Declaration of Rights and Grievances.[41]

Of the grievances listed in the resolutions, none disturbed John Sullivan more than the passage of the Quebec Act; in a letter to John Langdon he called it "most dangerous to American Liberties." Continuing, Sullivan described the threat which the Indians and French had been in the late war when they "Determined to extirpate the Race of Protestants from America." The extensive territory granted to Quebec would become a refuge for Roman Catholicism, Sullivan argued, and he saw no safety until everyone professed "that Holy Religion which our Sovereign has been pledged to establish." [42] Sullivan believed that a strong and hostile Catholic Canada, unsympathetic to the colonial cause, was a live threat to the northern frontier of the colonies. Following the grievances in this Declaration came the listing of rights. Although John Adams must be given major credit for the political theory denying parliamentary authority in all internal affairs, a theory advanced in the resolutions, Sullivan had offered the same opinion in his draft. Power to regulate internal polity rested in the individual provincial legislatures, he claimed.[43] This argument became the fourth resolution in the final form of the Declaration. Sullivan's draft had made no mention of the critical problem concerning the regulation of trade. The conservative feeling was that Parliament had the right to regulate trade, and that the right rested on "compact, acquiescence, necessity, protection, not merely on our (colonial) consent," as expressed by James Duane.[44] Adams really dodged the crux of the problem, and cleverly stated that the colonies "cheerfully consent" to allow Parliament to regulate external commerce.[45] No doubt the word "consent" played a larger role than Duane would have preferred, and Galloway was frantic, believing that the resolution hinted at independency.

After declaring the rights, and listing the acts infringing those rights, the Declaration concluded with a statement of determination by Congress to enter into a nonimportation, nonexportation, nonconsumption association, to address both the people of Great Britain and the inhabitants of British

North America, and to present a loyal address to the King.[46] Considering the fact that the more radical element controlled Congress, it is quite surprising that the Declaration was so mild in tone. But a mild tone merely showed the desire of Congress to avoid trouble if at all possible.

Time was running out. The radicals had won most of the rounds. Earlier in the session Congress had endorsed the Massachusetts "Suffolk Resolves." [47] Toward the end the delegates voted the adoption of the Association, designed for economic coercion, and dismissed Galloway's plan for imperial federation.[48] All signed the Association, the conservatives doing so to forestall more extreme measures. The men had been in deliberation since early September, and they wished to return home. On October 21 they resolved that seizing a person for transportation for trial for offense "will justify, and ought to meet with resistance and reprisal," perhaps to discourage seizure of themselves.[49] They decided to hold another Congress on May 10 should their grievances not be redressed by that time. On October 26 Congress dissolved itself. The delegates celebrated that night at the City Tavern. They had right to be pleased with their work, for they had taken a bold stand. Having rejected Galloway's plan of union that accepted British hegemony, although by a close vote, they insisted on control of internal polity as one of their rights, basing those rights on the English constitution, on the charters, even on natural law; and they had agreed to pursue a more extensive policy of economic coercion to achieve their ends.

The lines were being drawn. Sullivan and the others were prepared for the crisis that would come should King George and his ministers continue their unyielding ways. On November 8 Sullivan and Folsom reached New Hampshire and enjoyed a glorious welcome.[50] Immediately Sullivan threw himself into the task of getting the Association accepted. Late in November his own town, Durham, approved of it, then chose a committee of correspondence with Sullivan as a member.

The town meeting decided to send cattle and money to beleaguered Boston.[51] Thus Sullivan's Durham made firm its position. He liked this leadership and wanted to play a role that would send him back to Philadelphia should a new Congress convene. Folsom and he appeared in Portsmouth, undoubtedly to report on their activities in Congress and to press for acceptance of the Association.[52] The colony no longer was quite so docile as when it had succumbed to the charms of John Wentworth. Sullivan knew this was the time to take a firm stand, and he saw about him many men upon whom he could rely, perhaps most important of all the handsome John Langdon, Portsmouth's successful merchant. New Hampshire was falling in line and willing to follow the radical lead.

The leadership was waiting for some action to trigger an explosion. It turned out to be a short wait. News arrived that the King had forbidden the importing of arms into the colonies. This went too far, and on the afternoon of December 14, 1774, a group raided Fort William and Mary, situated on Newcastle, an island town at the mouth of the Piscataqua. Sullivan was not on this first raid, but he did lead a subsequent assault, thoroughly convinced that the action was justified. He had been arguing that military stores should be seized, and it is more than likely that he knew the raid would occur. On the night of the 14th he received a message from Pierse Long, one of the participants, telling him that some of the powder seized during the raid was being sent to him for safekeeping and asking him to bring a party to capture the cannon and munitions at the fort before the British ships secured them.[53] He did not delay and on the next day, December 15, hastened to Portsmouth with thirty or forty men.[54] Here he found a number of persons gathered ready to follow his lead. Sullivan and a few others waited upon Wentworth to ask whether British troops were coming. Although Wentworth had requested troops from General Gage, he denied that any were coming and suggested that Sullivan disperse the men. Wentworth's account of the conflict indicates that Sullivan said he would send the men away. Apparently Wentworth's statement that no troops were on the way, coupled with some assurance that the previous day's raiders might escape severe measures, calmed the men who then chose to go home.[55] But the crowd's "Demosthenes," undoubtedly Sullivan, persuaded them before they dispersed "to vote that they took part with, and approved of, the measures of those who had taken the Powder." [56] Obviously some of the men then must have gone home, but about seventy lingered with John Sullivan in the town into the evening. They retired to the taverns, most of them to Jacob Tilton's Bell Tavern on King Street, where Sullivan paid for the evening's entertainment. Wentworth's pleas had been in vain, for at about ten or eleven o'clock that night, the men left the taverns and went by water to the fort to remove as much as they could of the remaining military stores. They were there throughout the night and returned to Portsmouth the following day.[57]

If Sullivan in fact had told Wentworth that he would send the men home, then he doublecrossed the Governor when he led the raid. Possibly he intended to trick Wentworth into believing that all would remain quiet. Possibly the attempt of some to seek clemency for their part in the first raid irked Sullivan, for he would not want to see his fellow colonists knuckling under the will of John Wentworth. Perhaps the time spent in the taverns gave the men opportunity to see that it would be weakness if the Governor's will prevailed. Sullivan may have wavered throughout the day, but by evening, perhaps influenced by the conviviality of his surroundings, his mind became set. A persuasive man, he had the following of those who had tarried in Portsmouth. The planning, financing, and leading of this raid was John Sullivan's defiance of the Crown. Nathaniel Folsom later hoped to lead a group to complete the dismantling, but the arrival of two British ships prevented further action. In the meantime Folsom saw that the captured stores were sent into the country. Safely back in

Durham, Sullivan, assisted by his law clerks, Alexander Scammell, Peter French, and James Underwood, and a hired man and team, spent three days cutting through the ice taking those stores which had been entrusted to him to a safe place.[58]

Sullivan and the others had taken their stand. They had challenged John Wentworth and the monarchy which he represented. The die was cast. The irate Governor, frustrated because he could do so little and because he saw control slipping from his hands, and filled with injured pride because his popularity was on the wane, still displayed the marks of courage, no matter how futile such courage might be. He immediately singled out Sullivan as one of the instigators of the trouble. Although accusing the popular leaders in Boston of having stirred up the crisis, he believed that Sullivan must assume much of the blame. To him Sullivan was an ambitious man who wished so much to attend the next Congress that he took an ardent role in local affairs.[59] The Governor's proclamation seeking the arrest of the offenders got him nowhere. He even feared that he could not dismiss the civil and military officers who had taken part in the raid as it would simply make them martyrs. This decision, reversed later, shows his impotence at the time. He realized that he was contending against strong forces, for he soon learned that there was a plan to seize him should any of the raiders or Boston leaders be taken into custody.[60] Sullivan was the leader of the clique which was defying the authority of government. Instead of allowing tempers to cool, John Sullivan had gone ahead with the second raid, and his position was so secure that many people would have gone to his assistance had Wentworth tried to grab Sullivan and send him to England, an idea that he did entertain momentarily.[61]

The Durham leader was ready for anything that might happen. Although he stated late in December, "I am far from wishing Hostilities to Commence on the part of America," Sullivan must have been hoping that Great Britain would start a war.[62] There was no road upon which he could retrace his steps. He prepared for action, and under his leadership Durham trained a military company which usurped the usual role of the militia. Some in New Hampshire were moving toward warlike measures according to Wentworth.[63] Yet the Second Provincial Congress, meeting again at Exeter in late January, 1775, although under Sullivan's influence, refused to take action approving the raid on the fort. This group gave its blessing to the proceedings at Philadelphia and supported the Association; but at the same time the delegates told the people that they must "yield due obedience to the Magistrates within this Government, and carefully endeavor to support the laws thereof." [64] The Exeter delegates voted to send Sullivan and John Langdon to the next Continental Congress, urged the people to support the committees of correspondence, encouraged domestic manufactures, and suggested military training.[65]

In spite of the nod in the direction of law and order which the delegates made, Sullivan's more fiery point of view was noticeable. He moved that a petition be presented to Wentworth requesting him to call an Assembly and that he not dissolve it, regardless of the Assembly's activities. Men like the respected jurist Meshech Weare and the clergyman Paine Wingate, both from Hampton, disapproved, arguing that Congress had convened with the sole intent of reviewing the actions of the Philadelphia deliberations and of selecting delegates for the next session. To do more would be exceeding the purpose of their meeting. Sullivan, supported by John Langdon and Folsom, answered that the whole meeting was unlawful anyway, and that therefore they could do as they saw fit. They were the people, they had unlimited powers, he argued. The Continental Congress, an illegal body, had not failed to take action, he continued, and there was no reason why they in Exeter should be hesitant.[66] He got his petition.

Governor Wentworth, now fully aware of the effective hold Sullivan had over the Exeter Congress, saw the danger to his own government and realized he must take action. Not just the alarming activities at Exeter, but also the failure of his proclamation calling for arrest of the raiders, the opinion that the raid had been high treason, and the uneasiness of the situation in Boston, led Wentworth, evidently late in February, to dismiss the leaders of the December attacks on the fort from the offices that they held. Thus Sullivan lost his major's commission.[67] Wentworth moved even further and dissolved the Assembly until May. One third of the new House had consisted of December ringleaders, and he feared the Assembly would approve the actions at Philadelphia and might even take further measures. He was trying to show a firm hand and had hopes that assistance might arrive so that he could arrest some of the leaders. But aid never came, merely word from the Earl of Dartmouth that matters in New Hampshire were in a "disgraceful state." [68]

Wentworth knew that there was little that he could do to stem the surge of revolutionary feeling. Sullivan and John Langdon were elected to the Second Continental Congress, an act which the Governor could not prevent. On April 6, 1775, the two delegates left their homes and started the arduous journey to Philadelphia. By now Sullivan was completely enmeshed in the radical strategy, and already he was known within his own province as the leader of most of the trouble. The two men, along with a delegation from Rhode Island, met in Massachusetts and discussed the crisis with a group from the Bay Colony's Provincial Congress. They were in agreement that no decisive measure should be taken in that province without the consent of her New England neighbors.[69] Great Britain, however, by the march to Lexington and Concord threw down the gauntlet, and war began. Sullivan was missed in New Hampshire as the crisis came to a head. His law clerk, Scammell, wrote that his departure had "spread a general Gloom in Durham, and in some measure damp'd the spirit of Liberty through the Province." Upon the outbreak of hostilities Scammell told Sullivan that "the universal Cry was, O if

Major Sullivan was here! I wish to God Major Sullivan was here!" [70] But John Sullivan was in Philadelphia, renewing acquaintances, meeting new delegates, and relieved that war had come.

Sullivan soon aligned himself with the faction that believed Congress should face the fact that war had begun. The moderates, however, were able to get Congress to start out in a cautious vein. At first the strategy was defense, and when news came that Ticonderoga had fallen to Ethan Allen and Benedict Arnold, Congress chose to look upon the blow as a defensive action designed to prevent a "cruel invasion" from Canada. To bolster the argument, Congress voted to remove the stores from the fort to the south end of Lake George.[71] Sullivan, however, soon found himself attacking the stand taken by moderates, who, although accepting measures for defense, still yearned for reconciliation. Thus on May 26, 1775, Congress resolved not only to place the colonies in a state of defense, but also to present a "humble" petition to the King, obviously a victory for the moderates under the leadership of John Dickinson and James Duane.[72] According to John Adams, Sullivan attacked the petition "in a strain of wit, reasoning, and fluency, which . . . exceeded every thing I had ever heard from him before." [73] The scholarly Dickinson was fearful and argued with Adams outside of the State House. "What is the reason, Mr. Adams, that you New Englandmen oppose our measures of reconciliation?" he asked. "There now is Sullivan, in a long harangue," the Pennsylvanian continued, "following you in a determined opposition to our petition to the King." [74] Adams could expect, his critic warned, that a number of the delegates would break with New England if Adams and his adherents did not go along with reconciliation.

Dickinson's arguments met deaf ears. Adams took the position that Congress should recommend to the colonies that they call conventions to form "governments of their own, under their own authority." [75] These were startling words, but some of the delegates were pleased, "none more than Mr. John Rutledge . . . and Mr. John Sullivan." [76] Upon a request from Massachusetts, Congress told that colony on June 9 to set up its own government until the King was ready to govern Massachusetts according to its charter.[77] During the debate Sullivan gave Adams vigorous support. Later, when Sullivan had departed from Congress, Adams said that he had lost an "able coadjutor." [78]

Finally Congress could no longer delay facing the major problem, whether to take on the regulation of the army forming in Massachusetts. If this were done, chances for reconciliation would be dim. Congress plowed ahead, and if the delegates had misgivings, they rapidly lost themselves in their task. They had to supply powder, recruit riflemen, draft rules and regulations for the young army. They determined to have a commander, and George Washington was their choice. Next came the job of selecting the general officers, and here politicking was rampant. Conscientious Artemas Ward, already in Massachusetts, two former British officers, the maverick Charles Lee and Horatio Gates, New York's Philip Schuyler, popular Israel Putnam—all gained the approbation of Congress for the top ranks.[79] The brigadiers came from New England with the exception of the gallant Richard Montgomery of New York. John Sullivan was the seventh brigadier selected.[80] Possibly the belligerent John Stark or Nathaniel Folsom, both with more experience and seniority than Sullivan, deserved the commission. But Sullivan was in Congress, and his fiery attitude had impressed the delegates who had been observing at first hand his ardor, his enthusiasm, and his energy. Perhaps they hoped that he could transmit his zeal to the army facing the British in Massachusetts.

II: THE FIRST YEAR OF CONFLICT

JUNE, 1775–JULY, 1776

As an army gathered at Boston to challenge the British, Sullivan was in no mood for delay. On the morning of June 27, 1775, he rode from Philadelphia toward the scene of action, accompanied for a short distance by some light infantry and "gentlemen of the militia." [1] Then he was on his way. On July 10 he reached Cambridge and joined the siege against the British who were on Charlestown Peninsula and on Roxbury Neck, guarding the approaches to Boston proper. The rebel lines, drawn in a semicircle extending from the hills facing Charlestown Peninsula through the town of Roxbury, had to keep the British from moving into the surrounding countryside. Lines and redoubts had been thrown up between the Mystic River and Dorchester Point.[2] But to succeed in holding back the enemy, the motley army drawn from the towns of New England had to be organized and disciplined.

Sullivan, after a short trip to his home, immediately threw himself into the task of creating an effective force. Washington proposed forming the army into three divisions. Sullivan's brigade, along with Nathanael Greene's, went under Charles Lee's command on the left wing, with the brigades placed respectively at Winter Hill and Prospect Hill. Artemas Ward commanded one division on the right wing in the Roxbury area, and Israel Putnam commanded the third division, called the "Corps-de-Reserve." [3]

Sullivan soon had a chance to show his mettle, for Washington wished to take possession of Plowed Hill, between

Winter Hill and Bunker Hill, because he believed the British planned to seize the height for themselves. This action he hoped would bring about an encounter with the enemy. Accordingly on the night of Saturday, August 26, a party of 1,200 men under John Sullivan occupied the hill and secured the fortifications before dawn. On Sunday morning the British not only opened with a cannonade, which continued throughout the day, but also tried to enfilade the rebel position from floating batteries and an armed vessel. Sullivan's nine pounder forced the sloop to move away, damaged one of the batteries, and sank another. The lack of powder, however, prevented the Americans from taking advantage of their newly won position.[4]

General Washington, upset by the continuing stalemate, wished action, but a Council of War on September 11, at which Sullivan was present, advised against attacking Boston by boats along with a simultaneous land assault upon the redcoats in Roxbury.[5] Certainly the British had no intention of striking the American lines; instead they would await a rebel attack. In October Sullivan was still with those who advised against a thrust, but he and other officers suggested that winter might be the most feasible time for American action.[6] Meanwhile the British showed signs of activity elsewhere when on October 17 they burned Falmouth, Maine. Washington received the news that the British next planned to hit at Portsmouth, and he therefore sent on the energetic Sullivan to supervise the defenses—an assignment which he accomplished with dispatch.[7]

The fall wore on. Although the soldiers were growing restless, Sullivan remained as enthusiastic as ever. He knew that a firm stand must be taken to avoid abject surrender. For some time he had been urging New Hampshire to form a government, and when he heard that Congress had told New Hampshire to go ahead with a plan, early in December he wrote Meshech Weare, who throughout the war and early postwar years assumed the political leadership in New Hampshire, offering his thoughts on the subject. He prefaced his remarks by saying that government was for the good of the people; hence "that Form of Government is most perfect where that Design is most nearly and effectually answered." [8] Any form of government which had clashing interests was imperfect. This could be avoided, he argued, by having all branches of government controlled directly by the people. He wrote, "no Danger can arise to a state from giving the People a free & full Voice in their own Government, and that what are called the Prerogatives of the Crown, or Checks upon the Licentiousness of the People, are only the Children of ambitious, or designing Men." [9] Both those governing and the governed should have one end in mind: the good of the whole. He had no objection to a Governor so long as he was directly elected by the freeholders, but he would not allow him an absolute veto. He urged that there be annual elections, and that they be by secret ballot to avoid bribery.

Therefore, from the beginning of the struggle within the empire, Sullivan had become involved in the ways of political revolution. He had taken the extreme stand at Philadelphia in 1774; he had not faltered when the conflict came in 1775; completely disenchanted with authoritarianism, he now advocated a peoples' rule. Sullivan's star was shining bright, and he enjoyed his influential role in the army and in his native province. Later in December he recited to John Adams, rather egotistically, but altogether sincerely, his efforts in behalf of revolution. Winter's cold would do its work, he said, and soon a bridge of ice would open the way to Boston; either the Americans would "take possession of the town, or perish in the attempt." [10] He had complete faith, now was the time to declare independence he asserted. No room for moderation existed, he told the ardent Adams. Sending on his compliments to Hancock, Lee, and the other delegates whom he knew, he mentioned to Adams, certainly not tactfully, "that when an opportunity presents, if I should not have courage to fight myself, I should do all in my power to encourage others." [11] His enthusiasm impressed Abigail Adams who joined him for coffee on Winter Hill one December day. She described him as a man of "sense and spirit," a man whose countenance displayed "a warm constitution, not to be very suddenly moved, but, when once roused, not very easily lulled." He was "easy and social," suited for the army because he had "those popular qualities necessary to attach men to him." [12]

The time to attack finally came, but it would be abortive. In the early morning of December 29, Sullivan with a party of 300 men, supported by 1,000 men to the rear, attempted to seize the outbuildings and barracks on Bunker Hill. The weak ice evidently held him from crossing the creek, although some implied the attempt failed because the British became alerted when one American soldier fell and accidentally discharged his piece. No second try could come since obviously the British knew of the American intentions. Charles Lee, in Rhode Island at the time, was irked because he had wished to strike at Bunker Hill himself. Sullivan's failure now had ruined Lee's chances of success, and Lee's friends accused Sullivan of desiring to win glory during the absence of his superior officer.[13]

The year came to an end. The British remained in Boston; both armies merely glowered at each other. But Sullivan and the others feared that there might not be a patriot army as 1776 opened. Already the Connecticut militia had gone home, and more men were ready to leave. Their time was about up and no worthy cause could compel them to remain before Boston. In spite of Sullivan's pleas to his own men, he met with many rebuffs. Then he turned to chiding them for having "such Principles as would Induce them to Betray the Freedom of their Country, and Enslave themselves and Posterity Rather than Dispense with a Sight of their own habitations for a Month." [14] Yet somehow an army remained and the siege continued.

The impasse, however, could not last indefinitely, and Washington and his officers decided to seize Dorchester Heights, an action which might force William Howe to venture forth. On the night of March 4 General John Thomas occupied the Heights. Sullivan and Greene were holding back, yet poised for an attack against Boston should Howe challenge the Americans once they had Dorchester. General Howe now faced the threat of a cannonade; he either had to dislodge the Americans or withdraw from Boston. To attack the rebels would have been foolish, but Howe, having to save face, prepared for an assault. Fortunately for him, though, a storm came up on the night of March 5 and spared him the humiliation of sure defeat. He countermanded his orders and prepared to get out of Boston.[15]

On Sunday, March 17, the British embarked and fell down to the Castle. Some Americans feared an attempt upon Dorchester might still be forthcoming, but Sullivan, glass in hand, standing upon Plowed Hill saw the British boarding the ships and suspected the siege had come to an end. He galloped down to Charlestown Neck from where he could have a good look at Bunker Hill. There he saw the sentries with shouldered firelocks standing guard. The general paused, for the sentries remained motionless; putting his glass to his eye, he found they were effigies left by the departing enemy. Now convinced that the siege was over, Sullivan with a small party moved on and "bravely took a fortress Defended by Lifeless Sentries." [16] Washington ordered Sullivan to take possession of Charlestown and Israel Putnam to take possession of Boston. On March 18 Sullivan joined the party that accompanied the Commander-in-Chief into Boston. The months of waiting were over, and John Sullivan soon expected to be on his way to New York.

The joy of outlasting the British was somewhat dampened in Sullivan's case by a controversy with New Hampshire's legislature. In January, when the militia was threatening to leave, Sullivan had reenlisted as many of the New Hampshire men as would heed his persuasions, and had undertaken to appoint the officers—a prerogative which the legislators claimed to be their own. When Sullivan learned that he had been criticized, he was irate and shot forth a blast of patriotism. Remarking that he would soon be off for New York, he wrote that then "those persons will . . . have no more fear of the Destruction of their Liberties from a person who has Spent more money undergone more Fatigue and oftener Risqued his Life than any other person in your Province & all this to Secure that Freedom which those Gentlemen would perswade the world I am Endeavouring to Destroy." [17]

Toward the end of March he was writing New Hampshire once again, defending himself from the slurs of his critics. Nathaniel Folsom, who perhaps had hoped earlier for the command that went instead to Sullivan, had been most severe in his criticism, and Sullivan was striking back. In no way had he used money at the expense of the country, nor had he usurped more power than had been given him, he said. Folsom and the others, he claimed, were jealous because he had been given control over the defense of Portsmouth rather than they. Nor did the criticism end there; he was under attack because some in the legislature had suggested he be reimbursed for the expenses incurred when he had come to New Hampshire to supervise the defense. This charge angered Sullivan. "I sensibly feel my Obligation to those Gentlemen who actuated by motives of Justice & Humanity made the Motion without my knowledge or Consent," he wrote, "but at the Same time must beg leave to assure them that the loss of Interest and fatigues of War are what I expect nothing in Return for except seeing My Country freed from Slavery and those worthy Gentlemen and their posterity Enjoying the Sweets of peace and freedom." [18]

Already John Sullivan had established a pattern of behavior which would fit him for the rest of his military career. He was brave almost to the extent of folly. An ambitious man, he drove himself unsparingly; but at all times he considered the well-being of those under his command. He wished popularity, and on the whole gained it. Unduly sensitive, he often found himself embroiled in controversy which could have been avoided.

A certain arrogant manner led him to take on duties which tact would have left in other hands; yet he always was appreciative of civilian authority. Sullivan was a patriot and threw himself wholeheartedly into the revolutionary tussle. Often throughout the conflict, while many wavered, he showed determination and courage, and knew his duty. From the northernmost colony General Washington had gained a devoted, loyal, and hard-working lieutenant.

A testing period approached for Sullivan. Washington's army went on to New York City anticipating that the leisurely Howe might move in that direction. Late in March Sullivan left Boston for New York, but he was not to tarry long there. Soon he would be leading troops to Canada. No promising report had come from the American army to the north. General Richard Montgomery had fallen during the siege of Quebec in December. David Wooster had taken command before Quebec early in April, and Benedict Arnold had retired to Montreal. Late in April Washington told Congress that he would send Sullivan to Canada with six regiments.[19] The march north was slow and tedious, and it was not until May 27 that John Sullivan left Ticonderoga on the final stage of the move toward the enemy.[20]

Meanwhile the news from Canada did not augur well for success. On the day that he left Ticonderoga, Sullivan learned that an American force under Isaac Butterfield had been captured thirty miles above Montreal. Almost two weeks earlier General John Thomas, who had replaced Wooster, had raised the siege before Quebec after hearing that ships carrying British reinforcements were in the river below the city. He had gone on to Sorel.[21] Sullivan proceeded with his brigade toward a bewildered army in Canada, on the verge of collapse because of mismanagement and smallpox. Congress had two commissioners on the scene, Samuel Chase and Charles Carroll of Carrollton. They saw little hope unless discipline were restored. Nothing was working. Quite obviously Deschambault could not be held, and Montreal was being threatened from both sides. Smallpox ravaged the troops, and the men were terrified.[22] The able John Thomas, having succumbed to smallpox, returned his command to Wooster and retired from Sorel to Chambly. Wooster, however, did not have the approval of the Commissioners and left the front. Sullivan met him on May 31 at St. Johns, learned from him that there was no hope of Thomas's recovery, and that he must assume command.[23]

Sullivan was walking into chaos. Men were deserting, supplies were short, and the troops were so dispersed that often the colonels did not know the whereabout of parts of their regiments.[24] Wooster's final Council of War at Chambly on May 30 had determined that the army should try to stay in Canada and maintain a hold on Sorel.[25] Sullivan assessed matters for himself. Although he had heard a report that Sir Guy Carleton was advancing up the St. Lawrence, he chose to disregard it, preferring to believe another report that there was no sign of him above Quebec. "I am Surprized," he wrote, "that an Army Should Live in Continual fear of & Even Retreat before an Enemy which no person among them has Seen." [26] He planned to leave for Montreal to explore the situation for himself. There he quickly realized that almost everyone advised leaving Canada. This irked him because no one had seen the enemy, and he was itching for a fight. Soon he heard from Brigadier General William Thompson, who was at Sorel, that Colonel Allan Maclean and 800 British regulars supposedly had advanced as far as Trois Rivières. Possibly the nonexistent enemy was materializing after all. Now was the opportunity for Sullivan to show his spunk, to demonstrate to Washington and Congress that they had a general who was willing to fight. With no idea of a retreat in his mind, he hurried to Sorel where he immediately ordered the return of artillery that Thompson had been sending to Chambly and St. Johns in anticipation of retreat. His resolute ways pleased the Frenchmen. Men, women, and children lined the banks of the river, "Leaping & Clapping their hands for Joy to See me Arrive," Sullivan in no modest fashion reported to Washington.[27] Intelligence reached him on June 6 that about 300 British regulars, a fewer number than in Thompson's report, were at Trois Rivières. Encouraged by General Thompson, who earlier had sent a force under Arthur St. Clair to test Allan Maclean, Sullivan determined to move against Trois Rivières in force. He sent Thompson to join St. Clair's small force and to proceed with the raid.[28] Sullivan couched his orders to Thompson in careful words. Especial care must be taken to preserve the batteaux, and Thompson was to call off the raid if there were little chance of success as failure might easily mean the loss of Canada.[29]

Some optimism shone in the American camp. If the encounter at Trois Rivières turned out successfully, Sullivan planned next to secure Deschambault.[30] In a confident mood he wrote Washington to suggest that either Washington himself or Charles Lee should assume command in Canada. Should neither come, which Sullivan must have known would be the case, he asked to be relieved: "I beg That if any other officer is Sent to take it [the Command] That I may have Leave to Return as I am well Convinced that the Same disorder & Confusion which has almost Ruined our Army here would again Take place & Compleat its Destruction which I should not wish to See." [31] In effect John Sullivan, full of optimism, was asking to be confirmed in his command. But his optimism was not to last for long. Thompson, through either stupidity or treachery of his habitant guide, lost any chance of surprising the enemy who, well reinforced, threw back the assault on June 7 and even managed to capture Thompson himself. Carleton, in usual British fashion, did not press the retreating Americans, who began to filter back into camp by the evening of June 11.[32]

All American hopes were now shattered, but instead of ordering an immediate retreat Sullivan wrote, "I now think only of a glorious Death or a victory obtained against Superiour numbers." [33] Sullivan should have accepted some blame for the failure at Trois Rivières. He had quickly acceded to General

Thompson's understandable desire to join St. Clair and initiate the attack on the British, but Sullivan had not been aware of the factors any commander must know. He did not have reliable information as to enemy strength, nor did he accurately gauge the chances of maintaining the advantage if initially successful, especially by an army riddled with smallpox and unsure of immediate reinforcements from New York. Although Washington and Congress were both extremely anxious for success in Canada, Sullivan was on the spot, and they were not. Thompson never should have carried out the attack once chance of surprise had been dissipated, but Sullivan's unwarranted optimism had set the tone for the entire fiasco.

Now retreat had to come, a retreat hampered by the pursuing British. Still John Sullivan was reluctant to face the inevitable. He reported that he had 2,533 discouraged men with him to face an enemy force that was increasing rapidly; yet he told Washington he was "Determin'd to hold . . . as Long as a person will Stick by me." [34] His wild hopes, though, soon disappeared, and a Council of War, held the night of June 13, persuaded the zealous Sullivan to retreat. It began the next morning. Sullivan blamed his dispirited army, the desire of some officers to resign, and the chance his army would flee once the enemy appeared as forcing the decision upon him; but surely the man must have realized that he could not make an effective stand at Sorel. Although the British reached Sorel one hour after the Americans had left, they failed to exploit their advantage and did not undertake an effective pursuit.[35]

The retreat, surprisingly enough, was orderly and efficient although the agony of pain and illness which the unhappy army had to endure was a nightmare. On June 18 the army reached Isle-aux-Noix, lying in the narrow channel leading north from Lake Champlain, and here the stubborn leader decided to linger until ordered on by Philip Schuyler, Washington, or Congress.[36] A worse place for a retreating army to make a stand could not be imagined. Arthur St. Clair accused Sullivan of staying to protect the land of New Englanders whose holdings touched Lake Champlain—a reckless charge that could not be proved.[37]

Soon, however, Sullivan had to face facts and move on. Had he stayed longer he might not have had enough well men to move the sick. The men, "Owing to their Fatigue & Want of Fresh Provisions are daily dropping off like the Israelites before the destroying angel," he wrote, and so on June 24 he continued the retreat.[38] Late in the night of July 1 he reached Crown Point. He planned to fortify it and wrote John Hancock with pride that he had carried out a successful retreat from Canada.[39] Sullivan's self-confidence was soon to be dashed, for he learned that Horatio Gates had been assigned by Congress to supersede him.

Congress had been discussing the problem of selecting a proper commander for Canada, unaware of the fact that the Canadian campaign was rapidly collapsing. On June 17 Washington had sent on to Congress Sullivan's earlier letter in which he had strongly hinted that he would like the Canadian command. Washington made some interesting comments. Quite obviously Sullivan wanted the command he noted, then went on to describe Sullivan as "active, spirited, and Zealously attach'd to the Cause." But he had his foibles, also: "a little tincture of vanity . . . an over desire of being popular, which now and then leads him into some embarrassments." [40] Congress, however, preferred an experienced man and so chose Gates, who had been raised to rank of a major general in May. Sullivan was miffed. He wrote Schuyler that he did not like being replaced by a person who he claimed had not been his superior in rank from the beginning. Obviously, he thought, Congress no longer had faith in him, and he asked Schuyler to allow him to go to Philadelphia to resign his commission.[41]

Schuyler granted him permission, and the disgruntled John Sullivan left for Philadelphia. His anger is understandable. The Canadian debacle had occurred through no fault of his, although he had to accept responsibility for the foolish attempt on Trois

Rivières. He had conducted a retreat safely, assisted considerably, however, by the failure of the British to pursue. The decision of Congress to give the command to Gates is not surprising, for Sullivan lacked experience. His failure to gain the command did not mean that Congress blamed John Sullivan for the disastrous turn of events. He reached Philadelphia toward the end of the month and offered his resignation. His friends, however, fearing that Congress might accede to the impetuous Sullivan's resignation, urged him to reconsider, and he withdrew his petition on July 29.[42] John Hancock explained to Sullivan why Congress had selected Gates, and apparently Hancock's words soothed the ruffled Sullivan. Possibly Sullivan expected Congress to do some backing down, but if so, he misjudged the congressional temper, for Thomas Jefferson's report on Sullivan's petition, which Jefferson was prepared to submit to his fellow delegates, was critical. Because Sullivan had withdrawn his petition, the report never came to the floor, but in it Jefferson claimed Gates did have seniority. He was prepared to suggest that Congress accept the resignation.[43]

Sullivan fortunately was able to save face when he was allowed to withdraw his resignation, for Congress had intended to give him, in Jefferson's words, a "rap of the knuckles." [44] The episode does not do Sullivan credit. His reaction to Gates's appointment was petty, and Washington along with the other general officers was "much Disfected because Sullivan had left the northern department." [45] Congress still had use for Sullivan and sent him on to New York to await further assignment from General Washington.[46]

III: LONG ISLAND TO TRENTON
AND PRINCETON

AUGUST, 1776–JANUARY, 1777

The disgruntled and irate Sullivan did not have long to feel sorry for himself. The British and American armies were soon to clash on Long Island in one of the important battles of the Revolution, and he was to play a key and controversial role in that contest. In July, 1776, the British under William Howe landed on Staten Island, and as the days passed the enemy camp on the island totaled about 20,000 rank and file. Congress had already declared American independence; the die was cast. Now Howe had the initiative and threatened New York. Feverishly Washington prepared his army for the expected encounter; yet he was uncertain, for the attack could develop either on Long Island or on Manhattan.[1]

The reverses in Canada had not dulled Sullivan's ardor, enthusiasm, and optimism. He yearned for combat and was irked because as yet he had not been assigned a post or given a brigade. He soon got recognition, however, for on August 9 Congress raised him along with others to the rank of major general.[2] When Nathanael Greene, commanding on Long Island, became ill soon after and was unable to handle his assignment, Washington selected Sullivan to take the post until Greene could resume his duties. Sullivan had Washington's confidence, but Joseph Reed, the adjutant general, disapproved, claiming that Sullivan had no knowledge of the area.[3] Israel Putnam also disapproved because he had wished the assignment for himself.

When Sullivan reached Brooklyn, which the Americans had been fortifying, he found a series of redoubts and entrenchments running on his right from the marsh at the head of Gowanus Creek to the swamp at the edge of Wallabout Bay on his left. The direction of these works from the creek to the bay was southwest to northeast, covering about a mile. The strategic significance of the area was obvious since the heights in Brooklyn controlled the East River and New York City. About a mile and a half beyond the fortifications ran a ridge of hills, covered with thick woods, from the east side of the Narrows opposite Staten Island in a northeast direction for about five or six miles. Four roads penetrated the hills to the plain beyond. One, the Gowanus Road, went toward the Narrows. The next route, the Flatbush Road, was the main artery from Brooklyn through the ridge to Flatbush. The third one, the Bedford or Clove Road, ran from Bedford also to Flatbush. The fourth route, the Jamaica Road, from which the other three roads branched, led from Brooklyn through Bedford and eventually, about four miles from the fortifications, went through a low pass at the easterly end of the hills to Jamaica.[4]

On August 22 the British landed on Long Island at Gravesend Bay. This was two days after Sullivan had taken over the command from Greene. Some skirmishing occurred, and Washington sent on reinforcements. On August 23 Sullivan's men turned back a British probe at the pass on Bedford Road. The Americans, while chasing the British, burned some buildings which angered General Washington.[5] Apparently Washington had some misgivings about his choice of Sullivan for the Long Island command, for on August 23, after examining the ground for himself, he sent Israel Putnam to the island to supervise the defenses. He may have feared that Sullivan was too impulsive and might take the offensive whereas Washington preferred to let the British make the moves.[6] The scope of Putnam's command remains unknown.[7] Most likely Sullivan had command outside the Brooklyn defenses, although he denied this later,

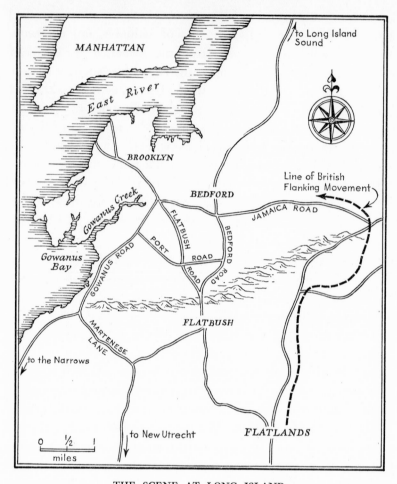

THE SCENE AT LONG ISLAND

Adapted from *A Book of Old Maps,* by Emerson Fite and Archibald Freeman
(Harvard University Press, 1926)

claiming that Lord Stirling had the honor, and that he had command within the lines under Putnam, but probably his memory
tricked him.[8] The confusion over responsibilities of the command on Long Island partially accounts for the disaster which
was to follow, since Putnam's and Sullivan's duties had not been
properly spelled out.[9]

The immediate problem facing the commanding officer on

Long Island was to defend the passes against any British move. The orders issued by Sullivan for August 23 indicate that regiments were being placed at the passes on Gowanus, Flatbush, and Bedford Roads.[10] In these orders he made no mention of the easterly pass on the Jamaica Road, the route of the eventual British attack, but later Sullivan claimed that he had posted a mounted patrol there at his own expense.[11] Although he did not know the terrain, at least General Sullivan recognized the significance of the Jamaica Road, and this admission caused him later embarrassment.

Colonel Samuel Miles's regiment, which had been posted on the Bedford Road, was the American unit farthest to the left or east. A number of years after the war, Miles claimed that Sullivan did not issue him a single order for four days, and that when Sullivan visited him on August 26 the general showed no interest in further protection on the left but rather devoted his attention to strengthening the redoubt before Flatbush village.[12] In the evening, during the same day, Washington, Putnam, and Sullivan rode to the front near Flatbush and examined the positions.[13] Washington's tour convinced him an attack was imminent, and he thought it best to continue stationing men on the roads leading from the British encampment to annoy the enemy when they marched.[14] Since Washington was on the line the eve of the battle, it is fair to assume that the defensive positions satisfied him. The generals saw the enemy striking their tents and evidently awaited a frontal attack. They had about 800 men at each of the three passes from the Bedford Road to the west, and east of the Bedford Road was Colonel Miles, who was expected to watch for British moves in that direction.[15] The orders of the 25th placed Lord Stirling in command of the American forces in the front line on the right along the harbor shore and also in command of the reserves.[16] Sullivan, himself, would take command of the center at Flatbush Pass. The defenders awaited the British move.

Toward morning of August 27 Sullivan knew that an engagement had begun. Earlier, at about 3:00 A.M., Putnam had informed Lord Stirling that the enemy was advancing from Flatbush toward the Red Lion Inn near Gowanus Bay. Was this the anticipated attack? By daylight Stirling was marching toward action with Haslet's and Smallwood's regiments. About one-half mile from the inn he met Atlee with his regiment; there he sighted the enemy between him and the Red Lion. At that time Stirling placed his forces and awaited the British assault under the notorious General Grant. In all there were about 3,500 American troops on the front.[17]

Just when Sullivan went to the front is unknown, but it must have been at some time after 8:00 A.M. One account says he sent down the Flatbush Road for information about the British activities, which might imply he was not at his post as soon as he should have been.[18] Sullivan later said he was to have commanded under Putnam within the lines and that, worried about the road along which he expected the enemy to come, he went to the front near Flatbush to reconnoiter.[19] When Sullivan wrote this statement, in 1777, he obviously meant that he expected an attack along the Jamaica Road, which is exactly where one did materialize. But was he expecting such an attack on Jamaica Road as he rode to the front on the clear, cool morning of August 27? It is possible that he did consider the importance of the road. It is also possible that the importance loomed in his mind only after the attack occurred. Perhaps that morning he thought the main assault was already unfolding against Stirling, and might soon commence against his center position, since the Hessians opposite him under General von Heister had approached and had been cannonading since daybreak.[20] Most likely Sullivan had confidence in Colonel Miles on his left and thought Miles would be able to patrol the area adequately. Also Sullivan had a party of five watching in the vicinity of Jamaica Road. To have maintained a permanent post at the Jamaica Pass would have been hazardous, since it was four miles from the Brooklyn lines, the only point of retreat, and two and a half miles through the woods from Bedford Pass.[21] Sullivan evidently assumed that Miles's detachment plus the patrol of five could give ample warning if the British moved in that direction.

On his way to the front, Sullivan heard that the main body of enemy was moving against Stirling on the Yellow Hook Road. He therefore hastened another battalion to aid Stirling.[22] Soon after he must have started to reconnoiter near Flatbush Pass.[23] What were the conditions at Flatbush Pass when Sullivan arrived on the scene? Near the junction of the Flatbush Road and the Port Road, which led from the Gowanus Road toward Flatbush Pass, stood the American center. Here was a redoubt which menaced the approach up the slope from Flatbush village.[24] Behind a line of abatis, under fire from the Hessians, the Americans waited for the enemy to come. At about 8:30 A.M. shots were audible from the direction of Bedford and the American left.[25] What Sullivan at one time had anticipated had now occurred. The British had flanked the American left, and had advanced on the Jamaica Road to Bedford. They were approaching on the American rear! Immediately the previous evening's activities in the British camp witnessed by the American generals became meaningful. The men seen withdrawing from Flatbush were under Lord Cornwallis, and had drawn back to Flatlands. At 9:00 P.M. British Light-Dragoons and a brigade of Light Infantry under Lieutenant-General Henry Clinton started the march through the new lots to the easterly end of the ridge. Following Clinton came Lord Cornwallis, then the main body under Lord Percy, accompanied by General Howe.[26] In all close to 10,000 troops were on this march. One of Clinton's patrols captured Sullivan's puny patrol of five and learned that the pass on Jamaica Road was unguarded. Howe had meant to turn the American left wing and had accomplished the flanking movement unopposed. The British Light Infantry and Light-Dragoons turned toward the woody ridge to oppose the retreating Americans from the left, who had finally dis-

covered that they were flanked.[27] Other British pushed on toward the Gowanus Road to block retreat from the American
center and right.

While the British were completing their surprise, Sullivan
probably was somewhere eastward of the redoubt at Flatbush
Pass reconnoitering with a picket of 400 men. Shortly after the
first shooting, at 9:00 A.M. came the report of two enemy signal
guns, likewise from the vicinity of Bedford.[28] The turning of
the American left was completed. Grant's assault upon Stirling
had been designed to absorb the Americans' attention until the
British reached Bedford. Now the Hessians, who had been cannonading from the plain before Flatbush Pass, began their onslaught against Sullivan's position at the center of the line. Colonel von Donop led his Yagers and Grenadiers in the first attack
on the ridge. With flags flying and bands playing, General von
Heister also moved forward up the slope.[29] To the rear of the
Americans were the British, and approaching from the front
were the Hessians.

Confusion ruled, and the ensuing events on Sullivan's portion of the field are in limbo. Most probably Sullivan and his
picket of 400 men were still somewhere east of Flatbush Pass
when the brunt of the attack from both British and Hessians
was felt. Already the regiments under Miles, Samuel Wyllys,
and Solomon Willis on the left were in retreat, trying to break
through the British standing between them and Brooklyn. Since
Sullivan was later captured probably at a spot east of Flatbush
Road, it is reasonable to assume he was unable to return to the
main body of his men at the center.[30]

Shortly Sullivan's men and the entire American front, except for Stirling's wing, were in precipitate flight. Pursued by
the Hessians, who gave little quarter, the Americans fled in confusion. But the British troops were the deciding factor, and it is
they who routed the Americans. The moment the Americans
fired the British pressed with bayonets before the rebels could
reload.[31] Each little group, isolated by the British and Hessians,

had to contend for itself. The main body of Sullivan's men retreated along the Port Road, since Flatbush Road was cut, and
those who were able to break through crossed Gowanus Creek
and made their way to the lines. Sullivan, however, was forced
to the plains most likely somewhere east of the Flatbush Road.[32]
Here he and his men waged a gallant fight. "What Resistance I
made," he later wrote, "with those 400 Men against the British
Army, I leave to the Officers who were with me to declare. Let
it suffice for me to say the opposition of the small Party lasted
from half past nine to twelve O'Clock." [33] At about noon, therefore, Sullivan was captured. A Hessian account records that he
was found hidden in a corn field by three Hessian fusiliers.[34]
Lewis Morris, Jr., wrote, "the last I heard of him, he was in a
corn Field close by our Lines with a Pistol in each Hand, and
the Enemy had formed a Line each side of him, and he was going directly between them.[35]

The battle soon ended. Stirling likewise became a captive
after his men had fought bravely against overwhelming odds.
Howe chose not to press his advantage, and Washington managed to retreat from Long Island to Manhattan. The few reports
from the regiments under Sullivan's command indicate that
many of his men made their way to safety. Their unfortunate
leader, however, not only was a captive but also was destined to
face criticism later on. "Upon the whole, less Generalship never
was shown in any Army since the Art of War was understood." [36] So wrote Lieutenant-Colonel Daniel Brodhead, one of
the participants, angered over Sullivan's charge that Colonel
Miles's failure to be aware of the British flanking movement was
responsible for the debacle. Brodhead replied that if Sullivan
and the other generals had been as vigilant as Miles, all might
have ended well.[37]

Was Sullivan responsible for the turning of the American
left? This is a question not easy to answer as it really hinges
upon the question of command. Did he have command outside
of the lines of the Brooklyn defenses? Probably yes, as already

mentioned. He realized the importance of Jamaica Road and made an error in judgment when he thought Miles's regiment and the patrol of five would be adequate. Certainly Miles accused Sullivan of negligence, but his criticism must be tempered because he was trying to counter an accusation made against himself.[38]

Washington must accept some blame. Because he had been at the front the night of the 26th, the measures taken for defense must have met with his approval. The entire concept of holding the ridge with attenuated forces against odds was questionable. Cavalry was needed. The patrol was inadequate, and here the militarily naive Sullivan must shoulder blame along with his Commander-in-Chief.[39] Perhaps the fact that he wrote no detailed defense of his action, to our knowledge—a practice to which he resorted when criticized at other times—indicates that garrulous John Sullivan was somewhat at a loss for words on this occasion. As he put it, "General Howe was too old for us." [40] Washington, Sullivan, and the others had been badly outgeneraled.

Had Howe been more ambitious for a quick victory, he might have nipped the revolt in the bud, but fortunately for the patriots William Howe chose the cautious road. Meanwhile Sullivan would have to bide some time as a prisoner of the British. His captors, delighted by their luck, described the reluctant guest. Frederick MacKenzie wrote in his diary: "Sullivan was bred to the law, and is said to be one of their best officers. He is a short-set, rough, ill-looking fellow." [41] Colonel von Heeringen called Sullivan a "man of genius." [42] The British took both Sullivan and Stirling aboard Lord Richard Howe's ship where they received the polite treatment so typical of eighteenth-century warfare. Every day they dined with Lord Howe, who was most anxious to serve as conciliator between the mother country and her rebellious colonies. He hoped, yet with little optimism, to bring the conflict to a speedy and amicable close.[43] Howe, assisted by his secretary Ambrose Serle, pointed out to the captives that England wanted a peaceful settlement, and evidently their persuasive ways bore fruit. At first the Americans argued that Great Britain wanted only colonial submission, but that America was much too strong to be forced to knuckle under. But the Britishers persisted and gradually Sullivan and Stirling "came down vastly in their Style & Air." [44] Lord Howe, if a later account of Sullivan's may be believed, spoke tellingly of his desire for peace and that his instructions allowed both him and his brother to settle matters between England and America. He wished to converse with Washington, or some members of Congress, on the possibility of arriving at some settlement, but since he could not recognize anyone as a member of Congress, he suggested that he meet the delegates as private gentlemen. [45]

Sullivan went for the bait. On the morning of August 30, while on parole, he entered the American lines to seek Washington's permission to travel to Philadelphia and relay Howe's instructions and desire for a talk. Rather reluctantly Washington gave his approval, but Sullivan failed to sense Washington's hesitancy. The permission itself was enough to remove all doubt in Sullivan's mind about the propriety of going to Congress. There was no reason for delay, and off he went. [46] His haste was understandable, for Howe was suggesting that Sullivan and Stirling be exchanged for two British officers. [47] On September 2 Sullivan gave a verbal report to Congress in which he stressed that both Lord Howe and William Howe had full power to negotiate. Sullivan went on to say that Lord Howe opposed the British taxation measures and thought the British had no right to interfere with American internal polity. [48] This was an important concession, and Congress asked Sullivan to submit his account in writing, which he did on the next day. His written report, however, made no mention of Lord Howe's denial that the British could interfere in American internal affairs, an omission that disturbed John Adams. [49] The members of Congress were not so gullible as the captured general; Howe's murmurings of peace did not convince them, and Adams was furious. During Sullivan's talk to the delegates, Adams leaned over to Benjamin Rush and remarked that he wished "the first ball that had been fired on the day of the defeat of our Army had gone through his [Sullivan's] head." He called Sullivan a "decoy duck whom Lord Howe has sent among us to seduce us into a renunciation of our independence." [50]

The unwitting Sullivan had opened Pandora's Box. If Congress did not sound out Howe, then many could say the rebels wanted nothing but further bloodshed.[51] Congress was not happy, but on September 4 that body agreed to comply with Howe's suggestion that Sullivan and Stirling be exchanged, and on September 5 resolved that Howe be informed by General Sullivan that Congress could not send members to confer with him privately, but that the delegates would send a committee to see whether Howe had any authority to treat with persons authorized by Congress. The members also went on record as opposing any overtures for peace unless submitted in writing and addressed to Congress. The delegates wanted to be recognized by Great Britain as being a legitimate body, and they wanted to avoid any similar embarrassment which Sullivan's errand had produced.[52] Sullivan, thinking that he had accomplished wonders, returned to his captors in blissful ignorance, but his hopes for peace were quickly shattered. Howe did meet a committee on Staten Island and claimed Sullivan had misquoted him by telling Congress that Parliament would give up taxation and control of internal polity. Howe's insistence that the Declaration of Independence must be rescinded before he could grant peace doomed the abortive efforts for reconciliation.[53]

Sullivan's role in these proceedings do not place him in the best of light, and his actions are not consistent with his earlier fiery ways. A desire to seek an honorable peace, however, is never censurable, and at this early stage of the war many did wish to return under British hegemony provided there were some concessions. It is hard to believe that Sullivan did want return of British control. His fault was gullibility. The suave Howe had painted too attractive a picture, and Sullivan, who never objected to being in the center of the stage, was willing to be his errand boy and try to do his part in bringing about a satisfactory conclusion to the conflict. But the wily, almost cynical, John Adams was not charitable in his observations:

The conduct of General Sullivan, in consenting to come to Philadelphia, upon so confused an errand from Lord Howe, though his situation, as a prisoner, was a temptation, and may be considered as some apology for it, appeared to me to betray such want of penetration and fortitude, and there was so little precision in the information he communicated, that I felt much resentment, and more contempt, upon the occasion, than was perhaps just. The time was extremely critical. The attention of Congress, the army, the States, and the people, ought to have been wholly directed to the defense of the country. To have it diverted and relaxed, by such a poor artifice and confused tale, appeared very reprehensible.[54]

General Sullivan's exchange came soon after, and by the end of September he had rejoined Washington's army which was hanging on to the northern tip of Manhattan at Fort Washington and Kingsbridge. On October 18 the army moved northward, leaving a strong garrison at Fort Washington. Sullivan's division took part in the flurries between Pell's Point and New Rochelle and at Chatterton's Hill near White Plains. Then he withdrew his division to North Castle where it was placed under Charles Lee's command.

William Howe, recently honored with the Order of the Bath for his victory at Long Island, turned his attention to Fort Washington and then New Jersey. This occasioned Washington to strike across New Jersey toward Philadelphia. The news was bad. Fort Washington had fallen, and Fort Lee had to be abandoned. Washington's men tumbled pell-mell toward the Delaware, and frantic word went to Lee to join the Commander-in-Chief. General Washington wanted Lee to hurry for he could not believe that Howe would close the campaign for the season. But the enigmatic Lee, accompanied by Sullivan, was in no hurry. At first he had been reluctant to leave his post, thinking it essential to protect New England; then when he did move, he lingered, always with the hope that he might aim a blow at the British.[55] On the night of December 12 Lee left his troops under Sullivan's command in Vealtown, near Morristown, New Jersey, and rode to nearby Basking Ridge for comfortable lodgings. General Lee's night may have been pleasantly spent at the Widow White's tavern, but the next morning brought only chagrin when he found himself surrounded by a party of British and became a prisoner of war. Sullivan heard the news that morning when Lee's aide, Major William Bradford, rode up to tell of the general's capture. Upon hearing the report "Sullivan rode through the line giving orders, to show that we still had a commander left, and did not appear to regret the loss of Lee." [56] Once General Sullivan realized that he had no chance of rescuing his superior, he did not hesitate to move; he pressed his men toward the Delaware and junction with Washington.[57]

By December 20 Sullivan had joined Washington above Trenton Falls.[58] The days ahead would test the mettle of the Americans, for the prospects were not auspicious. Yet the tide was to turn in their favor for the moment, and now Sullivan was to get his chance to redeem himself after the shambles on Long Island. General Washington wished to hit at the enemy in New Jersey, and Sullivan would be with him. By December 23 Washington had made his decision to attack Trenton where 1,400 Hessians were stationed under Colonel Johann Gottlieb Rall.[59] The plan was to have the main body under Sullivan and Nathanael Greene accompany Washington and attack before dawn on December 26, 1776.[60]

Sullivan had an important role in the approaching battle. Washington hoped to have the men over the river by midnight in order to attack before daylight, but ice impeded the crossing, and it was not until about 4:00 A.M. that the soldiers were in the line of march. A winter's storm raged, with the wind whipping the men's backs. Sullivan's division was to move along the lower or River Road toward Trenton, whereas Greene's division, accompanied by Washington, was to follow the upper or Pennington Road. Washington had ordered each division to force the outguard, then push directly into town endeavoring to crush the enemy before they had a chance to form. Sullivan was to hit the town from the south and Greene from the north. At Trenton the Delaware makes a slight turn from the southeast to the south, and running across the southern edge of the town toward the Delaware was the Assunpink Creek. A bridge across the creek, which James Ewing was counted upon to seize, led to Bordentown and provided possible escape. King Street, and to its east, Queen Street, ran north through the town for about half a mile until they ran into Pennington Road which entered Trenton from the northwest. Sullivan's line of advance was to place him at the southern end of town near the Assunpink Bridge, and Greene's was to take him to the head of King and Queen Streets.[61]

The men moved out. With Sullivan were the brigades of General Arthur St. Clair, Colonels John Glover and Paul Dudley Sargent, plus four batteries each led by a captain.[62] When the roads diverged, each division plodded along in the darkness, hoping to coordinate an attack soon after dawn. After a short halt, the men under Sullivan pushed on. Daylight came, and the storm now beat in the faces of the weary but hopeful soldiers. It was about 8:00 A.M. when firing was heard from the direction of the northern end of town indicating that Greene's van was on the attack. Three minutes later Sullivan's advance guard engaged the Hessian picket on the outskirts of Trenton on River Road and pressed it toward the town.[63] The picket retired, then stood for one volley, but, having no bayonets, the picket hastened by way of Front Street in the direction of Assunpink Bridge. Meanwhile the left wing of the Americans was hammering its way toward the mouth of the Pennington Road at the head of King Street.[64]

Artillery was soon brought into play, commanded the Hes-

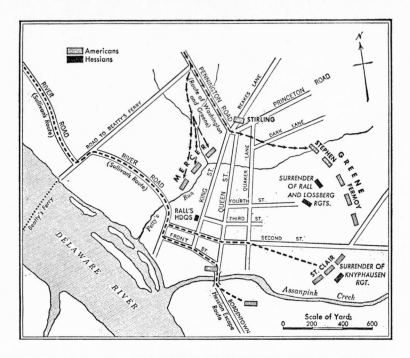

THE SCENE AT TRENTON
Reproduced from *Appeal to Arms*, by Willard M. Wallace (1951),
by permission of Harper & Brothers

sian position, and "in the twinkling of an eye, cleared the streets." [65] Small wonder that the startled Hessians were indecisive with the cannonading from the head of King and Queen Streets, with Sullivan's men hitting the southern part of town, and with Hugh Mercer, after deploying from the left wing, pressing in from the west. Some were able to flee over the Assunpink, because Ewing had failed to cross the Delaware and cut off the bridge, but the Americans were able to block any escape from the upper end of Trenton toward Princeton.[66] In Sullivan's sector, Stark, dealing "death wherever he found resistance," led his regiment at the head of St. Clair's brigade, with Moulder's battery, along Second Street toward the Von Knyphausen Regiment.[67] General Sullivan, with the rest of the first division, proceeded to Front Street, detached a group to seize the barracks, and then went toward Queen Street with hopes of closing off the bridge as an avenue of escape.[68]

The Von Knyphausen Regiment, under command of Major Friedrich Ludwig von Dechow, was unable to hold Sullivan's men from cutting off the bridge. In confusion the Hessians retreated before Sullivan and St. Clair eastward of the town just north of the creek. Soon General Sullivan, now placed at the intersection of Queen and Front, noticed the wounded Major von Dechow approaching him with the assistance of a corporal. The Hessian officer surrendered himself but not his regiment, which he had turned over to Captain Bernhard von Biesenrodt, who, in spite of von Dechow's desires, chose not to give up.[69] Captain von Biesenrodt, however, could not continue his heroics, and shortly Major James Wilkinson brought word to Sullivan that Von Biesenrodt had surrendered to St. Clair. This marked the end of the battle, since the other two regiments fighting toward the northern end of the town had given up to Washington moments before. This needed victory for the Americans over the Hessians had taken just thirty to forty-five minutes. The courageous Rall, a drunkard, had been negligent to an incredible extent, but the Hessian commander, who died from wounds received during the battle, never faced the court martial he so assuredly deserved.

The Battle of Trenton was the first encounter during the Revolution in which Sullivan enjoyed success. He must have been jubilant and anxious for another tussle with the enemy. Washington, now back in Pennsylvania, did not disappoint him, because he shortly decided to cross the Delaware once again to "beat up the rest of their Quarters bordering on and near the River." [70] He moved on December 30. This new thrust presented ticklish problems, because the British were assembling a force at Princeton. Washington chose to gather his forces at Trenton in preparation for a contest. As expected, on January 2, 1777, the British and Hessians under Cornwallis advanced toward Trenton, the head of the column reaching there about

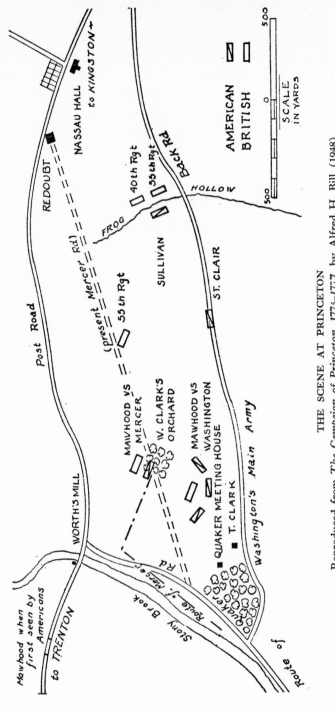

THE SCENE AT PRINCETON

Reproduced from *The Campaign of Princeton, 1776–1777*, by Alfred H. Bill (1948), by permission of Princeton University Press

4:00 P.M. Sullivan was among those Americans who harassed the enemy during their march from Maidenhead, which is now Lawrenceville. This delaying action allowed Washington's men to place themselves south of the Assunpink Creek, a risky spot because it might become a cul-de-sac. Darkness fell, and Cornwallis showed the same indecisiveness that plagued Sir William Howe's American career. His men were tired; he would bag Washington, "the fox," the next day![71]

A hasty Council held at St. Clair's headquarters determined to march at once, outflank the British, and proceed to Princeton. While campfires burned to delude the enemy into believing the American army remained in its position across the creek, the tired men during the early hours of January 3 moved in silence. If Cornwallis knew the Americans were leaving, he did nothing about it.[72] It was a motley group that marched—"half-starved, half-frozen, feeble, worn out men, with old fowling pieces for muskets, and half of them without bayonets." [73] Sullivan was placed somewhere toward the front. Washington planned to enter Princeton by a back road, which would enable him to turn the British, who had thrown up defenses only in the area of the Post Road leading from Princeton to Trenton. The army crossed Stony Brook, south of Princeton, at Quaker Bridge. The men followed the brook until they came to the Quaker Meeting House. At this point Sullivan wheeled his division to the right and took the back road toward the town. Hugh Mercer with about 350 men continued along the brook toward Worth's Mills, where they planned to cut off the bridge at the Post Road, which would prevent a retreat to Trenton and hinder any attempt by Cornwallis to come to the rescue.[74]

The morning was bright and cold, possibly another victory loomed ahead. As Sullivan's column slogged along the back road, Major Wilkinson glanced over his shoulder toward the west. There, across Stony Brook, moving up a hill in the direction of Trenton were some British soldiers. They saw the rebel forces at about the same time, for they turned and hastened back toward the bridge and Princeton. Later the Americans learned that these men were the 17th and 55th regiments, plus some Light Horse, on their way to Maidenhead, all under the command of Colonel Charles Mawhood. The 55th had lagged behind the 17th so that they were nearer Princeton, and Mawhood sent them word to scramble back into town to assist the 40th regiment, the sole force left there.[75] Sullivan, with the van, was well along the back road when he heard fighting. Mercer had been intercepted by Mawhood, but Sullivan could not return to help because the 55th Regiment had gained the heights between the Post Road and his position on the back road. Neither the 55th nor Sullivan could move for fear of exposing their flanks to the other. The fighting was fierce, and the British were routed only after Washington and Daniel Hitchcock came up from the rear. It was a costly struggle; the men were badly mauled, and the gallant Hugh Mercer was fatally wounded.[76]

When Mawhood's defeat became obvious, the 55th hurried to Princeton to join the 40th Regiment. Sullivan's men chased the British away from a ravine where they first had stationed themselves, and pursued them into the college yard. At this point some of the British surrendered to Sullivan; others who had sought shelter in Nassau Hall soon gave up when the artillery opened fire.[77] Washington then pushed on in the direction of Morristown hoping that from there he might be able to drive the British from New Jersey. He would like to have moved directly against Brunswick, but wisely decided that his men had had enough action.[78] At perhaps no other point during the war had the forces under Washington performed so brilliantly as during the days from December 26, 1776, through January 3, 1777. From a position where defeat seemed imminent Washington and his lieutenants had turned the tide. He had found in Sullivan a brave and tireless fighter.

IV: NEW JERSEY TO BRANDYWINE

$\mathcal{S}$*ullivan* entered the year 1777 with high hopes, particularly after the dazzling success at Trenton and Princeton. The nightmare of Canada and the debacle at Long Island were tucked away in the past; John Sullivan looked forward to new action. But now the rigors of winter were upon both armies, and Washington settled into safe quarters in the hills of Morristown, while the British occupied Brunswick and Amboy. Howe himself chose to remain in more comfortable surroundings in New York. The year 1776 had drawn to a close, but the campaign of 1777 was far in the offing.

The first part of 1777 was irksome to the New Hampshire general. Pained by illness, disturbed by lack of action, approached by the enemy, and engaged in controversy, John Sullivan found that the year's auspicious start was beginning to dull. He suffered from a digestive disorder during the winter, a chronic illness that bothered him on other occasions throughout his military career.[1] He received leave to return to his home for a while, but the trip was spoiled by news that Arthur St. Clair had been put in command at Ticonderoga, an assignment which Sullivan had coveted for himself.[2] The general, feeling slighted, wrote Washington a whining letter because he had gained no separate command. Telling his commander-in-chief that he should have been sent to Ticonderoga, he asked him to enumerate his failings "That I may Rid the Continent of an officer who is unworthy to Trust with command."[3] Washington rebuked the irate Sullivan, referring to "imaginary Slights." "No other

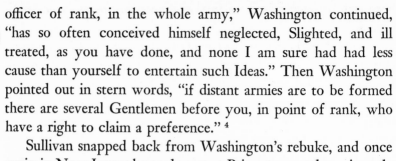

officer of rank, in the whole army," Washington continued, "has so often conceived himself neglected, Slighted, and ill treated, as you have done, and none I am sure had had less cause than yourself to entertain such Ideas." Then Washington pointed out in stern words, "if distant armies are to be formed there are several Gentlemen before you, in point of rank, who have a right to claim a preference." [4]

Sullivan snapped back from Washington's rebuke, and once again in New Jersey he took post at Princeton, ready to impede the enemy troops should they move toward the Delaware, or follow them should they march toward the Hudson. During June the British made a clumsy attempt to win Sullivan over to their side. General Sullivan was affected only indirectly, since the proposal was intercepted by Philip Schuyler and never did reach him. Peter Livius, who had known Sullivan in New Hampshire before the war, wrote him an anonymous letter from Montreal on June 2, urging him to retrace the steps he had taken in the revolutionary cause. His letter warned Sullivan of all the risks he was taking as an active participant in revolt; only ignominy and misery could result.[5] Undoubtedly aware that Sullivan had gone to Congress at Lord Howe's request the previous autumn, Livius had hopes that the New Hampshire man might waver. Burgoyne was about to start his march south, the British administration had picked out Sullivan as one who might be won over, and apparently the British thought Sullivan was in command at Ticonderoga.[6] Livius suggested that Sullivan's assistance be secretly given until the time when Sullivan would be able to bring all of New Hampshire with him back into the fold, a ridiculous presumption. Schuyler caught the messenger who was carrying this fanciful suggestion and then bungled the matter by sending a reply as though it came from Sullivan. When Sullivan heard through General Washington of Livius's overtures, he agreed to play along if it would help the cause, but he was unenthusiastic. Schuyler's letter to Livius had already been sent, however, and no further communications came from Canada.[7]

General Sullivan's ire over his failure to get the Ticonderoga post increased when he learned sometime during June that a Frenchman, Philippe du Coudray, had been promised a major-general's commission by Silas Deane, and command of the artillery and engineers. His sole superiors would be Washington and Congress. This time Sullivan had company in his complaints, for both Nathanael Greene and Henry Knox were furious. All three, angered at being outranked, chose to resign. Sullivan penned a curt note to John Hancock, president of Congress: "if This Report be True I Shall be under the Disagreeable necessity of Quitting the Service." [8] Congress did not like being dictated to by the three generals, but neither were the members anxious to lose their services. Nor was Congress happy over the arrangement with Du Coudray, but to back down on Deane's commitment now that Sullivan, Greene, and Knox were complaining would look as though Congress were abdicating control. The resignations were not accepted, but the hoped-for apology from the three generals never came.[9] The controversy revealed that the system of recruiting foreigners often meant injustice to the American officers, and that a sizable schism separated the general officers from Congress. The young, rebellious nation faced the problem of civilian control over military control during enemy occupation. At all times Congress maintained its authority; often, however, Sullivan questioned the ability of Congress to direct the war effort. During the summer Du Coudray's future plagued the American Congress, a problem removed only by his tragic drowning in September.

During this bickering Sullivan's illness became more bothersome. The symptoms indicate that he suffered from a peptic ulcer, certainly understandable in a man so excitable and mercurial as he. He complained to Washington that he bled on numerous occasions, and that the physician had cautioned him against solid food and alcohol. He wrote: "Spirits I must never again use but with the greatest Caution (if at all) as he (the Doctor) Conceives that the free use of them has in great measure assisted in bringing on my Complaint & if continued will always have the Same Effect." [10] His delightful threat to abstain from "spirits" was no more than a threat, for throughout Sullivan's life he drank, and William Plumer wrote that toward the end of it "he indulged too freely." [11] Washington hoped the physician's advice would soon bring Sullivan back to good health, but many other matters took the time of the Commander-in-Chief.

The summer was wearing on, and Howe's intentions could not be fathomed. In addition to being on edge over Howe's plans, the Americans faced the threat of Burgoyne's march from the north. The American task was complicated by St. Clair's evacuation of Ticonderoga, news of which reached Washington in the middle of July. Sullivan should have thanked the fates that he had not been put in command at Ticonderoga, for surely he would have fared no better than St. Clair. Yet John Sullivan chose to take a backhanded slap at the unfortunate Arthur St. Clair. He used the Livius episode as a chance to argue that the northern posts should be "in the hands of those who have the greatest attachment and the strongest ties to bind them to the cause of their country." [12] Sullivan had his comments published, and naturally they did not go unnoticed by St. Clair, who asked Sullivan to explain the insinuation that he had not been trustworthy for the Ticonderoga command.[13] Unfortunately Sullivan's reply, insofar as is known, does not exist. Soon, however, he had troubles of his own, for a few days earlier he had chosen to attack the British and loyalists on Staten Island. To his chagrin the attack failed. He had to face severe criticism, and the friends of General St. Clair were to have some revenge at Sullivan's expense.

Sullivan believed that he had reason enough for ordering the raid on Staten Island. The enemy had been sending small parties to harass the inhabitants along the Jersey shore and had seized some cattle. Sullivan made his plans for reprisal with the utmost secrecy, but British intelligence was aware that some activity was in the offing.[14] On August 21 he set out for Elizabethtown with men from William Smallwood's and Prudhomme de Borre's brigades, in addition to a group under the command of Colonel Matthias Ogden. Sullivan knew that the enemy forces were scattered at various embarkation points on the island and along the shore in the direction of Amboy.[15] He planned to cross his men at two different spots, hit the enemy units simultaneously at the embarkation points, then consolidate his force to meet those enemy units nearer Amboy. At first the raid, carried out on the morning of August 22, met with some success; but, as the morning wore on, the Americans began to face troubles. Strict discipline had not been maintained, and the men instead had straggled and had sought plunder. The attempt to cross back to New Jersey was accompanied by chaos. Enough boats were not available because the crossing back occurred at a different place from where the men had come over to Staten Island earlier in the morning and because those men bringing the boats to the new spot confused a boatload of Americans for British and so delayed. Confusion dominated the embarkation point at the Old Blazing Star Ferry. In spite of Sullivan's orders some of the cattle that had been plundered were carried across, and the picket left as rear guard to protect the crossing soon had to surrender.[16]

Sullivan, who had returned in an earlier boat for New Jersey to supervise activities on that shore, estimated his losses at about 10 killed, 15 wounded, and almost 140 captured. The Americans had seized about the same number, and Sullivan claimed enemy killed and wounded would total close to 400 men, much too high an estimate.[17] The execution of the raid had not measured up to the conception. In many ways the attack showed Sullivan at his best, both daring and imaginative, for at other times he lacked both initiative and imagination in handling the problems of command, but on this occasion he threw caution to the wind and almost achieved a brilliant success. But his men were tired and had not had enough rest before crossing to Staten Island. Lack of discipline made a shambles of the efforts on the island, and failure to have enough boats on hand for the trip back to New Jersey sealed the raid's doom. The misfortune which accompanied Sullivan's endeavors throughout his military career continued to plague him on August 22.

On the very day of the Staten Island raid Washington had written Sullivan from Bucks County in Pennsylvania ordering him to join his army, since he had learned William Howe was in the Chesapeake.[18] General Washington marched south through Philadelphia to meet the invading army moving north from Head of Elk, and by early September Sullivan was with him in Wilmington. Washington talked with him about the Staten Island assault and told him that some military inquiry would be necessary. Sullivan recognized that he would have to face the music, but he asked for delay so that he might call upon the testimony of William Smallwood, who by now was in Maryland.[19] Any Court of Inquiry would have to be delayed anyway, for as Howe pushed on in his usual lackadaisical fashion, the Americans had to look about and prepare to seek battle with the invader, whose goal was Philadelphia.

The stand would be made at the Brandywine, a narrow river of many fords, which, after its east and west branches come together about seven miles northwest of Wilmington, flows in a southeasterly direction parallel with the Schuylkill into the Delaware. Once again Washington was ordering Sullivan to carry out a key assignment—command of the right wing. By September 9 Washington had moved most of his force to the east side of the river and had taken post on the high grounds near Chad's Ford.[20] Sullivan, who would be commanding the right above Chad's Ford, came to Washington's Headquarters on the night of the 10th for his instructions. He was told to position himself at Brinton's Ford, just above Chad's Ford, and

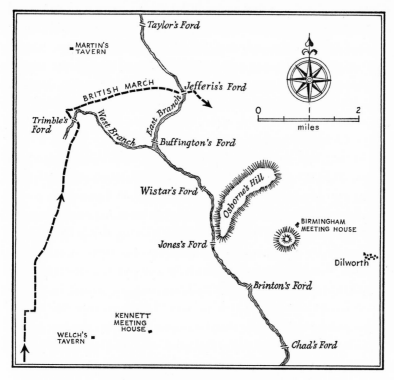

THE SCENE AT BRANDYWINE

Adapted from *The Marquis de La Fayette in the American Revolution,*
by Charlemagne Tower (Lippincott, 1901)

to send parties to the north as far as Buffington's Ford, which
was at the fork where the east and west branches of the Brandywine met. Sullivan had not as yet examined the ground for himself and asked Washington whether there were any fords beyond Buffington's. He got incorrect information that there was
none for twelve miles, and that any crossing made at that point
by the enemy would necessitate "a Long Circuit Through a
very Bad Road." [21] He was told not to worry about the fords to
the north of the junction, therefore, since light horse were reconnoitering in that direction to warn of any surprise flanking
move. The Americans rapidly were lulling themselves into a
sense of false security.

The morning of Thursday, September 11, found Washington's men awaiting the next move from the British, who were encamped near Kennett Square. As morning dawned, a heavy fog rolled over the countryside, a prelude to disaster. Sometime after 8:00 A.M. the Battle of the Brandywine began when British troops, supported by cannonading, engaged units under William Maxwell on the west side of the stream near Chad's Ford. Sullivan, impatiently waiting in his sector for the events to unfold, had to bide his time while he listened to the noise of artillery puncturing the sky below him. He was expecting a British flanking move, at least so he later claimed, but unfortunately he did not take the initiative to scout the ground beyond the fork. Instead he relied upon the light horse that were meant to be in that direction. But he thought some flanking move was coming, because at two separate times during the morning he sent word on to Washington, once that he expected it, and later that Colonel Moses Hazen reported it actually was occurring. Two messengers were sent on to Washington with this information: Lewis Morris, Jr., and John Eustace.[22] Eustace later commented that both Washington and Henry Knox laughed when he brought in the information that the enemy intended to turn the right flank. The laughter probably indicated that they thought Howe was committing an error by dividing his force. Washington most likely had already received similar intelligence from Lieutenant-Colonel James Ross, who reported that an enemy force was on the road leading to Taylor's and Jefferis's Fords, both north of Buffington's.[23] Since Washington believed incorrectly that this march would take the enemy at least twelve miles north of the fork, he thought he had a perfect opportunity. He must take advantage of Howe's daring risk. He would have time to strike at the force opposite him at Chad's Ford, then regroup and wait for the blow from this reported flanking movement. Washington was making a bad error, for he was relying upon inadequate intelligence. Whether Sullivan knew of Ross's report remains unknown. Certainly if he had

NEW JERSEY TO BRANDYWINE

seen it, he should have sought out the fords north of the fork to see whether they were as remote as Washington thought. If Ross's report had gone directly to Washington, and the report exists in Washington's papers, obviously the Commander-in-Chief should have informed John Sullivan. One senses paralysis and a lack of coordination between headquarters and the right wing.

Washington made his decision. He would attack. Sullivan got orders that he was to cross with his division and attack the left of the enemy's stationary force, not the flanking force as is commonly assumed.[24] General Washington would cross at Chad's Ford, and Greene and Benjamin Lincoln were to go over with Sullivan. Just as John Sullivan was about to order his men to move, Major Joseph Spear of the Pennsylvania militia rode up with intelligence that there was no sign of the enemy in the vicinity of the branches of the Brandywine. Was the previous activity merely a feint to induce Washington across, then face him not with what he supposed would be merely a segment of the army, but rather with the entire force? Spear's report presented problems, for it ran counter to Sullivan's own opinion and previous intelligence of some flanking march. Yet if Spear were correct, it would be suicidal to attack across the river. The general was in a quandary, but he quickly decided that Washington must have the information immediately.[25] To allay his own doubts he sent a sergeant for more details from the northern direction, then wrote Washington:

Brinton's Ford, 11 September

Since I sent you the message by Major Morris I saw some of the Militia who came in this morning from a tavern called Martins on the forks of the Brandywine. The one who told me, said he had come from thence to Welches Tavern and heard nothing of the Enemy above the forks of the Brandywine and is Confident that [sic] are not in that Quarters. So that Colonel Hazen's Information must be wrong. I have sent to that Quarter to know whether there is any foundation for the Report and shall be glad to give your Ex'y the earliest information.[26]

Sullivan later claimed that he was unwilling to accept Spear's report, although his statement, "So that Colonel Hazen's Information must be wrong," might indicate otherwise. The confirming proof which he sought unfortunately happened to back Spear's account. Sullivan ought to have been more decisive at the time. He was correct in forwarding Spear's account, but he should have told Washington to be wary. Instead he chose to pass the responsibility of evaluating intelligence on to Washington. There is a good chance, though, that General Sullivan accepted Spear's news and was no longer so sure of the flanking march as he later asserted. Spear was sent on to Washington to fill in Sullivan's written report. General Washington dared not order an assault if there were the possibility that the enemy faced him in full strength across the Brandywine. The waiting and cannonading continued.[27]

Close to 2:00 P.M. a messenger rode up to Sullivan with a communication from Colonel Theodorick Bland, who had been sent out earlier by Washington to scout for any flanking. Bland's message was short and alarming:

¼ past one o'clock

Sir,

I have discovered a party of the enemy on the Heights just on the right of the two widows who live close together on the road called the forks road, about half a mile to the Right of the meeting-house. There is a higher hill in their front.[28]

Sullivan hastily scratched a note to Washington:

Dear General   Col⁰ Bland has this moment Sent me word that the Enemy are in the Rear of my Right about two miles Coming Down— there is he Says about two Brigades of them.
2 of Clock p m
he also Says he Saw a Dust Rise back in the Country for above an hour [29]

The inept Americans had allowed Howe to pull off another successful flanking maneuver like the one on Long Island. Once again the rebel wing had been turned. Those men who were responsible for intelligence from Generals Washington and Sullivan on down were at fault. Why did Bland delay his report if, as he says, he saw dust rising for more than an hour? It does seem strange that the first communication to Washington was sent as late as 2:00 P.M., especially since Colonel Elias Dayton, who was on his way, if not already there, to Birmingham Meeting House, northeast of Brinton's Ford, said intelligence received about 1:00 P.M. indicated that the enemy had crossed above. Sullivan appears to have handled his command almost in a daze as he waited for Washington's orders. In spite of his earlier belief that Howe would attempt to flank, it actually happened, and unknown to General Sullivan for sure until too late! [30]

At 2:30 P.M. orders came from Washington for Sullivan, still at Brinton's Ford. He must move his division to join the two divisions under Lord Stirling and Adam Stephen; then with Sullivan in command this force of about 3,000 to 5,000 men must oppose the enemy.[31] General Sullivan was puzzled. Where was the enemy? Unless one knew the ground, Bland's message was vague. By what route were Stirling's and Stephen's divisions joining his troops? At that time he did not know that Washington earlier had ordered them to go to Birmingham Meeting House. Sullivan whirled into motion. He set out in a northerly direction and in less than a mile met Moses Hazen's regiment which had been at Wistar's Ford, three miles above Brinton's.[32] Hazen quickly told Sullivan that the enemy was nipping his heels, and that apparently it was the principal part of the British army. Until Sullivan had talked with Hazen he thought he was moving against just two brigades. Immediately the Americans saw hostile troops in the road about forty rods from the rebel advance guard. Sullivan turned to the right and started to deploy his men when he soon discovered Stirling's and Stephen's troops on a height near Birmingham Meeting House to his rear and right. To join them he had to move his men on a diagonal line toward the hill. First went Hazen, then the artillery, then the rest through a hollow way approaching the height. Sullivan was desperately trying to form his lines before the enemy, already in position, moved into action.[33]

About 7,000 men, perhaps fewer, led by Cornwallis and accompanied by Sir William Howe, faced the Americans. The climax of the Battle of the Brandywine neared. At daybreak, covered by the heavy fog, the British had left Kennett Square and marched north toward the West Branch of the river. Here they crossed at Trimble's Ford, proceeded to Jefferis's Ford on the East Branch, and since 2:30 P.M. had been facing the frantic rebels, who were scurrying to ready themselves for the impending attack. For an hour the enemy fortunately did not move, because Cornwallis wished to give his men some rest after their seventeen-mile march.[34]

This hour of grace, during which Sullivan was moving his men, gave Stirling and Stephen time to form on Meeting House Hill and the immediate vicinity. They were well placed, for the Britisher, Captain John Montresor, noted: "This position of the Enemy was remarkably strong, having a large body advanced, small bodies still further advanced and their Rear covered by a wood wherein their main body was posted with a natural glacis for ¾ of a mile." [35] Sullivan had time to put his men in a line with the other divisions, but half a mile to their left. When it appeared that the British probably would try to flank the Americans' right, Sullivan realized he must close the gap between his men and the other divisions and move all farther to the right. While this shift was occurring, the enemy pressed forward near 3:30 P.M. from Osborne's Hill.[36] Three columns moved out to the tune of the *Grenadiers' March*. As yet Sullivan's division had not formed, and one of General Stephen's brigades was badly placed as a result of the shifting to the right. Certainly by 4:00 P.M. the attack had become general, but still John Sullivan's men were not placed, and the enemy's rapid approach was throwing the division into panic.[37]

Sullivan rode over to the center of the line on the hill to direct the artillery fire, hoping that this would allow his broken troops time to reform to his rear. He wrote that his actions were "all in vain no Sooner did I form one party but that which I had before formed would Run off & Even at times when I though on Horseback and in front of them apprehended no Danger." [38] With faint hopes that the disarranged men might be rallied by their officers, he returned to Meeting House Hill, which commanded both the right and left of the American center. There General Sullivan realized that should the hill be carried, it would mean total rout and would hinder a retreat. Both Stirling and Thomas Conway were with him on the hill; Stephen was to the immediate right, and Dayton's, Hazen's, and Ogden's regiments were to the immediate left. If only the artillery could support these troops on the hill until the rest of the division had a chance to rally, but the hopes were futile.

Terror and confusion pervaded the whole scene—"infernal Fire of cannon & musketry, most incessant shouting. . . . Trees cracking over ones heads. . . . The leaves falling as in autumn by the grapeshot." [39] The extreme American wings, General Prudhomme de Borre's brigade on the right and Sullivan's own division on the left, collapsed. For close to fifty minutes Meeting House Hill had been disputed, almost muzzle to muzzle on the summit, but then the right and left of the center gave way. The hill had to be abandoned, "but not till we had almost Covered the Ground between that & Bremingham meeting House with The Dead Bodies of the Enemy," Sullivan wrote.[40] Now the rebel position was grave, since the enemy line was stretched and threatened a flanking of the right wing, especially after the flight of De Borre's troops. The line had to break to prevent its being surrounded.

The bitter fight ended in retreat to the east toward Dilworth. Nathanael Greene arrived on the line of retreat in time to give invaluable assistance to Sullivan's disorganized men. Sullivan himself joined George Weedon's brigade and fought valiantly, although his horse was shot from under him, to cover the retreat until darkness fell.[41] With the fading light, the Americans also retired from the action near Chad's Ford where Anthony Wayne, William Maxwell, and Thomas Proctor's corps of artillery had been withstanding an assault by a larger part of the enemy's forces, launched simultaneously with Cornwallis's blow.[42] The weary and battered army made its way toward Chester. No accurate count of casualties exists. One Hessian officer said they lost about 500 men, killed and wounded, and the Americans over 1,000, including prisoners. Howe placed his own losses at 89 killed, 488 wounded, and 6 missing.[43]

The Battle of the Brandywine had been a critical one. Some British, including William Howe, believed the American cause might have been scotched that day, had the invader been given another hour of daylight.[44] But the history of the British military endeavors during the Revolutionary War is a long catalogue of "if's." It was unfair to expect Washington to win when facing a full enemy force, for his successes had come only when he had utilized the element of surprise. The men of Congress were quixotic when they expected not only a head-on struggle with Howe, but also a victory. A scapegoat had to be found, however; there had to be an explanation for the rout, and John Sullivan was the explanation. Demands came from some members of Congress for his removal for what seemed to be poor performance at Staten Island and Brandywine. North Carolina's Thomas Burke was candid and damning in his criticism, although some weeks passed before Sullivan learned the identity of his critic. Sullivan, according to Burke, was "the Marplot of our Army." [45] Faulty intelligence and incompetent placing of his troops marred Sullivan's performance, Burke claimed.

Burke's criticism, although he had witnessed parts of the battle, was on the whole unfair. He thought Sullivan had been posted on the right for three days and that he had enough troops for reconnoitering. It is true that Sullivan had been in the area for a few days, but he did not assume his post at Brinton's Ford until the eve of the battle. Just what role the Light Horse played, which General Washington had sent off to the right, remains unknown. The reconnaissance was poor, and it is unfair to throw all the abuse in Sullivan's lap; certainly Washington never censured him, and the Commander-in-Chief took full blame upon himself for the inadequate information about the fords above the fork of the Brandywine.[46] Burke likewise lambasted General Sullivan for having forwarded Spear's mis-information—a ridiculous charge, although Sullivan may have been remiss by not challenging its accuracy. Washington said that Sullivan by all means should have sent on the report, and the false information may have saved Washington from a disas-trous walloping had he continued with his idea of striking across the Brandywine, which he countermanded only upon hearing Spear's report that no flanking march apparently was taking place.[47] The error which both Washington and Sullivan made with Spear's message was their failure to pin down the time of his reconnaissance. He could have made his trip from Martin's Tavern to Welch's Tavern and still not see the marching col-umn. His information, therefore, was not so much misleading as misinterpreted.[48]

Burke's second major complaint, that Sullivan improperly handled his troops, was unfair. He said that Sullivan brought his division into action after an unnecessary circuit of two miles, whereas "one quarter in the direct road would have brought him to his grounds." [49] It is true that Sullivan made a circuit, but he did not know where Stirling and Stephen were located, and un-til he met Hazen he did not know that a considerable body of the enemy was in the area. Admittedly he was confused, but the collapse in coordination was not his fault. The circuit move did make him late in getting ready for battle, but his reaction to the events as they unfolded was logical.[50] Nor was the reckless charge that he insisted upon coming up on the right of the American line, the place of honor due him because he was in command, true. Burke said that Sullivan was trying to gain that position and therefore added further confusion to the scene.[51] Sullivan did come up on the left; De Borre held the right of the line.[52]

The disposition of the troops was by no means perfect, but perhaps all that could be accomplished under stress and confusion. Raw troops are easily disarranged when changing ground during action; even so Sullivan desperately tried to salvage an uncomfortable situation. Plagued by the chaos within his own division, he never lost composure; at all times he fought courageously regardless of the odds. No one can be blamed for the loss at Brandywine. To pull off a victory would have been close to a miracle, for the Americans were inferior in discipline, in arms, and perhaps in numbers.[53] The encounter did little credit to American generalship, it is true, but out of harsh failure came experience.

General Sullivan, now embroiled in controversy, did not even know whether he would be used for any further defensive operations about Philadelphia, for on September 14 Congress recalled him from the army until after the inquiry which had been ordered earlier.[1] A clique in Congress was out to get him: the Maryland delegates, who disapproved of the way he had handled the Staten Island raid in which many Marylanders had taken part; James Wilson, who disliked Sullivan's slurs against St. Clair; James Duane, who was a partisan of Philip Schuyler; and some of the Southern members, particularly Thomas Burke.[2] Wilson insisted that if St. Clair had to face an inquiry, Sullivan should also.[3]

Washington persuaded Congress to delay Sullivan's recall until the military picture cleared. A new action loomed ahead, and he feared the loss of top officers. General Washington might have offered Sullivan more vigorous defense at this time, for surely he more than Sullivan had been responsible for the rout at Brandywine. Instead he was merely asking for a delay of recall, not a reconsideration. Congress obliged the Commander-in-Chief, although Samuel Chase of Maryland and George Read of Delaware asked that troops from their states be placed under someone else's command. Fortunately Congress would not go that far, for surely had such a resolution been passed John Sullivan would have left the army.[4]

Sullivan was furious, and with good reason. He asked Washington to come to his defense, but General Washington was unwilling to commit himself at the time, arguing that he could not take part in the inquiry since he had not been in Sullivan's sector at Brandywine. His words offered small comfort: "Some have condemn'd your disposition tho' time perhaps wd. not allow a better but none have accused you of want of bravery, and exertion, that I have heard of." [5] Adam Stephen, shocked over Sullivan's treatment, thought he was being condemned without a chance to present his story. "Undeserved calumny" was what another officer called it.[6] Matthias Ogden, who had had a key role at Staten Island, saw no reason whatsoever for an inquiry.[7] The sensitive Sullivan had justice on his side. He wanted an early decision, but Washington's request for a delay was more compelling. All Sullivan could do for the time being was to unburden his grievances. He thought his troubles had resulted from the complaints of a few "Disaffected & Mutinous & worthless officers" who had been on the Staten Island raid.[8] His Brandywine performance was being questioned by one man who "Don Quixot Like pranced at a Distance from the fight & felt as Little of the Severity of the Engagement as he knows about the Disposition of our Troops or that of the Enemy—." [9] But if Congress would listen to such unwarranted charges, he told Hancock, he was ready to resign from the army to defend his reputation. "I am the butt against which all the darts are levelled," he wrote.[10]

Any slight chance for a speedy inquiry, however, disappeared when the wily Howe slipped unopposed into Philadelphia on the 26th, after having feinted Washington to shift his troops in the direction of Reading. The only cheering news came from the north with the defeat of Burgoyne at Freeman's Farm; his total destruction now appeared certain. Washington held his force at Pennypacker's Mills, northwest of Philadelphia on the Perkiomen, waiting for another opportunity to battle with William Howe. Soon he learned that Howe had detached part of his army to the New Jersey side of the Delaware. The time seemed proper to move against the remainder of the British troops stationed in Germantown—a suggestion concurred with by his council on the night of October 3.[11]

Germantown was about five miles from Philadelphia on the road leading northwest to Reading. The town extended for two miles along this road, called "Main Street" in Germantown proper. Stone houses lined the street, behind which the fields and orchards, separated by fences, spread for a considerable distance. The Market House stood in the center of the town with Mount Airy a mile to the north and Chestnut Hill still another mile beyond. Here the road branched, the left fork leading toward Bethlehem, then soon branching northwest along the Skippack Road to Washington's position at Pennypacker's Mills. At Market House leading out of Germantown at right angles to Main Street were two roads, Church Lane to the east and School House Lane to the west. Church Lane ran into Lime Kiln Road at Luken's Mill, then ran east of Skippack Road in a northern direction. School House Lane went west toward the Schuylkill where it met the Manatawny or Ridge Road, which in turn ran in a northern direction toward Reading.[12]

The British, encamped in Germantown, had lines extended across the village at right angles, the left reaching westward toward the Schuylkill, the right resting on Lime Kiln Road with a flanking wing even farther to the east.[13] General Washington had three approaches to the town: a frontal assault from Chestnut Hill, and two flanking movements along Lime Kiln and Manatawny Roads, entering the town via Church and School House Lanes. Once again John Sullivan received a major assignment, command of the American right wing. This time, however, Washington chose to accompany Sullivan's troops, perhaps to keep the ill-fated New Hampshire man from misfortune and adverse criticism.[14] Nathanael Greene had independent command of the left wing. Washington's plans were elaborate, more elaborate than usual in Revolutionary War fighting, since they called for a long march followed by a simultaneous attack by various columns over a four-mile front. The terrain, "intersected

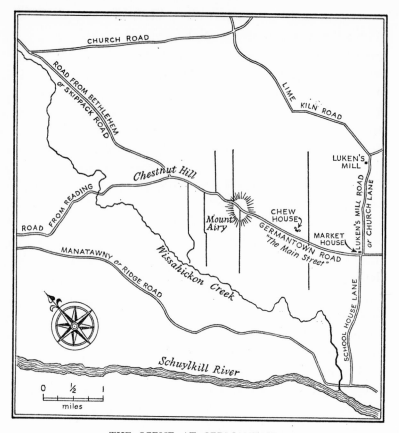

THE SCENE AT GERMANTOWN
Adapted from "The Battle of Germantown," by Alfred C. Lambdin,
The Pennsylvania Magazine of History and Biography, 1877

with hills and ravines," hindered proper communication.[15] Although the American attempt was courageous, it had an element of the foolhardy because Howe's men were well placed with rough country in front of both wings.[16] The complicated plans were anything but helpful, for some units were delayed or even failed to arrive. In brief Sullivan's wing, composed of his own division, Wayne's division, and Conway's brigade, was to enter Germantown from Chestnut Hill. Greene and Adam Stephen on the left wing, assisted by McDougall's brigade, were to approach via the Lime Kiln Road. To Greene's left General William Smallwood and Colonel David Forman had orders to push with a flanking wing to get at the enemy's rear. The western approach to Germantown was given to Armstrong, who with his militia was to move along the Manatawny Road. Lord Stirling was to form the reserve. The troops, maybe as many as 11,000 including militia, were to move on the evening of October 3, preparatory to coordinating at 5:00 A.M. the next morning a surprise attack on the pickets, with Armstrong on the right, Sullivan closing in at Mount Airy, and Greene slipping in from the left. The pickets were to be bayoneted; there must be no outcry.[17]

According to plan, therefore, Sullivan's column moved out of its camp on Metuchen hill at 9:00 P.M. on the start of its twelve-mile march; already the other units were in motion as they had more ground to cover. The men moved in silence in a night threatened by rain. General Sullivan rode near the advance in front of Wayne and behind Thomas Conway, who was leading the wing and whose instructions were to file off to hit the enemy's left flank.[18] Just as the sun rose the column descended into a valley near Mount Airy, but the soldiers were not to see much sunlight that day, for later a heavy fog rolled over the contested area to tantalize the embattled men.

Now, with the rising of the sun, Sullivan detached two regiments to fall upon the pickets in Mount Airy. His attack came later than Washington had planned and not to the complete surprise of the British. At first the redcoats gave way, but soon Light Infantry positioned in an orchard reinforced the pickets, thereby compelling Conway, in the lead, to take a stand rather than continue with his flanking maneuver. John Sullivan immediately formed his division to give Conway support; the Battle of Germantown had opened. The sun no longer shone, the fog rolled in. Forty-five minutes were to elapse before Greene would be ready to commence his attack to Sullivan's left.[19] The fog and Greene's delay were portents of trouble.

Sullivan's first task was to thwart an attempted flanking

movement on his left. From his position on the west side of the
road, he ordered Colonel Benjamin Ford's regiment to move to
the east side to stem the British flanking and to wait until
Wayne's division could come up into position. Quick decisions
had to be made to form proper lines, and when Wayne came up,
Sullivan sent him on the east side of the road to attack the
enemy's right. Then he ordered Conway's brigade to go to the
rear where the troops were to file off and flank the entire division. But General Sullivan soon found he could not wait for
Conway's men to get to their new position; the fog was cloak-
ing the British moves and as yet there was no indication that
Armstrong was on his right. Hurriedly, therefore, he pushed
one of Wayne's regiments along with one of his own to keep
the enemy from turning his right.[20]

One-half hour possibly had elapsed since the troops hit the
pickets at Mount Airy. Now deployed, the Americans began to
push the redcoats back into the town, at times using the bayonet, with the enemy retiring and then reforming. Sullivan and
Conway were sweeping down the west side of Germantown,
and Wayne down the east side.[21] This drive meant severe fighting; soon Sullivan forced the Light Infantry and 40th Regiment
to give way. With this break, General Sullivan sent his aide,
Major Lewis Morris, Jr., to Washington to let him know that
the British left wing was falling back and to urge that he order
Wayne, whom he did not know was already pushing on, to advance against the British right. The Commander-in-Chief detached part of the reserve to go forward on the flanks and told
Wayne to continue with his advance. Soon Sullivan had passed
the home of Chief Justice Benjamin Chew, one mile from Mount
Airy; another mile lay between Sullivan and School House Lane.
By now Wayne's division was abreast with him.[22] All was confusion, with fog and smoke from muskets and from the stubble
fired by the British denying any proper visibility. One could
see fifty yards, perhaps less. The retreating enemy took aim
from the cover of every house and every hedge to harass the

Americans, who also had to remove the fences that stood in their path.

Sullivan kept on pushing. When he had advanced about 300 to 400 yards beyond the Chew House, Adjutant-General Timothy Pickering rode up to tell Sullivan that General Washington wanted him to preserve ammunition. The Commander-in-Chief feared that the impetuous Sullivan was wasting ammunition on an unseen foe.[23] By now Sullivan must have noticed that he was not getting the assistance for which he had hoped. Maxwell had not as yet come up, but for good reason, since some of the British Light Infantry under Lieutenant-Colonel Thomas Musgrave had barricaded themselves in the Chew House. Now, in effect, a fortress blocked part of the American advance. Upon General Knox's advice some of the Americans delayed for a time in an unsuccessful attempt to dislodge Musgrave and his men.[24]

An hour and a quarter had passed. Sullivan had been in the thickest part of the fighting with hopes of meeting success. But shortly he sensed trouble on his left, although the fog prevented him from having an accurate picture. Apparently, however, Wayne was falling back, thereby exposing Sullivan's left flank. The fighting must have been frantic on the left, since about half an hour earlier Stephen and Greene had come up to their positions. Fate once again teased the rebel troops, for in the fog Wayne's and Stephen's men, the latter having come up to Wayne's left and rear, mistook each other for the enemy and opened fire. Sullivan later learned that Wayne drew back because of Stephen's men and because he thought the firing behind him at the Chew House meant Sullivan had been defeated. Until that moment Wayne believed that Sullivan was abreast of him to his right.[25]

Although his left flank now was exposed, Sullivan continued his advance against the British left. But the resistance stiffened. Against him the enemy hurled fresh troops, the 15th, 17th, and 44th Regiments.[26] Sullivan had penetrated to the center of town at School House Lane, but the attack had spent itself. Unsupported, with cartridges exhausted, fearful that they were surrounded, Sullivan's men began to retreat, but not before the retreat had started on the left. The officers tried to halt the scampering troops, but had no luck.[27] At the Chew House General Sullivan saw Washington "Exposing himself to the hottest fire," upon which Sullivan rode over to the Commander-in-Chief and asked him to retire. But Washington soon returned and waited until the remainder of the troops had retreated. The battle had lasted under three hours.[28]

Howe, in his usual way, made only a token pursuit which enabled the Americans to retreat in safety back to Pennypacker's Mills, but what had started as a partial withdrawal soon became a general retreat because the raw troops were not used to breaking ranks and rallying again. The Americans blamed the fog for their misfortune, and so did Sullivan, who claimed both the fog and cannon smoke "prevented our Troops from Discovering the motions of the Enemy or Acting in Concert with Each other." [29] General Sullivan was not responsible for the retreat; it had started to his left, but his men, once their ammunition was gone, had joined the rush to leave the field. Adam Stephen, later dismissed for drunkenness during this battle, was accused of ordering the retreat on the left wing; but the pathetic Stephen claimed that he had begged his men not to run from victory.[30] Some have suggested that Sullivan changed the plan of battle when he ordered Wayne to the east of Main Street; and that, although circumstances justified the move, it meant that Wayne got in front of Stephen, which opened the way for confusion and disorder.[31] The charge is not fair. General Sullivan had to advance on both sides of the street, and he had every reason to believe that Stephen would come into the battle to the left of Wayne.[32]

The Americans were frustrated because they sincerely believed victory had been within their grasp. The loss was a mockery, they thought. Fog, the delay at the Chew House, a drunken general, and spent ammunition had combined to deny them their win. Washington even claimed that the British themselves were prepared to retreat, having already assigned Chester as the place of rendezvous.[33] But the enemy had to contend with the same fog, and reinforcements were on hand. Colonel Louis du Portail later observed to General Washington: "Your Excellency in that instance really conquer'd General How [sic], but his Troops conquered yours." [34] For Sullivan the day had been an unhappy one. Two of his aides, Majors Edward Sherburne and John White, received mortal wounds. In spite of his own brave advance, insinuations were in the air that his division had been the first to get out of the battle, but Washington spoke highly of Sullivan's performance, doubtless to appease the members of Congress who had little faith in the New Hampshire general.[35]

While the Americans tried to salvage what respect they could out of Germantown and licked their wounds, Sullivan faced the Court of Inquiry which examined his raid on Staten Island. The Court under Lord Stirling met on the 10th but did not begin proceedings until the next day. As the evidence unfolded it soon became apparent that justice was on Sullivan's side. On the morning of October 12, the members of the Court gave as their unanimous opinion that the expedition had been well planned and had offered chances of a stunning success. The weariness of the men, failure to carry out Sullivan's orders properly, and misbehavior of some of the troops, all were beyond John Sullivan's power to control and had brought about the calamitous result. The Court acquitted him of the charges, and Washington's general orders of October 16 published the findings.[36]

The whole affair had irritated Sullivan, and rightly so. In spite of his exoneration he preferred to keep harping on the attempt of some of the men under his command to embarrass him. He said they used the Staten Island raid to strike back at him for the rigorous duty he had made them perform the previous

August. Full of wrath, he believed this clique had been circulating rumors that he no longer had the confidence of his officers.
In a letter to the President of Congress, written on October 17,
Sullivan showed his anger and with a sense of injured pride offered these final words in which he referred to the loss of his
aides at Germantown:

The Last Action Took off half my family perhaps the next may
Sweep the Residue and Involve me in their Fate & what is Still more
Terrible to me my Reputation may unjustly perish by my Side.
This Sir is a poor Encouragement to Sacrifice that Life which I have
often ventured in my Countrys Cause & to Exchange Domestick
Ease for the Dusty field of Mars. But as Every American Looks up
to Congress for Justice I cannot perswade myself that Congress will
Refuse Either to approve my Conduct publickly or grant me Leave
to Retire from the army.[37]

The desired approval was forthcoming when on October 20
Congress resolved that the action of the Court was pleasing, and
that the opinion should be published "in justification of the injured character of that officer." [38] Sullivan's troubles were not
over, for he had become embroiled with North Carolina's
Thomas Burke over the Battle of Brandywine. On October 12
Burke had written Sullivan a letter in which he detailed his criticism, discussed above, of Sullivan's behavior and performance
during the battle. Now Sullivan knew the identity of his ac-
cuser. Burke did not mince his words:

I urged your recall with all the force I could, and thought it, and
still do think it necessary for the public good because, in all your
Enterprises and in every part of your Conduct, even as represented
by yourself, you Seem to be void of Judgement and foresight in
concerting, of deliberate Vigor in Executing, and of presence of
mind under Accidents and Emergencies—and from these defects
Seem to me to arise your repeated ill Success.[39]

He then took exception to Sullivan's letter to Congress in
which Sullivan had castigated his anonymous critic who had
witnessed the battle. Now that Sullivan knew who his detractor
was in Congress, there arose a feud between the two men that

lasted until 1781. Pleased by complimentary remarks sent on by
Eliphalet Dyer, indicating that Sullivan had considerable support within Congress, and likewise cheered by favorable comments offered by his brother officers, Sullivan felt much better
and late in October wrote Burke that he would not explain his
earlier missive to Congress and the slurring remarks he had
made. Nor was he upset over Burke's criticism, he wrote, because he was sure Burke lacked the capacity to judge. The entire dispute was unseemly, but it does reveal the tensions under
which the members of Congress and the officers were working.
The lines were drawing. John Sullivan thought he had ample
reason for being critical of Congress for not backing him early
enough or vigorously enough until he had suffered some damage. Sullivan's pride had been wounded also when Washington
was late in coming to his defense over the Brandywine matter.
A letter of October 24 cleared Sullivan of any negligence insofar as the Commander-in-Chief was concerned, but surely Sullivan must have thought he deserved earlier support from the
man he idolized.[40]

The fall of 1777 was a time of recrimination, and the officers
faced severe criticism. Benjamin Rush, fearful of military control, viewed Washington as the idol of America governed by a
small coterie, chiefly Greene, Knox, and Hamilton, but also
Sullivan, Stirling, and Stephen. Rush had little to say that was
kind. Sullivan was "weak—vain—without dignity—fond of scrib-
ling—in the field a madman." Greene was a "sycophant" to
Washington, "timid," "speculative." Stirling was "vain," also a
"drunkard." Stephen was "a sordid, boasting cowardly sot." [41]
Rush's carping, courts-martial of various officers (one leading to
the dismissal of Adam Stephen for drunkenness), the ire of
senior officers over criticism leveled against them by their
juniors, all added to the unhappiness of Washington's army,
which, having been defeated twice by Howe, saw its reputation
suffer when compared to the accomplishments of Gates's force.
Some members of Congress, jealous of Washington and his mili-

tary entourage, preferred to entrust the cause to the militia and republican virtue. Now people heard Gates's name more frequently, and Washington discovered that in some quarters his abilities were being questioned. Into this situation entered the aspirations of Thomas Conway. A native of Ireland who had found his career in the French army, Conway had come to America the previous spring to further his fortunes in the rebel cause. Although Congress had seen fit to honor him with a brigadier's commission, Washington never had any use for Conway, and Conway in turn violated all propriety when he questioned the competency of the Commander-in-Chief.

For a time Sullivan liked Conway, probably because the latter had spoken highly of Sullivan's efforts at Brandywine.[42] Conway wished promotion, and Sullivan in a letter to John Adams argued in his behalf.[43] It was ironical that Sullivan was arguing the cause of the man who had attacked Washington, for throughout his military and later political career Sullivan maintained an unswerving loyalty and devotion to George Washington. Here he was backing the fortunes of the man around whom was centering the rising distrust of Washington as commander. Congress was appointing a new Board of War, and two of the members, Gates and Thomas Mifflin, former quartermaster and critic of Washington, were not to the Commander-in-Chief's liking. A further irritation was the promotion given to Conway on December 13. Whether Sullivan's letter to John Adams had inspired the promotion cannot be determined; but the fact was that three critics of Washington—namely Gates, Conway, and Mifflin—were in the ascendancy. Many have claimed that a definite attempt was made during the winter of 1777–78 to make Gates commander in Washington's place. Since Conway apparently emerged as the center of controversy, this so-called conspiracy has become known as the Conway Cabal. For lack of proof one should doubt the existence of a cabal, and there is not one shred of evidence which would indicate that Sullivan ever wavered in his support of Washington. If any plot existed to remove Washington, John Sullivan had nothing to do with it.[44]

Sullivan's attitude, though, does appear somewhat equivocal. Early in January, 1778, he represented nine brigadiers when he forwarded to General Washington their memorial to Congress protesting Conway's rise in rank.[45] Later in the month he once more thought Conway merited promotion, however, although his letter to Henry Laurens is remarkably noncommittal. Sullivan was disturbed, he wrote Laurens on January 20, because officers were complaining over James Wilkinson's and Conway's promotions. He had no opinion of Wilkinson, but he thought Conway well suited for the office of Inspector-General. He did not wish to see Congress deviate from the principle of promotion on the basis of seniority, however, save for exceptional ability. Sullivan, although he still argued Conway deserved promotion, readily admitted that his word stood against the word of the nine brigadiers. Rather inconclusively he suggested that a committee "Inquire into the Grievances Respecting Rank . . . & to Redress them and . . . to fix a Regular Line of promotion not to be Departed from but in Cases of Extraordinary merit or upon political principles." [46] With this letter Sullivan seems to have disentangled himself from a ticklish problem. Apparently he offended neither his Commander-in-Chief nor Thomas Conway, the officer who had praised his actions at Brandywine.

In the midst of this intrigue and bickering the Americans had gone into winter camp at Valley Forge. To attack the British seemed plausible to Sullivan, he perhaps being more agreeable to the idea of a fight than some of his brother officers. "I am so weary of the infernal clamor of the Pennsylvanians," he wrote of the inhabitants who wished the army to engage in battle, "that I am for satisfying them at all events, and risking every consequence in an action." [47] But nothing came of the idea; instead the forlorn troops remained at Valley Forge.

The story of Valley Forge is a twice-told tale of misery,

starvation, and fortitude. John Sullivan was there during that
winter of trial, freed for a time from the mundane duties of
camp life because he was building a bridge over the Schuylkill.
When he had completed that task in February, he sought leave,
arguing that he found it essential to try to recoup some of his
financial setbacks.[48] Washington's refusal, saying that he could
not spare his general officers, had little effect, for the over-sensi-
tive Sullivan replied:

I Reallize my Command as high in The Army at the Same time
Consider it as arising from mere Fortuitous Circumstances & not
from any notice that has been taken of my Constant & faithful Services—In fact I have never yet had a post assigned me where there
was Even a probability of Acquiring Honor Those posts are Either
Reserved for older or for younger officers (more in favor Than
myself) I have often Sensibly felt The Degrading prefference given
to others & have Suffered it So far to operate upon me: That I am
now unhappy in the Service—I am willing as heretofore to Live
upon my own fortune in the Service a Campaign or Two Longer
provided I can have an opportunity of putting my affairs in Such a
Situation as will afford me the necessary Subsistance but if I might
have my Choice it would be that Some more Suitable person Should
fill my place in the Army & I be permitted to Retire.[49]

Sullivan was adamant; once more he wrote for leave, professing that his real desire was to quit the service. His financial
situation would not allow him to continue, he wrote. During the
various campaigns he had lost or had stolen from him suits of
clothes, linen, camp equipage, a military library, and three
horses. No recompense had been forthcoming. He must leave
to prepare himself for "greater Fatiques & Losses." [50] He might
be tired, but he still had energy enough to complain. The same
time that he wrote Washington for leave, March 2, he also
wrote him a second letter, this one in behalf of his brother
Ebenezer, who had been captured at the Cedars in 1776 and
just recently exchanged. He thought his brother entitled to certain financial remuneration, but evidently Congress thought dif-
ferently unless the exchanged officers had remained in the serv-

ice. Sullivan's comment was sharp: "I think the Conduct of Congress with Respect to those Hostages would Disgrace a Senate of Barbarians." [51]

Washington's reply of the 6th gave Sullivan little comfort. He could do nothing for Ebenezer, and Sullivan was not to get leave.[52] But Washington cushioned the disappointing news in this letter with an offer, sent on March 10, of command of the post in Rhode Island.[53] Congress wished a major-general to take the post to succeed Joseph Spencer who had resigned both his command at Rhode Island and his commission. Neither Heath nor Putnam suited Congress for the assignment. Washington had little other choice except Sullivan. Yet he had confidence in the general; it would be an independent command, something which Sullivan had always wanted; and it would give the dissatisfied officer a chance to go home before assuming his new post. Perhaps, too, Washington saw this as an opportunity to rid himself for the time being of a chronic complainer.[54]

His new assignment delighted Sullivan. Late in March, 1778, he informed Rhode Island's Governor Nicholas Cook that he hoped to take over the command in a fortnight, but that first he was going to visit his family in New Hampshire.[1] The Britisher, Frederick Mackenzie, upon hearing that Sullivan was assuming the command at Rhode Island, noted, "he is an enterprizing spirited fellow."[2] Enterprise and spirit would be needed, for John Sullivan knew he had to collect an army. On April 17, after his trip to Durham, he arrived in Providence where an escort met him and led him to the State House. There the Governor and Council received him before he moved on to his headquarters. On the next day the Rhode Island Council of War placed all troops within the state under his command.[3]

Eager for action, Sullivan was ready for anything and even threatened Thomas Burke, his old adversary, with a duel. But that fight could wait, he said.[4] Soon he received from General Robert Pigot, British commander at Newport, the Parliamentary plan for reconciliation which had come before the House of Commons in February. Pigot trusted that Sullivan would distribute the copies throughout Rhode Island.[5] Sullivan's answer was blunt. The proposals had been printed in the Providence *Gazette*, he told Pigot; but he said in no uncertain terms that they had come too late.[6] Positive word that France had allied herself with the United States brought to an end the attempt at reconciliation. Therefore the task facing him was obvious: he must build up the strength of the army under his command. He estimated the enemy at Newport to be about 3,600 strong, "Busy in Fortifying the Island & . . . much afraid that we are about to attack them." [7] Sullivan hoped that the deception might continue, as he was lacking the strength to withstand a British blow. With practically no troops on hand, he had to guard the shore from Point Judith to Providence on the west, and from Providence to Seconnet on the east.[8] On May 9 he wrote Jeremiah Wadsworth, the new Commissary General, congratulating him and trusting that some attention would be paid to Rhode Island; for as yet no purchasing commissary had joined his command.[9] As the days slipped by, he still was not being properly supplied so that he sought assistance from the Marine Board in Connecticut, the Navy Board at Boston, the Board of War, and from General Heath. The latter, in command at Boston, agreed to forward him provisions and some munitions.[10]

While Sullivan grappled with the problems of his new assignment, events unfolded elsewhere which soon would lead to a campaign in Rhode Island against the British. Now that France had allied with the Americans, active military assistance could be expected; in fact, a fleet under the Comte d'Estaing had left Toulon for American waters on April 13, 1778. Arriving in Delaware Bay only to find Lord Howe's fleet no longer in the area, D'Estaing sailed for New York. With this naval assistance soon available, Congress advised Washington to utilize the welcome force either at Sandy Hook or at Newport.[11]

Shortly Sullivan learned that his command in Rhode Island would likely play an important part in the strategy for the summer of 1778 when on July 22 or 23 word came from Washington telling Sullivan that D'Estaing was off Sandy Hook, that an attack was imminent upon either New York or Rhode Island, and that Sullivan must prepare for the latter possibility. He must raise his troops to total 5,000 by applying in Washington's name to Rhode Island, Connecticut, and Massachusetts.[12]

Reports varied about the size of the British garrison which was increasing in Newport. Between July 18 and 22 Sullivan raised the estimate from 6,000 to 7,000, with expectations of its rising to 11,000.[13] But as he now had only about 1,600 men at hand, he was being an alarmist simply to frighten the New England states into forwarding troops as soon as possible. These efforts were timely, for D'Estaing, having decided to suspend operations against the British in New York because the channel was too shallow, sailed for Rhode Island. Lieutenant Colonel John Laurens brought positive word from Washington to Sullivan on July 24 that the French were proceeding toward Newport to cooperate with him in an attack upon the enemy.[14] Thus almost immediately after he had been ordered to make preparations, Sullivan learned that the French actually were on their way. Washington's letter told him that he was not limited to raising 5,000 men, but that instead he should try to procure as many as needed to guarantee success. "You will I am well assured," the Commander-in-Chief wrote, "pursue every measure in your power that can render the enterprize happy and fortunate, and as its success will depend in a great degree on the promptness and energy of its execution, I trust the conduct will answer the spirit and hopes of the expedition." [15]

Two brigades were on their way, detached on July 22 under Generals James Varnum and John Glover, both under the command of the Marquis de Lafayette. A detachment under Colonel Henry Jackson would follow.[16] This was the first independent command Sullivan had enjoyed since the retreat from Sorel two years earlier. The old jealousies of the previous winter began to appear, and the flamboyant Lafayette, still envious of the adulation Horatio Gates had received at the expense of Washington, wrote Sullivan:

had G¹ Gates or any other gone there [i.e., Rhode Island] I had already express'd that I did not choose to go, but I confess I feel the greater happiness to cooperate with you to our glory and the common advantage—for god's sake, my dear friend, don't begin any thing before we arrive.[17]

Nathanael Greene, though restricted by the more mundane

duties of Quartermaster General, was most exuberant when he wrote Sullivan:

You are the most happy man in the World. What a child of fortune. The expedition you are going on against Newport I think cannot fail of success. You are the first General that has ever had an opportunity of cooperating with the french forces belonging to the United States. The character of the American Soldiers as well as that of their officers will be found from the conduct of the Troops and the success of this expedition. I wish you success with all my Soul and intend if possible to come home to put things in a proper train in my department and to take a command of part of the Troops under you. I wish most ardently to be with you . . .

A certain Northern heroe [i.e., Gates], gave His Excellency several broad hints that if he was sent upon the Newport expedition great things would be done. But the General did not think proper to supercede an officer of distinguished merit to gratify unjustly a doubtful friend. Had it been necessary my little influence would not have been wanting to have prevented, such a piece of injustice from being done you.

The good agreement that has ever subsisted between us; and the prospect of a noble opportunity of acquiring reputation together with the certainty of your doing justice to every man who distinquished himself in any manner what ever induces me to wish to join you upon this occasion. Not as a Northern Heroe to rob you of your Laurels; but to share them under you.[18]

Greene concluded in a more ominous vein. He warned Sullivan that he could not afford to fail:

I was an advisear [sic] to this expedition and therefore am deeply interested in the event. I wish a little more force had been sent. Count de Estaigne will block up the Harbour and you may wait until your plan is ripe for execution. I hope you wont precipitate matters until your force gets together. Every thing depends almost upon the success of this expedition. Your friends are anxious, your enemies are watching. *I charge you to be Victorious.* The Marquis de la Fyette is coming to join you, trust to your own judgement for forming the plan as you have every thing at Stake; and pray give your orders positive for the execution.[19]

John Sullivan had no intention of failing; he must have realized that to fail would so hurt his reputation that his military usefulness would be at an end. While awaiting the arrival of D'Estaing, he made preparations for an offensive. Many letters went from his headquarters to the New England governments urging that troops be speedily forwarded.[20] In addition he wrote William Heath at Boston for flat-bottomed boats, a regiment of artillery, and 40,000 flints.[21] Nor was this all he requested; in fact his appetite for military supplies was voracious.[22]

In the midst of his preparations for the conflict, Sullivan on July 25 wrote D'Estaing that he was delighted that such "an officer as the Count" was arriving to cooperate with the forces under his command; but at the same time he made it quite clear that there would be some delay in combining operations. His troops were thin at present, and a British raid in May had destroyed the boats he might have used for transporting his men. He assured D'Estaing that he was preparing for action as rapidly as possible.

In the rest of the letter he outlined his plan to the French commander. He wished to cross with his men from Tiverton onto Rhode Island proper, and then to proceed south toward Newport. He would bypass the enemy redoubts scattered throughout the island. Before Newport, however, the British had redoubts crossing the width of the island, and these he would have to storm. He went on to suggest the role D'Estaing might take. At least the French should station three ships at the mouth of the East Channel and four at the entrance to the West Channel. Three of these could capture the two small enemy frigates in that channel, and then sail toward Rhode Island around the northern tip of Conanicut Island. The rest of the fleet should stay at the mouth of the Middle Channel, which separated Conanicut from Rhode Island. At the time the Americans would be crossing from Tiverton, Sullivan suggested that the French pretend to land troops at Newport to mislead the enemy. This would give the patriots an opportunity to gain possession of the island and then move to attack the redoubts in

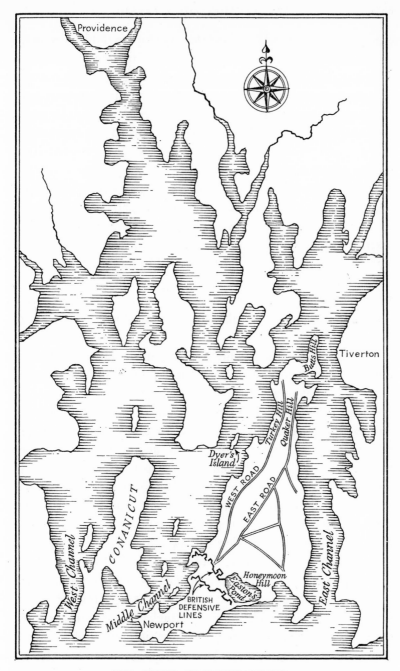

THE SCENE AT RHODE ISLAND
Adapted from "The Siege of Newport," by Thomas C. Amory,
The Rhode Island Historical Magazine, 1884–85

front of Newport itself. The French ships would then sail up
to fire upon the town before landing men to cooperate with the
American attack. Later on they could reduce at leisure the other
redoubts which had been bypassed at first. The large fleet in the
Middle Channel would prevent the arrival of reinforcements
from New York, and the ships which turned the northern tip
of Conanicut would prevent the three enemy regiments on that
island from crossing to Newport.[23]

A Council of War held the same day, July 25, advised
unanimously against an attack before the arrival of Lafayette's
force.[24] In the meantime while waiting for the appearance of
both D'Estaing and Lafayette, Sullivan still had a host of problems concerning troops and supplies. He must try to get food
for D'Estaing.[25] He asked Massachusetts, in addition to the
1,000 troops already sought, to send an extra 2,000 to be drafted
preferably for six weeks, although he thought he would be able
to release them after service of only ten days.[26] So anxious was
he to meet his needs that he became embroiled in an argument
with Heath. The Boston commander, in short, charged that
Sullivan had empowered his aides to impress supplies that were
at Heath's disposal. Those orders must come from him, not
Sullivan, but General Heath chose to excuse Sullivan's action
as "Zeal for the Service, and not any design to treat me indeli-
cately." [27] Sullivan was impetuous; it was part of his nature. He
was not lazy, and, now that he had independent command, he
showed much initiative. He had to get additional troops by
goading the states into forwarding quotas; he had to provide for
his own supplies by seeking the assistance of the head of the
Eastern Department, General Heath. Some aid did come from
the main army; in fact the continentals from that army provided
the core for Sullivan's force. In the last analysis, however,
organizing the army, planning the attack, and procuring supplies
were left to the initiative of the general in command.

Nothing went undone. Washington sent on Dr. Thomas
Tillotson and two assistants to establish a medical unit under

Dr. Isaac Foster, director of the Eastern Department.[28] A few days later, on July 29, Sullivan asked Heath to send four or five "Emminent Surgeons . . . with Instruments & Every Necessary for Restoring Broken Limbs & Raising men from the Dead." [29] He needed entrenching tools, wanted the thirteen-inch mortar at Boston, and requested shells and fuses.[30] He issued orders to seize boards and planking, if they could not be bought, for building flat boats, capable of carrying 100 men, and a few days later he sent to Boston and Marblehead for boatmen, each to be offered $3.00 per day as wages.[31]

In the midst of his preparations the General informed Washington on July 26: "Every Effort of mine to prepare for Executing your Excys orders has Succeeded beyond my most Sanguine Expectations & Every thing now promises Success. . . . I find I shall have a Sufficiency of Stores of Every kind & I hope Boats & troops Enough to make the attempt with a moral Certainty of Success the moment the Marquis & Admiral arrive." [32] This optimism does not ring true when considered in light of the previous day's letter to D'Estaing advising that some delay might be necessary, but Sullivan appeared loath to exhibit anything save a sanguine mood whenever he wrote Washington about the operations under his own separate command. He did the same when he had faced insuperable obstacles in Canada. Plagued by his previous ill-fortune, by the humming of criticism which surrounded him after the Staten Island raid and Brandywine, he did not wish to seem like Cassandra, thus perhaps shaking Washington's confidence in him. The Rhode Island campaign had to succeed, but the optimistic Sullivan was relying on troops that had not as yet put in their appearance.

A letter arrived from Washington saying that he was sending on Nathanael Greene, which meant that Sullivan would have two divisions, one under Greene, the other under Lafayette. Somewhat distrustful of the militia, Washington wished to distribute Varnum's and Glover's continental soldiers, originally placed under Lafayette's command, amongst the militia in both divisions. Should troops be debarked from D'Estaing's fleet, Washington suggested that they be placed under a commander agreeable to the Count's wishes.[33] As the end of July approached, John Sullivan awaited the arrival of Lafayette, Greene, and D'Estaing in an anxious mood, hoping to gain a stunning victory. His confidence augured well for success.

On July 29 the French arrived when twelve ships of the line and four frigates anchored off Point Judith at noon.[34] Because they lacked water and were weary after many days at sea, the French wished to go into immediate action; but delay, as Sullivan had warned in his communication with D'Estaing, was inevitable.[35] Enough troops were not on hand, and Sullivan had had only a few days' notice that the French were coming. To expect him to have increased his force from 1,600 to many times that number in about one week, when D'Estaing appeared, was to have asked the impossible. Weare could promise him nothing from New Hampshire, because a number of the militia were already in the service, and more than a few were privateering. Massachusetts had hired at least 500 New Hampshire men for her own battalions; as it was, too few remained behind to cultivate the land.[36]

Massachusetts was more optimistic. The Council wrote Sullivan that they were meeting his request for the 3,000 men, but the word from Connecticut was not so encouraging. Jonathan Trumbull had written that he was sending seven companies of infantry and one company of matrosses; but since they were scattered throughout the state, their departure would be delayed. Connecticut could send no more. The men under Lafayette had not as yet arrived, and General Greene did not leave White Plains for Rhode Island until July 28. Sullivan had done all he could to gather a sufficient number of troops, although he overestimated the strength of the enemy.[37] He still hoped for speed and informed Massachusetts that, as soon as both Lafayette and D'Estaing were on hand, "the attempt will be immediate." [38]

Upon the fleet's arrival, on July 29, John Laurens went aboard to outline Sullivan's plan of attack, which on the whole met with D'Estaing's approval. On the evening of the 29th two small frigates and a brigantine entered the East Channel, and the next morning two vessels of sixty and fifty guns respectively entered the West Channel. During the succeeding days the British burned a number of their ships to prevent capture, a desperate measure which proved the value of the French fleet.[39]

Sullivan, anxious to welcome the French, went to board D'Estaing's ship, the "Languedoc," on July 30. Before boarding, however, Laurens met him with a letter from the French Admiral, dated that same day. D'Estaing was not too enthusiastic about Sullivan's plan, particularly the suggestion that he should place most of his fleet in the Middle Channel between Conanicut and Rhode Island in Newport Harbor only to wait until time came to cooperate with the American assault. He also disapproved of sending three of his ships to turn the northern tip of Conanicut and sail down the Middle Channel. This was too impracticable, D'Estaing argued, because of the uncertainty of the winds. Instead the French wished to seize Conanicut, and D'Estaing, through Laurens, proposed that the American militia assist in storming that island.[40] It was obvious that the two commanders must come to some agreement. D'Estaing was desperate. "The position in which I find myself," he wrote, "cannot be ended too soon; my need of water demands it and every instant gives the enemy one more advantage." [41]

Sullivan received a warm greeting when he went aboard the "Languedoc" to meet the French. The effulgent D'Estaing, writing at a later date to Washington, observed that the New Hampshire general was "full of that spirit of activity and combination, with which you inspire all those who have served under your orders." [42] Sullivan still wanted the Americans to land on the east and then have the French second the attack by crossing over from Conanicut.[43] The problem of controlling Conanicut was solved for the two men, however, when the British

unexpectedly withdrew from the island. Forcing the Middle
Channel, therefore, was not necessary until the time for combined operations. On the 31st D'Estaing sent a party ashore to
investigate, and on August 1 he landed on Conanicut with a
detachment. Since it appeared that the British were concentrat-
ing their force about Newport, the allies could look forward
to landing on Rhode Island with comparable ease.[44]

Waiting was all that could be done until enough troops were
available, much to the regret of the French. Sullivan was hopeful; all the British were on Rhode Island, and the ship in the
East Channel was destroyed, thereby leaving "nothing now to
obstruct our Landing, but a Battery upon the Shore, which can
be easily silenc'd by the French Shipping." [45] He saw no reason
why he could not commence the offensive sometime during the
first week of August.

His optimism may have suffered a momentary setback when
he received from Washington a letter which urged caution after
the Commander had heard of Sullivan's intentions to take the
enemy position by storm. Washington wrote:

I will only say, that as I would not, on the one hand wish to check
the Ardor of our Troops, so I would not, upon the other, put them
upon attempting what I thought they could not carry but with a
moral certainty of success. You know the discipline of our Men and
Officers very well, and I hope you, and the General Officers under
your command, will weigh every desperate matter well before it is
carried into execution. A severe check may ruin the expedition,
while regular and determined approaches may effect the work, tho'
perhaps they may take something longer time. Upon the whole, I
will not undertake, at this distance, to give orders, I submit every
thing to your prudence, and to the good advice of those about you.[46]

On August 4, Lafayette, finally on the scene, went aboard
the "Languedoc" to speak with his fellow countryman. Out of
that conference emerged changes in the plan of attack. Sullivan's original idea, as described above, called for the 4,000
French troops to land after the Americans had crossed from
Tiverton and were ready to storm the enemy position; but ac-

cording to John Laurens, Lafayette, eager for a glorious role in the encounter, persuaded D'Estaing not only to place the French under the Marquis's command but also to ask that some American troops join with the French. A simultaneous attack would be more honorable to the French than having them merely feint a disembarkation to confuse the enemy. The French did not wish to wait to go into action; they wanted to land before the Americans came into position. D'Estaing suggested to Sullivan:

This marine manoeuvre [i.e., a feint], as you remark, might draw off the attention of the enemy. The Marquis de la Fayette will describe to you the peril in which we should find ourselves if I were obliged to reembark to resist a maritime enemy. This purpose, and that of dividing the forces of the English by presenting to them a more imposing front than we could otherwise do, make me desire that you might deem it suitable that a wing or at least a portion of your army should attack at the same time and in the same place as our men. You would be still more certain that all would act at the same instant. Should your choice fall then on Monsieur the Marquis de la Fayette the unity of the movement would be assured; he would always command your troops and he would find himself in my absence naturally at the head of the French.[47]

Sullivan was unhappy over this proposed shift in plans and criticized Lafayette. D'Estaing tried to absolve Lafayette of the blame, stating that he was the one who had pushed the idea, although at one point he had suggested that Lafayette should accede to Sullivan's wishes; but at heart he still desired a detachment to cooperate with him. He won out and Sullivan gave Lafayette the coveted assignment after all, but Sullivan could not have been too pleased by this change in tactics.[48] Any detachment taken from his army to be placed under Lafayette naturally would weaken the American force which had only a small number of tested troops. The American division could then be exposed to a vigorous challenge, but, according to John Laurens, the "private views" of Lafayette "withdrew his attention wholly from the general interest." [49] The plan now was to have the French land on the west side of Rhode Island above

Dyer's Island, and the Americans on the east side about opposite.[50]

The time for action approached. Yet as late as Thursday,
August 6, Sullivan complained to Henry Laurens that the militia
was tardy. He could not expect many from Connecticut, but
he hoped the New Hampshire and Massachusetts men would
arrive shortly. The army that was on hand, mainly the Continental troops, marched for Tiverton on that day, and early the
next morning, August 7, General Sullivan left his headquarters
in Providence and proceeded to join his men at the place of
rendezvous.[51] The militia of New England began to pour into
that area. John Hancock, a later arrival, was to command some
of them, and two of Sullivan's brothers, James and Eben, were
to be on hand for the campaign. The spirits of the militia were
high, the French were impatient for battle; only a brilliant victory could be in the offing.

The anxious D'Estaing informed Sullivan in a letter of August 7 that two vessels would be at his disposal in the East Channel to cover the crossing. D'Estaing, himself, would lead the
major part of the squadron and force the Middle Channel the
next day to carry out the double diversion of attacks by land
and by water. He had every desire for prompt action, and to
some degree seemed to be forcing Sullivan to commit himself
before the latter wished to. D'Estaing merely stated, "I flatter
myself that the moment for action will not be deferred." [52] He
went on to remind Sullivan that he expected a detachment of
American troops to go into action with the French, couching
his terms in no uncertain words:

I dare hope that Your Excellency and the General Officers who
serve with you, will put it in my power to give an account to the
King and to the Congress of the Number and goodness of the troops
that you shall have joined to the French—This detachment . . . is the
first occasion on which the Generals of the United States have it in
their power to give an authentic proof of the value which they set
upon the alliance of His Majesty and the satisfaction with which
they join their troops to his.[53]

During the afternoon of August 8 the French fleet forced its way into the Middle Channel and anchored in a line off Conanicut. Sullivan, who had received D'Estaing's letter on August 8, detached Jackson's regiment and some militia, about 1,000 men in all, under Lafayette's command to operate with the French. At first he planned to cross on the 9th, then sought a delay, but found that D'Estaing had forced his way into the harbor; so they agreed to land at daybreak on the 10th.[54]

The situation soon changed; for when the British realized the threat to the northern part of Rhode Island, once the French had forced their way into the Channel, General Pigot ordered the forts evacuated. Pigot had to take care that his troops not be cut off by a landing to the south. Hence the quick evacuation. On the evening of August 8, General Pigot's troops retired into the redoubts immediately before Newport, and into the town itself. On Sunday morning, August 9, Sullivan learned of the British evacuation and in order to prevent the enemy from possibly repossessing the forts, he ordered an immediate crossing to seize the works without waiting for the Count to land his forces.[55]

Though Sullivan would have preferred to delay action until he had sufficient numbers, the course taken by D'Estaing and the British retreat from the northern end of the island caused him to take immediate steps. Therefore he sent across the "indigested Body of Militia & regulars which composed [his] little Army."[56] After the men possessed the British works on Butts Hill and Quaker Hill, Sullivan sent word to D'Estaing to land his troops on the opposite side of the island. But even before he had his army entirely across from Tiverton, he learned that a British fleet of about thirty sail was standing for Newport.[57]

Were all his plans, all his expectations, to go awry? His only chance for success was to receive help from the French. Surely he held hopes that D'Estaing would continue the offensive before contending with the British fleet under Lord Howe. "However unexpected, surprising, and miraculous General Sullivan found the appearance of this fleet, as he did me the honor to inform me . . . " the Count wrote, "its existence was not the less certain." [58] Certainly there was no question in D'Estaing's mind as to what he should do. Reembarking the men that had already started ashore, on August 10 he "cut all his cables, and came firing through the harbor, as if the very Devil was in him." [59] The Count said that with his forces split he feared the British fleet might have possessed Conanicut, thereby exposing his ships in the Middle Channel to two fires from land. He knew he had some chance of success against Howe if he gave chase; but he had no desire to risk being bottled up in the harbor. It was essential also that he maintain freedom of action for his squadron so that he might supply protection for the French West Indies.[60]

D'Estaing did not choose to leave the Americans out of spite just because Sullivan had gone ahead on his own in crossing from Tiverton. Though the French leader showed surprise when he heard that Sullivan had done so, he admitted that such action merited only praise.[61] Sullivan was frustrated, for the French had forced him to move before he was ready; then when he did move, the fleet put out to sea to give chase. Now he had to cool his heels while itching for a fight.

Sullivan's troops, by no means fully reinforced, sat at the northern end of Rhode Island in the Portsmouth area opposite Tiverton. Placed in the mouth of Narragansett Bay, Rhode Island, today called by its Indian name, Aquidneck, is about fifteen miles long and three miles wide, with its vertical axis running north and south. Leading south from Butts Hill, at the northern end of the island, were two roads. The West Road proceeded to Newport, which was tucked in the southwest corner of the island, protected on the south by Brenton's ledge and facing west across its harbor to Conanicut. The East Road, running from the other side, joined the West Road before Newport. To the north of the town stands Tonomy Hill, and to the east on the southern shore lies Easton's Pond. The British defenses ran in an arc from the pond to the hill so that the enemy lines faced to the east and to the north, protecting the southwestern corner of Rhode Island.

The morning of August 10 found Sullivan watching the British "fly before" D'Estaing with obvious pleasure. He soon would have misgivings; for later in the same day he realized that, since he had no idea when the French would return, he would have to delay the attack.[1] Sullivan trusted the delay would only "Retard my movements in Some Respects," he wrote, "& Render our opperations more tedious if nothing worse."[2] An army finally was gathering; he found militia on hand "with a number of Gentlemen of the first Character."[3]

Sullivan decided, therefore, not to wait. His motley, undisciplined, and growing force, gathered from the towns and hamlets of New England, must be put in motion. Accordingly on August 11 he determined to march toward Newport the following morning at six o'clock. His general orders for the day returned "his most cordial thanks to the brave officers, volunteers and soldiers, who have with so much alacrity repaired to this place to give their assistance in extirpating the British tyrants from their country." The army having a "sacred regard" for American liberties, "fired with just resentments against those barbarians," with an "exceeding promising" prospect before them had "everything to animate and press them on to victory." The General himself, he claimed, "is ready to venture his life in every instance where his country calls for it." [4]

The wind was from the northeast that Tuesday, August 11; it blew hard, and the day was cloudy and rainy. In spite of the weather John Sullivan paraded his army in the afternoon in preparing for the next morning's march. Once more the ill-fortune that had accompanied Sullivan's military adventures mocked him. For on that August day the storm increased in its intensity, and on the 12th, the day assigned for the march, the gale violently swept across the sea. The people in Boston might be "anxious beyond description," and thousands might be on "tiptoe to join" Sullivan, as Heath wrote the harassed general; but no army could march in such a tempest.[5] Through the 13th the storm raged causing Sullivan to write:

The Situation of my army is now miserable beyond Description most of my troops without any kind of Covering & those who have tents but Little better Guarded against this violent and uncommon storm my ammunition mostly ruined & arms rendered useless.[6]

He could not consider retreat, should it be necessary, since the river was "Rendered impracticable"; hence "our Safety must therefore Depend upon Bravery & the Point of the Bayonet." [7] Nor were these his sole worries. Word had come to headquarters that the British admiral, John Byron, was on the coast and in all probability would make his appearance before the return of D'Estaing, who undoubtedly had been blown to sea.[8]

The General was determined to surmount these unforeseen difficulties. Writing Governor William Greene, Governor Cook's successor, of his desire to succeed in his mission he said: "Should I fail to accomplish it or perish in the attempt I wish you & your assembly to witness for my Character against a Censorious world who will take pleasure to Blast my Reputation for being unsuccessful Even though they know it to be unavoidable." [9] Toward daybreak of the 14th the wind veered to the southward, the storm had run its course. The battered army turned out to examine the arms and spent the day drying clothes and renewing cartridges. A raging sea still made retreat impossible; histrionically Sullivan informed Henry Laurens that a militia unable to retreat may find "the only remaining alternative is to conquer or die." [10]

From Providence Governor Greene wrote that he would do all he could to renew cartridges, some of which he sent immediately, and reassured Sullivan that in no way could he be blamed for the course of events. Neither the storm nor the departure of the French fleet could have been avoided. "I can truly say," he continued, "that I have Often heard with pleasure that You have from the beginning of Your making preparations for the present Expedition, done everything and a great deal more than couᵈ reasonably have been expected in so short Space of Time for the forwarding the Expedition." [11] Now that the storm had abated, the Governor trusted the assault would be launched and with success.

Sullivan's general orders for August 14 announced that the army would move forward on the next day, Saturday, at 6:00 A.M. In the first line James Varnum's brigade was to move along the West Road, John Glover's along the East Road, both of which ran from the northern end of the island toward Newport, with Ezekiel Cornell's and Christopher Greene's brigades in the center. The second line, reserve, and flanking parties were to preserve a proper distance for deploying.[12] The 15th dawned. At 6:00 A.M. from the right came the signal gun for the troops to parade, and by 6:30 the army had formed in columns ready to advance. Forward went the first line in four columns, the second line in two. The flanking divisions and flanking parties likewise advanced, and to the right the light horse went out to reconnoiter. At the head moved the "pioneers" to tear down the walls in the way of the marching men.[13] Out of a rabble, howbeit respectable, Sullivan had managed to create something resembling an army. Earlier he had referred to his troops as a "dissaranged Chaos of Militia," needing to be organized "if any Power less than the Almighty fiat" could do so.[14] By 2:00 P.M. the army had advanced to within a mile and a half of the redoubts before Newport in the vicinity of Honeyman's Hill east of Easton's Pond. Here they encamped. General Sullivan still had his problems. Writing to the Governor, he asked for more men, since he feared that D'Estaing might not be able to join him. Besides, some of his volunteers had already departed, and he had no guarantee others would not follow them.[15] He had not only to organize an army; he had to keep it together. Sullivan's plan was to take the town by regular approaches, and for the next five days the army stood before Newport erecting works. Throughout this time the British maintained a rather steady cannonading, with the Americans returning some of the fire.

Faced with the problem of desertion, Sullivan issued a proclamation on the 16th urging the neighboring towns to apprehend and return to camp all persons leaving the island who lacked a proper pass. The militia, in particular, he complained were "so base as to Desert the Army, tho engagd in the most glorious Cause, and in the Fairest prospects of Victory." [16] Word went out to the New England states to send on additional men. Even without adequate troops, General Sullivan decided to commence the approaches on that night, the 16th.[17] A trace of his earlier confidence returned, and once more his vanity and his optimism served to encourage him. On the 17th he wrote Washington that "by timely addresses to my men [I] have exhilerated their spirits & reconciled them in a great measure to the vicissitudes of war." [18] The British had best beware, he wrote, for he would be able "to keep up so warm a fire upon them as to render the properties of a salamander essentially necessary to their existence."

By August 19 he reported that some batteries were already within musket shot of the enemy, indeed one was within half that distance. All this accomplished in defiance of unceasing, though inefficient fire! A lingering fog had assisted his approaches without the loss of a single man. This day, he acclaimed, he would accost the enemy in "accents of Thunder." As yet he had no word from D'Estaing, but in the distance the faint sound of cannon gave him hopes that his allies were off Block Island waiting for the fog to rise. [19]

Perhaps now he would have battle. Irritated because he had been unable to provoke the enemy to action, he sought to storm the British works. [20] In his opinion only the arrival of a British fleet and reinforcements could save the enemy; even then the size of his army would enable him to retreat without loss, a possibility which he was loath to consider. [21] There was some reason for optimism. That morning a battery of four eighteen-pounders had silenced an advanced redoubt of the enemy. The next day, the 20th, another four-gun battery opened. [22] More troops were promised from Massachusetts; and Rhode Island, wishing to enlist in the army the seamen who in their small boats swarmed in Narragansett Bay seeking plunder, placed a one week's embargo on all vessels. [23]

Soon Sullivan's fortunes were again to cloud. Though some of the French fleet reappeared off Rhode Island on the morning of August 20, unpleasant news came from the Count de Cambis who was off Point Judith aboard the captured corvette, "Senegal." Since the "Languedoc" and "Marseillais" had suffered considerable damage in the storm, D'Estaing had decided he must go on to Boston.[24] Howe had left for New York to refit his ships which had been battered by the storm that had prevented a major engagement between the fleets. No news could have been more shattering than D'Estaing's announcement. Sullivan was beside himself and saw all his hopes for a successful campaign collapse about him. Nathanael Greene, John Langdon, and Lafayette went aboard the fleet to remonstrate with D'Estaing, whose ship, the "Languedoc," limped into Rhode Island waters because the Count had promised to return; but all efforts to persuade him to remain were bootless.[25]

Early on the morning of August 22 the fleet stood well to sea. A campaign that had augured success appeared doomed, cracked by chance and by circumstance beyond the control of John Sullivan. Perhaps to ask him to remain calm was to ask the impossible, perhaps not, but all military leaders should prepare themselves for unavoidable contingencies. Sullivan's reaction to D'Estaing's departure revealed him at his worst—petulant, quite intolerant of an opposing point of view, and unappreciative of the importance of proper relations between the Americans and their new and sensitive allies. Considering Sullivan's overweening ambition and his extreme fear of failure, it is understandable, though censurable, that he became almost uncontrollable in his fury. As the French sails dropped over the horizon, General Sullivan's chances for the victory he so cherished for both himself and for the cause of independence dimmed.

He made one further attempt to induce D'Estaing to return by penning a letter which outlined to the Frenchman the ruinous consequences which must follow in the train of his departure. Since the fleet had already sailed, Sullivan and his officers also drew up a remonstrance which they sent by John Laurens after the French on August 22.[26] Sullivan believed D'Estaing was reluctant to leave, but he had little hopes that the French fleet would turn about. The remonstrance viewed the French action as violating an agreement and argued that the honor of

France was involved. Quite naturally Lafayette, upon being called to headquarters, refused to sign the protest and was considerably irritated.[27]

On August 23, Laurens returned from his fruitless chase. Now convinced that the French were not going to come back, Sullivan sought the advice of his officers. On hand he estimated his strength at 8,174 rank and file, excluding 628 matrosses and artillery men, with an expected reinforcement of 3,000 men due shortly. The British strength he placed at about 6,000 including the artillery, but, in the absence of the French, Newport was open to reinforcement. He told his officers that there were three alternatives: continue the siege, attack, or retreat. The officers were not in agreement. Just the day before, on the 22d, Sullivan had hoped he could continue the siege provided that he received support from the militia.[28] Yet indecision was reflected in his orders of August 24 in which he said he hoped a retreat would not be necessary. He could not curb his pique against the French and, in an inexcusable fashion, stated that the Americans would procure by their own arms that which her "Allies refuse to assist in Obtaining." [29] Trouble was in the offing; such aspersions cast against the French might easily disrupt the new and valued alliance. Lafayette quickly came to his countrymen's defense, lamenting rather priggishly that he had had an "occasion of seeing so ungenerous sentiments in American hearts." Rumor circulated that he even had challenged Sullivan to a duel.[30]

His complaints to Sullivan bore fruit, for on August 26 the General, his fury somewhat cooled, tempered his earlier indiscreet remarks. These new orders read in part:

It having been supposed by some Persons that by the Orders of the 24th Inst. the Commander in Chief meant to insinuate that the departure of the French Fleet was owing to a fixed determination not to assist in the present enterprize—As the General would not wish to give the least colour for ungenerous and illiberal minds to make such unfair interpretations, he thinks it necessary to say that as he could not possibly be acquainted with the orders of the Admiral he could not determine whether the Removal of the Fleet was absolutely necessary or not and therefore did not mean to censure an act which the Admirals orders might render absolutely necessary— He however hopes that the Speedy return of the Fleet will show their attention and regard to the Alliance formed between us and add to the obligations the Americans are already under to the French nation. However mortifying the Departure of the Fleet was to us at such a time of expectations we ought not too suddenly to Censure the movement; or for an act of any kind to forget the aid and Protection which had been offered by the French since the Commencement of the present Contest.[31]

Soon Sullivan made up his mind; he would maintain the siege but withdraw from before Newport. Then he would wait for the fleet's return from Boston, for without naval support Sullivan could not hope to assault the enemy lines. He was not properly placed for an onslaught against Newport anyway, for a deep ravine separated him from the enemy, a ravine at the bottom of which was Easton's pond and its inlet. Any sapping approach down its slope from where the Americans were placed would have resulted in disastrous enfilading fire from the British, and an attempt to turn the British right by crossing the defile between the pond and the sea would have met with failure, since artillery placed in the British inner redoubt controlled the area. An alternative approach, which Sullivan either did not consider or decided against, was from the north, to the west of the position he took. Here there was no ravine to cross, and he might have met success.[32]

Be that as it may, at present Sullivan saw before him the enemy upon advantageous ground. Their entrenchments were extensive, and behind them stood a series of redoubts lined with cannon. Guarding these lines were professional soldiers before whom stood an army of perhaps 8,000, mostly inexperienced militia "unaccustomed to the noise of arms." [33] Other factors entered the situation. His force was melting away, and on the night of the 24th he had heard from Washington that naval reinforcements might be coming to Newport's assistance. To retreat was the proper decision under the circumstances. Accordingly on the night of August 28 the army was put in motion.[34] By about 2:00 A.M. the Americans had encamped on Butts Hill, their right extending to the West Road, their left to the East Road. Further toward the water on either side were the flanking parties, and on a redoubt in advance of the right of the first line was posted one regiment. The light corps under Colonel Henry B. Livingston in the East Road and a detachment under John Laurens in the West Road were both posted three miles in front.[35]

Early in the morning the enemy came out of their lines and advanced down both roads toward the rebel positions. For the first time in his military career, Sullivan now would have the overall direction of a battle. At Long Island, Trenton, Princeton, Brandywine, and Germantown he had been responsible to a senior officer, but here he was in command, and accordingly took his position somewhere on Butts Hill.[36] At 7:00 A.M. the British encountered the American advanced units under Livingston and Laurens. Sullivan, considerably to the rear of the action, most likely had just fragmentary information about the fighting in this sector. Pigot had sent Brigadier General Smith with two regiments and the flank companies of two others by the East Road. Major General von Lossberg proceeded along the West Road with the Hessian chasseurs and two Anspach regiments.[37] The enemy met warm reception from Livingston and Laurens, who were supported by the army picket. Sullivan sent forward two regiments to assist them, but at the same time gave orders that all were to retire to the ground where the main army stood. Although Nathanael Greene at the time urged a general action, Sullivan chose not to follow his advice, and Greene later admitted that the General's decision to pull back his troops was the prudent course to take.[38]

The withdrawal was not precipitate, but rather regular and leisurely. Sullivan's orders were strictly followed, and the general later spoke highly of the way in which his men retired while giving the enemy resistance. At Quaker Hill, on the eastern side of the island south of Butts Hill, the Americans put up a stiff fight as they fell back, now reinforced by the two regiments. Here they were well posted and twice repulsed the enemy on their left. Sullivan sent John Trumbull to Colonel Edward Wigglesworth, who commanded the rear guard of the advanced units, with orders that the men must retire.[39]

To Sullivan's left he saw the enemy approaching, but General Glover's brigade was on hand to hurl them back toward Quaker Hill. In this vicinity the British took their position about one mile from Sullivan's front line, but Sullivan had his troops placed and ready. The front line, consisting of the brigades of Varnum, Cornell, Christopher Greene, and Glover, was before the works on Butts Hill. Titcomb and Lovell in the second line were behind Butts Hill, and the reserve under William West was one-half mile behind the front line.[40]

Meadowland, interspersed by a few trees and a small copse, separated the American front line and the British on Quaker Hill. The action until now had been prelude to the battle fought that Saturday, August 29. At about 9:00 A.M. the British cannonading began, a fire that the Americans returned. The grumble of cannon continued throughout the summer's day, an accompaniment for the actions of the sweating men. Some skirmishing occurred between forward units, but any advance would have to come from the British, because Sullivan preferred to wait. About 10:00 A.M. Sullivan noticed firing to his right, and learned that two ships of war and some small armed vessels which had gained his flank had commenced to fire. Evidently the advanced redoubt on the American right was the British target. Sullivan could expect pressure in this area and took measures to prevent that flank from being turned. Here the enemy bent their whole force in a conflict that was bitterly contested.[41]

For a number of hours the enemy in this struggle tested the American right. Nathanael Greene, who commanded that wing, later commented that a cannonade lasted for some hours while skirmishing continued in front of the lines with two British attacks driven back in great confusion. Then about 2:00 P.M. the enemy tried another advance, this time hurling forward more troops than before and apparently with greater determination.[42]

The enemy gained against four regiments ordered up by Greene, who himself advanced with two more regiments and one brigade of the second line, Lovell's militia. This brigade was the sole unit of the second line to see action. Sullivan ordered Henry B. Livingston with his light troops, who had been resting in the rear, to advance.[43] For perhaps an hour the men struggled for control of the ground, but gradually the enemy began to give way. Sullivan believed that the British attack would have succeeded if no timely aid had been sent forward. Now the enemy was routed, Sullivan attested, tumbling back in confusion to the lines on Quaker Hill. Nathanael Greene claimed the British ran in worse disorder than the retreating troops at the Battle of Monmouth.[44]

The battle ended as it had begun, with cannonading and skirmishes. Sullivan wrote that the musketry had been firing for about six hours, the artillery throughout the day. He wished to press toward the British line, believing that the enemy could be routed. His men had not rested for thirty-six hours, however, and had nothing to eat either the night before or during the day of battle. The condition of his troops and the strong position of the British caused him to cease fighting—a wise decision, because the British were not outnumbered. Neither is it likely that their retreat was so precipitate as both Sullivan and Greene reported.[45] General Sullivan claimed a complete victory, although he admitted that his loss had been considerable, Varnum's brigade suffering the most. He was lavish in his praise of both officers and men. American losses in killed, wounded, and missing totaled just over 200. Pigot put the British casualties at 260.[46]

The next morning, Sunday, August 30, disquieting news came from Washington. Howe evidently was on his way to relieve Newport.[47] Also Sullivan found out that D'Estaing's fleet would not show up so soon as expected, although the Marquis de Lafayette who had sped to Boston on the eve of the battle to urge D'Estaing's return reported back to Sullivan the next night, after the conflict, that D'Estaing was willing to march overland with his soldiers to offer what assistance he could to the American cause.[48] The decision to retreat from the island, however, had already been reached before this news came from D'Estaing; but without the aid of the French fleet, no further action against Newport was possible. The Council of War was unanimous for retreat. In fact the enemy fleet was seen in the distance, and three ships had already arrived. The Americans also may have known that Pigot was bringing up artillery from Newport and would renew his efforts to dislodge them.[49]

Accordingly at 6:00 P.M., on August 30, Sullivan gave orders to retreat. During the day the army ferried the heavy baggage and stores across to the mainland. Sullivan had a number of tents pitched forward in sight of the enemy to mislead them. Night fell. The remaining tents were struck, and the light baggage and troops were all safely across on the mainland by the early hours of the next morning. The British were unaware of the American withdrawal until too late.[50] The Americans got out none too soon, for Sullivan reported that one hundred enemy sail appeared in the harbor the following morning. Sir Henry Clinton had come with about 4,000 men. Contrary winds in Long Island Sound had delayed his arrival, but it is possible, had he appeared earlier, that he might have been able to cut off the retreat.[51]

Thus ended a campaign that had commenced with high hopes. The British still held Newport. Although Sullivan had failed to accomplish his goal, the campaign was not a discredit to him, for all he could do was to withdraw, and that he did with a minimum amount of effort and without much loss.

Safely on the Tiverton shore, John Sullivan soon found that he was once more in the midst of controversy, because his harsh criticism of the French was straining the new alliance. The officers' unfortunate protest and Sullivan's general orders of August 24 rankled the sensitive allies, although Washington tried to soothe the irate Lafayette by excusing Sullivan's comments as "uttered perhaps without Consideration, and in the first transport of disappointed hope." [52] Washington and Congress had quite a problem on their hands, but the delegates chose to thank Sullivan for his efforts against the British rather than censure him for insulting D'Estaing.[53] Certainly General Sullivan received far more praise than blame, and he was far from contrite. Although he had toned down his remarks in his general orders of August 26 upon Lafayette's insistence, he was too obtuse to realize that he had violated etiquette, and he never got it through his head that his remarks and the protest had been insulting. He minimized the whole affair and continued to argue that D'Estaing could have given him naval support for forty-eight hours, which in his opinion would have allowed victory.

Although D'Estaing himself tried to calm the waters by writing Sullivan that his feelings had not been offended, still as late as October 1 he hammered away at the General's overbearing manner.[54] He had reason to be irritable, because he believed that the Americans were completely unready for a campaign in Rhode Island, which made Sullivan's arrogance uncalled for and gave him no license for the abuse heaped upon the French.[55] It hurt D'Estaing to see unfavorable feeling in New England toward him and his men, typified by one person's comment that the French had "made a most miserable figure," cursed by all ranks of people.[56] Gradually, however, more sensible opinion began to gain ground, and many pacified D'Estaing's ruffled feelings.

As the crisis over the French eased, some found time to assess Sullivan's efforts as commander during the Rhode Island fight, and, on the whole, compliments came his way. Nathanael Greene said that any attempt to storm the British lines after the French departure would have met with disaster. Describing Sul-

livan as "sensible, active, ambitious, brave, and persevering in
his temper," Greene pointed out that the general would have
tried any means to achieve victory, if such had been at all possible.[57] Even Lafayette offered some praise when he wrote that
Sullivan "retreated in good order; he opposed very properly
every effort of the enemy; he never sent troops but well supported; and displayed great coolness during the whole day." [58]
Yet not all extolled the virtues of John Sullivan. Pennsylvania's
Joseph Reed, who did not like him and never showed much
confidence in his ability, claimed that the outcome failed to
disappoint him because he had expected nothing, and that Sullivan never would shine as an officer. Writing off both Sullivan
and D'Estaing as prima donnas, Reed said that Sullivan should
have bottled his criticism of the French leader, since he ought to
have known "that God almighty may have made some other
Creatures in the same mould with himself." [59]

Earlier Reed remarked, somewhat bitterly, that the expedition had ended "with little real Advantage to the Publick." [60]
Perhaps that must be the judgment; but if so, in no way can
Sullivan be blamed for the failure. Washington had not given
him enough time to get ready for a campaign; yet, considering
the inadequacies and irritating matters which faced him, it is
surprising Sullivan accomplished what he did. He got an army
together, he had boats built or brought from the Eastern Department to transport his men, he crossed over to Rhode Island successfully, and he stood before Newport. Then that adversity
which had bedeviled his career showed up again. Delays that he
could not have avoided allowed the British fleet to make its appearance. D'Estaing had to give chase. The storm was the crush-
ing blow; D'Estaing's decision, this time to go to Boston, was
correct, but without French naval assistance any hope of cap-
turing Newport was sheer nonsense.[61] George Washington believed that success at Rhode Island might have meant the end
of the war, and if that were the case, it would be impossible for
a man of Sullivan's temperament to sit by idly and watch such

a chance for gaining renown slip out of his grasp.[62] Regrettably, but possibly because the man was merely human, he had carped at his allies. His ambition, which failed to let him adjust to events whenever they affected him adversely, was a flaw in his character. Nathanael Greene advised Sullivan good fortune may be followed by reverses, and that one should be prepared. He wished Sullivan might be spared reverses; "But Fortune is a fickle Jade," he said, "and often gives us a tumble when we least expect it." [63] If John Sullivan had learned anything out of his experience, he had learned that fortune indeed was fickle.

The disappointing campaign put General Sullivan in a peevish frame of mind, and he found it difficult to stay calm. He had to keep an army together, because the British moves were an enigma and he had no idea where they might strike next. General Washington kept Sullivan as well informed as possible about the enemy moves. The worried Commander-in-Chief considered sending Horatio Gates to assume command of the Eastern Department from Heath, a prospect which brought the captious side of Sullivan to the surface. Nathanael Greene reported: "I hear General Sullivan declares, by all that is sacred, that he never will submit to an order of General Gates's." [64] When Washington wrote Sullivan, late in October, of the impending shift in command, his letter brought a reply from Sullivan affecting injury, but surely by now Washington must have been inured to the General's complaints. Sullivan said: "I am at a Loss to know Either the Reason or the meaning of it—how far his Command will Interfere with mine his Conduct will Explain & point out the path I ought to pursue—in Every Step I take I Shall Earnestly wish for your Excellenceys approbation to follow my Conduct which whether in publick or private Life I Shall Esteem more than The Inconsiderate Disapprobation or unmeaning applause of millions." [65]

Sullivan, however, soon became involved in new controversies and did not hassle over the protocol of command. Instead he got into a dispute over what he considered to be a lack of supplies. During the fall and winter months his arbitrary point of view and his begrudging compliance with the civilian authorities show the least attractive side of Sullivan's personality. His impulsive nature made him criticize legislation, which he said made it more difficult to procure supplies, and to chastise the Commissary Department, which he claimed was grossly inefficient, for as yet he had not acquired the wisdom and restraint that can come with maturer age. Also the fatiguing, frustrating campaign of the summer added to his unreasonableness, but this is no defense for his overbearing actions when he tried to arrogate to himself powers that others were reluctant to allow him.

The entire fall and winter found Sullivan in almost constant argument with the neighboring states over supplies, and with the commissaries, particularly Jeremiah Wadsworth. Fluctuating prices were playing havoc with the supply system, a brutal fact which infuriated Sullivan. Purchasing commissaries often found that sellers could obtain in other markets higher prices than the commissaries themselves had been instructed to offer. He could not obtain forage from Massachusetts, which had a surplus, because the inhabitants of the Bay State would not sell at his price. Sullivan wanted the forage masters to impress what they needed, but out of a begrudging awareness of civilian control he hoped to get permission from the Massachusetts authorities. The Massachusetts Council, however, would not agree with his position, saying that there was a difference between a marching army and one in quarters, and that only in the most extreme cases would the Council grant authority to impress.[66] General Sullivan then appealed to Congress, claiming that the alternatives were clear: "Either impress Hay at a reasonable Rate, purchase it at the most extravagant Price demanded by the Country People or loose [sic] all the Horses of the Army." [67] Little comfort was forthcoming, however, for Congress was unwilling to place that much power in the hands of the forage masters. On November 30 Congress, however, did resolve that, when forage could not be obtained at reasonable rates, the state might interfere and offer assistance. Yet Massachusetts had shown little disposition to help, and Sullivan had not gained his point.[68]

Even more annoying than the shortage of forage was what he considered a glaring deficiency of supplies for his troops, especially in flour. He took matters into his own hands, particularly after hearing that Washington was sending on three more brigades, when he decided—unwisely—to hire his own purchasing agents. This action bypassed the Commissary Department and caused a price rise, because Sullivan's agents were competing with the commissary buyers at public sale. Upon receiving complaints from Peter Colt, deputy commissary general at Hartford, Sullivan said he would stop buying flour through his own agents just as soon as regular channels would supply him, and these assurances quieted Colt for the moment.[69]

Sullivan then began to bombard Washington with letters defending his actions. He continued the flow of letters even after Washington advised him that Jeremiah Wadsworth was complaining and that his actions had gone around the law.[70] Sullivan did not blame Wadsworth for failing to get supplies to his army, but he did blame his deputies. Wadsworth, quite naturally, was displeased and asked for an inquiry, but Washington tried to avoid one.[71] Wadsworth "would wave [sic] the matter of the enquiry," the Commander-in-Chief informed Sullivan, "which would involve all parties concerned in a tedious and disagreeable dispute." [72] General Sullivan, nevertheless, seemed not to be in a conciliatory mood. He denied that he had ever misrepresented the situation in Rhode Island, and suggested that Wadsworth would not want an inquiry since Sullivan could prove that only through his own buyers' exertions had his army been saved.[73] Wadsworth was furious, particularly because Sullivan had gone over his head to General Washington, but he ordered Colt to get the flour to Rhode Island, even to fetch it "from the ends of the earth if necessary." [74]

General Wadsworth, however, was in no mood to let the matter rest here, for he argued that Sullivan had made misrepresentations to Washington about supplies in his command, and that Sullivan had denied all. The Commissary General was most irate because Sullivan had implied a complete breakdown in the supply system under Wadsworth's command, when, except for a paucity of flour, there had not been much of a shortage. Sullivan did have a tendency to dramatize and most likely overstated the conditions in Rhode Island; yet he refused to accept any blame, but instead argued that there should be a Court of Inquiry to examine the behavior of Peter Colt, who had been the cause of his troubles. From the time Sullivan had hired his own buyers he had placed himself in a delicate situation, but he had no intention of backing down.[75] The Commissary Department did not care to back down either and prosecuted Captain Amasa Sessions, who, while purchasing for Sullivan in Connecticut, had violated a Connecticut embargo when he tried to take supplies to Rhode Island.[76] Washington still was trying to bring about a compromise, hoping to avoid any trials of the commissaries, in particular Peter Colt, if the Commissary Department would not proceed in its action against Sessions. The Commander-in-Chief seemed to be quite helpless in this embroilment.[77]

The outcome of the controversy is clouded. A Court of Inquiry took place under General Glover in Rhode Island, beginning March 1, 1779, but the proceedings remained secret, perhaps so that Sullivan could use them to advantage at Sessions's trial. The Court of Inquiry, certainly not an impartial body, determined that a shortage had existed, that the commissaries had been deficient, and that their actions had been dictated by their own private interests.[78] Naturally Sullivan now felt justified in having circumvented the Commissary Department. Although Colt had looked upon the inquiry "as Essential to fix our Characters, & free us from the wanton aspersions of General Sullivan or any others in the Quarter," the commissaries made little effort to defend themselves before the Court.[79] Only one purchasing commissary had attended, for the department evidently did not consider the proceedings would be or could be impartial. No further action occurred against the commissaries.[80]

Sessions finally appeared for trial in Pomfret, Connecticut, on March 11 after one postponement. Sullivan was on hand, surely hoping to show that there was no cause for the action. Sessions was acquitted. Nathanael Greene wrote Wadsworth later in the month, wryly indicating that Sullivan might have been better occupied. He commented:

> General Sullivan I find has turnd Lawyer again. I wonder what fee he had. Methinks he has gave a fine opening for some satirical pen—Suppose the Enemy had surprisd his post while he was playing the Cicero in Connecticut.
>
> I am Sorry he interests himself so deeply in that affair; and I still more so that he gives his tongue a latitude of reflection.[81]

Shortly the General's attention was to turn elsewhere, for a letter arrived from Horatio Gates, dated March 16, enclosing one from General Washington. Washington was offering Sullivan another command, should Gates refuse; this time to lead an expedition against the Six Nations.[82] Since time was precious, Washington dared not wait for Gates's reply; hence he had enclosed this letter in his original offer of the command to Gates in expectation of the latter's refusal, which is exactly what happened.[83] Sullivan first had doubts. Ill health, financial worries, and his desire to see his family all argued against acceptance, nor had Washington's letter been entirely explicit. Also he did not wish to leave Providence without settling the accounts of his command. He wrote Gates: "A years pay will not Support me & my family [i.e., military staff] to Head Quarters & Back again & Even if my health & all other Circumstances would admit I could not think of Leaving a Department where I have Commanded a year without Settling my Accounts & Securing myself ag^t after Demands." [84] He decided to write Washington about his hesitation, and let Washington's reply determine his decision.

Six days later, however, he had made up his mind to under-

take the leadership of the Indian expedition without waiting for
Washington's letter. Too much valuable time would be lost unless he set out immediately for headquarters at Middlebrook,
New Jersey. A friend had loaned him some money so that he
would be able to make the trip; the public chest, he said, had not
a farthing.[85] He planned to leave Providence on Monday, March
28. Thanks came in from many quarters to Sullivan, sincere
statements from officers, from the town of Providence, and
from his brother Freemasons, one of whom wrote: "May the
great grand Master of the Universe take you under his particular Guidance and Direction, cover your Head in the Day of Battle, and crown you with Success, equal to the Square of your
most Sanguine Wishes." [86] Monday arrived. Thirteen cannon
saluted the general. John Glover, James Varnum, and other officers, all accompanied by a band, and many of Providence's
respectable inhabitants escorted Sullivan as far as Johnston,
where after an elegant dinner "he took a most affectionate Leave
of them, and pursued his Journey." [87]

VIII: PLANNING FOR THE INDIAN CAMPAIGN

APRIL–JULY, 1779

Once more Sullivan was taking on a separate command, but, as he rode toward headquarters at Middlebrook, he knew only that he was to lead "an Expedition of an extensive nature agt. the hostile tribes." [1] Washington wanted Sullivan to hint that a blow against Canada was in the offing, for this would confuse the enemy and hide from them the intent to move against the League of the Iroquois, or the Six Nations, to use the English name. No one must know why Sullivan was going to headquarters, Washington warned; because if it became known that an officer of Sullivan's rank was to command in the west, the enemy would find out that the Americans were planning a major campaign in that direction.

The idea of a campaign against the Indians was not new. Most of them had sided with the British, because they realized that the land-hungry American was a rival for their domain. The savages had taken the offensive and during 1778 had carried out two brutal raids at Wyoming and Cherry Valley. In November, 1778, Washington had considered thrusts against Detroit, Niagara, and the area around Lakes Erie and Ontario to curb the ravages of the Indians.[2] A few weeks later Washington even thought of the possibility of a drive toward Canada along with a blow at Niagara, for an invasion into Canada would have pleased Congress.[3] By the beginning of 1779, however, the Commander-in-Chief had fairly well determined in his own mind that a drive against the Six Nations would be enough, and that a push toward Canada might overtax his strength. In Washington's opinion three alternatives in strategy for 1779 faced the Americans: to expel the British from their present posts on the seaboard, to launch an attack against Niagara, thereby opening the door to Canada, or to remain entirely on the defensive, except for smaller operations against the Indians.[4] He preferred the third scheme, because the first two would require too much manpower and expense. Once he had made up his mind, Washington acquired as much information as possible about the country to be invaded.[5] He already had anticipated the wishes of Congress, for the delegates passed a resolution on February 25, directing him to take effective measures to protect the inhabitants of the frontier and to chastise the Indians.[6]

Sullivan was not a popular choice for the command, and Washington had to defend his appointment. John Armstrong, representing Pennsylvania in Congress, would have preferred Daniel Brodhead, but Washington assured Armstrong that Sullivan had not been appointed from partiality or from haste. After long consideration of the people involved, the circumstances, military rules, and propriety, he could do no better. "I must work with such means as I have," he wrote.[7] Earlier he had told John Jay that Schuyler would have suited him, but that the New Yorker was too uncertain of remaining in the army. Seniority required that he offer Gates the assignment, and the latter's somewhat curt refusal irritated the Commander-in-Chief.[8] Almost by default, then, the command had fallen on Sullivan. Upon learning that Sullivan had been appointed, Pennsylvania's President, Joseph Reed, despaired of success for the expedition. Nathanael Greene did his best to persuade Reed that Sullivan had been chosen after long and mature deliberation, but Reed still had no confidence in Sullivan's ability.[9]

After his arrival at Middlebrook early in April, General Sullivan immediately conferred with Washington, and learned that the campaign was to be no more than a punitive expedition.[10]

The patriots wished to quell the Indians and loyalists under John Butler and his son Walter. They wanted to bring a welcome peace to a molested frontier; far too often the Indian war cry had pierced the soundless night, causing the men of the eighteenth century to look upon the Indian as a savage who deserved no quarter. The immediate problems facing Washington and Sullivan were to determine which route the army would take to enter the land of the Six Nations, and the best way of moving a large army, well supplied, into a wilderness.

Washington had given much thought to the campaign and undoubtedly explained his reasoning to the eager Sullivan. He wanted the main thrust to go along the Susquehanna by way of Tioga, because the Mohawk route struck him as being too circuitous, particularly as the Senecas to the West were to be the primary objective.[11] This does not mean that Washington thought there should be a strike from just one direction, but instead he saw the offensive as a combined operation. One army would also move from the Mohawk in conjunction with the main advance from Tioga; in fact, as events unfolded, there were subsidiary moves, one against the Onondagas in New York, and another into the Indian Country from Fort Pitt.[12] Since General James Clinton had command of the troops operating from New York, the offensive has rightly been called the Sullivan-Clinton Campaign.

Into John Sullivan's hands Washington placed all the information he had collected: detailed descriptions of the Indian country, the best routes, maps, and the ways of transporting supplies.[13] Sullivan studied the materials, and on April 15 sent his opinion to Washington. He though Schuyler was underestimating the strength of the enemy when he placed their numbers at about 2,000, and Sullivan went on to claim that a larger force would stand against the Americans, because loyalists would join the savages.[14] If the main American force assembled on the Susquehanna, the enemy would then know that any attempt on Canada had been suspended, Sullivan argued. Therefore the

enemy would throw their entire attention first against the secondary force proceeding by way of the Mohawk, and then
against the major force coming from Tioga. Instead he urged
that the main body, consisting of 4,000 men, enter the Indian
country by the Mohawk. Such a force could march "with that
necessary firmness which consciousness of superiority seldom
fails to inspire." [15] An army moving this way had a better
chance of cutting off an Indian retreat than did an army advancing along the Susquehanna; but Sullivan did not choose to
slight the Susquehanna route, however, for he suggested that
2,500 men go that way as a subsidiary force.[16]

In asking for so many men, Sullivan justified his demands by
arguing that the expedition must not fail. The purpose of the
campaign, he said, was to cut off the alien nations and to convince others that the Americans had the power and means to
carry war into their land. Unless the blow be sure and fatal, he
continued, the campaign might best be forgotten, because to
fail would merely swell the confidence and insolence of the
savages.[17]

The next day he had changed his opinion about the routes.
Philip Schuyler had written that the main body going by way
of the Mohawk toward Lake Cayuga could not be provisioned,
and therefore Sullivan accepted the Susquehanna route as the
main one. Since the opinion in Council suggested that opposition
would be met between Wyoming and Tioga, Sullivan raised his
request to 3,000 effective men for the Susquehanna route, after
making deductions for guards and boatmen. Although the
Council had estimated that the force opposing him would not
amount to more than 1,400, General Sullivan wanted a large
force. He observed that Indians familiar with the wilderness
would be "no Despicable Enemy." [18] He added that underrating
the number of the enemy had been a constant fault throughout
the war, and that he wished to be ready for any eventuality,
particularly in case the British reinforced Fort Niagara. His request for more men was unrealistic, and Washington, although

willing, could not satisfy his whims. As matters stood the main army was strained enough in supplying the necessary troops for the expedition, but, insofar as was possible, Sullivan's request for specific corps was met.[19] Fortunately for him the units assigned to his command were Continentals, because the militia could not be recruited for a long enough period of time.

A decision came some time in April that the army would move on May 15 and rendezvous at Easton on May 20. Almost immediately they were to press on because success depended upon both secrecy and dispatch.[20] Soon Washington admitted that other matters pressed him for attention and that Sullivan should handle the details for the campaign.[21] Jeremiah Wadsworth, still not overly fond of Sullivan, hoped he would be fortunate. "I sincerely wish General Sullivan may have success in his Expedition. I really do not wish him any Evil." [22] Wadsworth feared that the want of money endangered the smooth running of his own department, and the next day Greene admitted to him that preparations were not proceeding as well as might be either hoped for or expected.[23]

Already the first part of the campaign had taken place when on April 24 Colonel Goose Van Schaick had returned to Fort Schuyler from an expedition into the land of the Onondagas and reported complete success in destroying some villages. Now the threat to the flank had been removed, and his success was a good omen.[24] About this time Washington determined that it would be too difficult to coordinate Brodhead's march from Fort Pitt with the march of the main body so that he decided to forego an attack from that direction.[25] The expedition would be entirely in the hands of Sullivan and Clinton.

On May 4 Washington ordered Sullivan to Easton to prepare to enter the Indian country by way of Tioga.[26] Upon his arrival in Easton on May 7 Sullivan found that boats and stores were not ready at Wyoming, and that he would have to delay most of his troops at Easton. The outlook was bleak. No work had been done on the road through the swamp to Wyoming, although earlier Washington had ordered that a route be cleared. All hopes of maintaining some degree of secrecy were idle, Sullivan discovered, for in Easton the purpose of the expedition was well known. Intelligence arrived that the enemy, aware of the intended expedition, was ready to destroy communications on the Susquehanna. Word went to General Edward Hand at Wyoming to speed on the provisions, to hire guides and, if possible, some spies.[27] Meanwhile, Sullivan worked at a feverish pace in Easton. He asked President Reed to allow the quartermasters to impress wagons and sent a letter to Washington asking for more clothing and suggesting that the remaining troops reach Easton by May 20. By then Colonel Robert Hooper, deputy quartermaster general at Easton, expected to have 1,200 to 1,400 pack horses available for the march, although both forage and money were scarce.[28]

Sullivan's demands seemed insatiable, but he would not move until all his needs had been met. Problems mounted. Word came from Major Richard Claiborne, who had gone to Estherton late in April to expedite the movement of supplies from that area, tossing aside any hopes of speeding the campaign because few of the boats for carrying provisions to Wyoming by the 20th had been built. Some were being built, he commented, and he was hiring boatmen.[29] Even had the boats been ready, though, the supplies would not have been. The Board of War wrote that the stores were on hand, but that there were not enough wagons; three fourths of the provisions had not as yet been put in motion.[30] Sullivan then heard from Reed that the quartermasters could not impress wagons—that might lead to abuse of power—but Reed was placing at Sullivan's disposal wagons from Bucks, Berks, and Northampton Counties.[31]

Meantime, a further report came in from General Hand at Wyoming. He complained that he was short of ammunition, and that, since he had only 424 rank and file available, he could not detach men to escort ammunition coming up the Susquehanna to Wyoming. In fact he questioned whether there was any ammunition to escort.[32] Sullivan said he would send troops and reassured Hand that provisions were on their way up the river.[33] His continual request for supplies began to fray the nerves of some, and Alexander Hamilton wrote: "General Sullivan appears to be very anxious to have his supplies of every kind forwarded to him, that he may begin his career—He is in his usual pother; but dispatch is certainly very desireable." [34]

On May 29 Sullivan set out to examine the road that was being built to Wyoming and found that the road builders had pushed it to within twenty-three miles of that place. Since the Indian path could not be followed, the road had been cut through wilderness. Sullivan wrote that he had never seen such country, and that only by moving along on hands and knees could he find his way through the laurel. Now the road was passable for a coach, he commented, and the men needed only five more days to complete the route.[35]

Back in Easton on May 30, he received the detailed instructions from General Washington outlining the course of the campaign. Sullivan must destroy and devastate the Indian settlements. His force would include the brigades of James Clinton, William Maxwell, Enoch Poor, and Edward Hand, in addition to whatever independent companies Pennsylvania might add. From Tioga, Sullivan was to take the direct route into the Indian country. Washington had certain advice to offer:

I beg leave to suggest as general rules that ought to govern your operations, to make rather than receive attacks attended with as much impetuosity, shouting and noise as possible, and to make the troops act in as loose and dispersed a way as is consistent with a proper degree of government concert and mutual support. It should be previously impressed upon the minds of the men when ever they have an opportunity, to rush on with the warhoop and fixed bayonet. Nothing will disconcert and terrify the indians more than this.[36]

Only after the settlements had been destroyed should Sullivan consider making peace if the Indians expressed willingness. Even then they should give evidence of their sincerity by putting Butler or the Mohawk, Joseph Brant, in the Americans' hands, or perhaps even by seizing Niagara by some stratagem. But in no wise was he to consider peace until the settlements had been demolished. The troops should travel as light as possible and move with speed. Sullivan asked for clarification; if the enemy made concessions which would enable the Americans to control Fort Niagara and the lakes, he wished to know whether he must proceed with the destruction of their country. Washington answered that such offers would be illusory, and that they would result only in delay and unhappy consequences.[37] The capture of Niagara was not a primary objective, but was looked upon as a possible target, only if the Indians could be persuaded to assist in its capture. Pennsylvania's John Armstrong a few days earlier had written Horatio Gates that neither the capture of Niagara nor Detroit was contemplated; retaliation against the Senecas and their allies was the main object.[38]

Sullivan was impatiently waiting to be off, although he did not want to have to draw upon the supplies being gathered at Wyoming until it was time to push into the Indian territory.[39] On June 11 he sent orders to James Clinton. Clinton's point of embarkation would be Lake Otsego, and since no pack horses were to be taken, all troops would be embarked. At Otsego Clinton was to await further orders before continuing with his army.[40] Although Sullivan still waited for more supplies, and although the Pennsylvania companies had not yet been raised, he told Washington that he would not wait for them since he had already delayed too long.[41] Finally, on June 18, John Sullivan ordered his men on their march to Wyoming, from where they would enter the land of the Senecas.[42]

The day after leaving Easton the troops went through the Wind Gap, a pass in the Blue Ridge below the Delaware Water Gap. On the 21st they entered the Great Swamp, twenty miles of "horrid rough gloomey country," and on June 23 reached Wyoming, which was about 65 miles from Easton.[43] One diarist wrote that Wyoming was a beautiful place, "through which

runs the Susquehanna, in a swift delightful course." [44] He spoke
glowingly of the fertile lands and the river plentiful with shad,
trout, and pickerel. General Maxwell also delighted in the
country and noted that the settlement would have been flourish-
ing if it had not been for the cruel enemy who raided it the
previous summer.[45]

The army expected to remain at Wyoming for a short time
only, but Sullivan delayed his march toward Tioga until the
end of July. He wanted the supplies to catch up to him. On
June 25 he wrote Washington the familiar story that the provisions were still down the river, that scarcely a barrel of the
salted meat was edible, and that most of the bread was too
moldy. He hoped that he could save the meat by smoking it, but
he did not know what to do for bread. The troops were not up
to his expectations, and he did not think a single Pennsylvania
man would arrive. Thoroughly disgusted, he wrote; "I have
every possible disappointment and difficulty to grapple with. I
will endeavor to surmount the whole, but I cannot look upon
myself answerable for Consequences which are but too likely
to follow an inattention to this department." [46] Sullivan continued his bitter complaining when he wrote Colonel Charles
Stewart, one of the commissaries, that only great exertions could
save the expedition, and that he needed provisions immediately.[47]
Ironically, General Greene was writing Colonel Hooper on the
same day, the 26th, saying how delighted he was to hear that
Sullivan had moved his army. "This will relieve us from numerous applications," he wrote. "I think his Army was liberally supplied and I hope his success will be equal to the preparation for
the expedition." [48] Greene soon realized that his hopes were
premature.

Over the next few weeks Sullivan waited while his army
strained for action. Charles Stewart replied to Sullivan's urgent
request of June 26 and said that he would try to meet his
needs.[49] Sullivan's answer was testy: "I have been Long Living
upon promises & cannot Say whether Ever they will be per-

formed." He then curtly noted that he had only 700 barrels of flour and about the same of salted provisions. Only about 200 of 1,000 promised cattle had arrived, and other cattle had been left at Sunbury, because they were too weak to stand.[50]

Sullivan had the additional problem of coordinating his moves with those of James Clinton. On the 28th he learned that Clinton had the necessary provisions and was awaiting further orders.[51] The news that a detachment under Lieutenant Colonel Albert Pawling would join Clinton was encouraging. Because Sullivan had heard the enemy was gathering nineteen miles above Ononquaga, the place where Pawling would meet Clinton, he thought it best that Clinton move only after Sullivan had reached Tioga. Then, if Clinton were threatened, a force from Sullivan at Tioga could speed to his assistance. He wrote Washington that Clinton and he had only 3,511 men. He feared he would have just 1,500 by the time he reached Tioga because he would have to leave men to guard the rear.[52]

Washington disapproved of Clinton's carrying many supplies, and wrote Sullivan:

My intention, and which I thought had been sufficiently explained and known to you, was, that the Troops under the command of Genl. Clinton should be at Connajoharie and the vicinity with Boats ready to proceed up the Mohawk River or across to Otsego as you should, under a full consideration of all circumstances and information, resolve on; and that, if the latter should be the choice he was to move rapidly over quite light, and with a sufficient Stock of Provisions and Stores only, to serve him till he could form his junction with you at Teoga, where every thing was to be provided.[53]

Clinton had so many provisions and boats, Washington continued, that he lost any chance of making a secret junction. In fact the Commander-in-Chief thought the entire expedition was over-provisioned. You cannot depend, he advised Sullivan, on salted provisions or hard bread. They would spoil, and transporting them would delay the army and expose it to risks. If Sullivan thought otherwise, however, he was not going to interject his own views. He approved of the plan to reach Tioga before Clinton left Lake Otsego, but he believed that Sullivan underestimated the number of men he would have available as his main force. In his opinion General Sullivan planned to use too many men as guards on the supply line to his rear.[54]

The overly sensitive Sullivan thought Washington was censuring him for ordering Clinton to be fully provisioned. He tried to justify his actions. All his troubles, he said in a lengthy letter to Washington, emanated from the failure of those responsible for collecting the necessary stores. His army remained at Wyoming, consuming precious stores, thus forcing him to order Clinton to provision his own army.[55] Greene wrote Hooper the same day that he was sorry to hear of Sullivan's embarrassments, but that he hoped the General would not allow his army to become too unwieldy for a wilderness campaign. Greene recognized that Sullivan liked to do things in abundance. "He is a friend of a Soldier," he wrote, "although it may be a bane upon the Citizen." [56]

So the army waited. Life in camp was routine. During some of his spare time Sullivan discussed religion. The Reverend Samuel Kirkland wrote that the General and his military family often argued about the authenticity of Scripture and the nature of deism. Evidently Sullivan tried to persuade many of the deists present among his officers that the Scriptures were of divine origin, "at least the doctrinal and perceptive parts." [57] Late in the night of July 4 and during the early hours of the next morning, Sullivan had read to Kirkland a thirty-page treatise, written by him in less than a day, "to prove the existence of a Supreme Being, the truth of the Bible, and that Jesus is the promised Messiah and Saviour of the World." [58] His arguments impressed Kirkland. During their discussion Sullivan had confided to the missionary that at one time he had been an atheist, then a deist, before he "became convinced, by fair and impartial reasoning, of the existence of the Supreme Being, and the perfection of His character." [59]

General Sullivan could not delay indefinitely at Wyoming, in spite of shortage of provisions and what he considered to be an inadequate force. He had three brigades organized under New Jersey's William Maxwell, New Hampshire's Enoch Poor, and Pennsylvania's Edward Hand.[60] President Reed thought this force was larger than could be properly fed once the men went into the Indian country. In a letter to Washington, in which he answered Sullivan's criticism of Pennsylvania's exertions, Reed, miffed because Sullivan had complained to Washington and not to him, said the Council had not heard from the General since he had departed from Easton. "But we cannot change the Course of Things & Order of Providence," Reed observed, "to advance Genl. Sullivans Views be they ever so apparently salutary—and we hope his Recollection of past Periods wherein he has seen you rise superior to Disappointments & Deficiencies far more important, will strengthen his Mind to obviate those which may occur to him." [61]

Those close to Sullivan refused to criticize him for the troubles the army was encountering. He considered himself blameless and persisted in his complaints, particularly to the Board of War. He wrote a long letter to John Jay, president of Congress, because he believed it his duty to both the public and his own reputation to explain to Congress the reason for his delay. He then gave a detailed description of the failure of the supply system. In order to excuse himself should misfortune overtake both him and the expedition, he made it clear to Jay that he did not have as many men as he thought necessary. Only 2,312 rank and file were with him. The 720 rangers and riflemen promised by Pennsylvania had not arrived. After deducting men to serve as boatmen and for garrison duty, the General estimated that he would have only about 938 rank and file as his operating force. This against an enemy supposedly 2,000 strong and lately reinforced! [62] Washington took exception to this letter of Sullivan's and likewise wrote Jay. To him Sullivan's claim that out of a force of 2,312 he could muster only 938 as a fighting force was ridiculous. "If almost the whole of the 2,300 men are not effectually serviceable in action, it must be Genl. Sullivans own fault," he commented.[63] He admitted that the number was lower than it ought to be but believed that little was to be feared once Sullivan and Clinton had joined forces. The Board of War likewise took exception to Sullivan's letter when Timothy Pickering wrote Congress that by and large the demands had been met, but that the Board had found Sullivan's demands difficult to satisfy because they were so vague. Because his demands were on the large side, the Board believed "some caution necessary in granting him supplies." [64]

The provisions began to come through. On July 24, 134 boats arrived from Sunbury.[65] On the same day, a Saturday, the orders stated the army would start toward Tioga on the following Wednesday. All public horses were to be turned in by Tuesday morning. At that time the officers entitled to horses were to be on hand to make their selection. Those appointed as pack-horse drivers were to prepare their loading Tuesday afternoon, ready to leave the following morning. The general orders of the 25th outlined the procedure for marching. Hand's brigade, serving as the light corps, would move in three columns less than a mile in advance of the main body. Maxwell was to advance by his left, Poor by his right. Flanking guards were to be on both the right and left. To the rear of Poor's brigade were to come the pack horses and cattle, and one regiment, taken from both Maxwell's and Poor's brigades, would serve as the rear guard. Colonel Thomas Proctor and his artillery were to go by boat. The main army was told to stay abreast of the boats, which, in turn, were to sound horns frequently to give their position. On the west side of the river scouts were to stay one mile in front watching for ambuscades.[66]

The next day Sullivan made further efforts to defend his decision to delay the expedition until this time. Admitting that he disliked having his reputation attacked, he wrote Henry Laurens and enclosed several letters which outlined the condition of the army. Professing great confidence in Laurens, the General asked that he publish the letters should anything happen to him or his army.[67] This, he hoped, would quiet adverse criticism.

The time approached for departure. Fortunately the rise of the Susquehanna made it easier to transport the boats.[68] Sullivan still was not pleased and whined that "the wretched condition of many of the Soldiers makes it cruel to exact the necessary duty from them." [69] Because supplies were yet to arrive, he announced on July 27 that the army was not to move on the 28th as previously ordered. He expected flour coming by pack horse from Carlisle and by wagons using the road from Easton.[70] He moved the date of march to Saturday, July 31, and on the 29th ordered the brigadiers and field officers to have everything in readiness for the trek to Tioga. He assigned 400 men to the fatigue which was to load the boats and pack horses.[71] On the next day, Friday, word came that the enemy had attacked Freeland's Fort, fifteen miles from Northumberland up the west branch of the Susquehanna. Northumberland likewise was expecting a raid. At about the same time news arrived that Joseph Brant had fallen upon Minisink. Quite obviously the loyalists and Indians were trying to divert Sullivan's attention.[72] But the General would not turn from the march. He replied that, although he would like to offer Northumberland aid, to do so "would Effectually answer the Intention of the Enemy, and Destroy the Grand Object of this Expedition." [73] He believed that by marching into the Indian country his army would draw off the enemy from the frontiers. Rather sarcastically he suggested that those who needed help should turn to the Council, claiming that, since Pennsylvania had not supplied him with troops, the state should be able to defend her own frontiers.[74]

Sullivan's rather blunt refusal to assist brought on criticism. Colonel Matthew Smith called Sullivan no friend of the state, and said "the People of this County is petitioning in very Strong terms, & will Request a hearing against the Genl." [75] President Reed insisted that Sullivan should have detached some men to the frontier posts, because this would have put the Indians be-tween two fires. Instead Sullivan moved away, he wryly com-mented, and chose to leave no ammunition behind.[76]

Sullivan was adamant and wrote Washington that he was marching the following morning, the 31st, as previously de-termined. He boasted, "I have at length surmounted every ob-stacle." [77] Orders went from Sullivan to James Clinton telling him to set out on August 9, and that once Sullivan reached Tioga he would send some light troops "to favour and secure your march." [78] Also he had asked Washington to put Colonel Pawling in motion so that he might make his junction with Clinton on time.

No one could argue that General Sullivan chose to march too soon. Nathanael Greene, who dubbed him the "Duke de Sully," believed he had delayed much too long. He thought it ridiculous that the frontiers should be ravaged when Sullivan had so many men on hand. In fact he feared Sullivan's inaction to date would merely confirm Reed's unfavorable opinion that the general was "a child of disappointment" and would never succeed in any undertaking. Instead of proceeding, Sullivan had been attacking the departments responsible for supplying him, and Greene feared the General would find himself in another dispute with Jeremiah Wadsworth.[79] The army was finally about to move, though, and Sullivan now could turn his atten-tion to other directions.

IX: THE MARCH AGAINST
THE SIX NATIONS

AUGUST–DECEMBER, 1779

The day of departure toward Tioga at last had arrived, and only a small garrison under Colonel Zebulon Butler remained at Wyoming. On July 31 at about noon a cannon fired from the fort, signaling the start. The fleet, commanded by Proctor and carrying the artillery and stores, saluted the fort. About 1,200 pack horses and 700 beef cattle accompanied the army, as Sullivan's men started on their journey from Wyoming to Tioga.[1] They went about ten miles that day, through pleasing wilderness and past some homes burned the year before, with occasional glimpses of the river. Toward nightfall a heavy rain began, and it was not until late that the rear units arrived at the place chosen for camp. The fleet did not reach the site until the middle of the following afternoon, and then the second day's march began.[2]

Just how much did Sullivan know about the enemy as he led his army toward strange country? Before leaving Wyoming he had strong reason to believe that a force was massing to fall upon either him or Clinton before a junction could be made at Tioga.[3] Washington sent on extracts from two of Schuyler's letters which speculated upon enemy strength, and the Commander-in-Chief mentioned that Colonel Brodhead was going into Indian country after all, because a thrust against the Mingoes could serve as a diversion in Sullivan's favor on his left flank.[4] Shortly after, on August 1, Washington relayed further intelligence which he was inclined to credit. The entire force the enemy would be able to assemble, including both whites and Indians, would not exceed 1,500 men, but these the enemy considered equal to twice that many Americans. John Butler, commanding officer of his own rangers of British Provincial Troops, was reportedly at Canadasaga with 300 to 400 men. At Chemung and adjacent towns were 200 or 300 warriors, and there they planned to give battle. If they were unsuccessful, they intended to retire toward Niagara and harass Sullivan as much as possible. As yet no reinforcements had come from Canada, but Brant reported men would be sent. On the whole Sullivan could expect the principal strength of the Indians to be centered in the Genesee towns.[5]

In his later report to Congress, upon the completion of the campaign, Sullivan complained about the poor knowledge he had of the country which he had to traverse. The army lacked proper guides, the maps perplexed rather than enlightened, and not a single person was able to take the lead whenever the army wished to leave the Indian path. The guides' ignorance arose from the fact that the Indians had done all in their power to prevent their country from being explored.[6] Sullivan's information must have been somewhat better than he was willing to admit, however, for he had details on distances and terrain which Washington had carefully assembled. Scouts and spies had been infiltrating into the land of the Six Nations for many weeks and months, and their information must have helped in determining the route the army should take; but Sullivan did not hesitate to say that the maps were poor. They probably were inadequate because the area had never been surveyed.[7] Colonel Charles Stewart had given Sullivan detailed information about the best camping sites between Wyoming and Tioga, although information about the lands beyond Tioga would have been more vague because of limited knowledge.[8]

The army plodded on, making a few miles during a day's

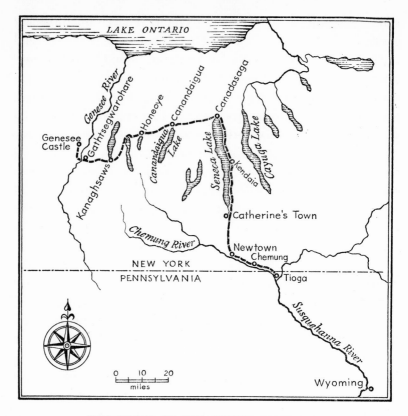

THE SCENE OF THE INDIAN CAMPAIGN
Adapted from "New Sources on the Sullivan-Clinton Campaign in 1779,"
by Alexander C. Flick, New York State Historical
Association *Quarterly*, 1929

march, at times remaining stationary because of rain. The
women accompanying the army had to leave the boats and proceed by horseback, since that would cut down the number of
drivers needed.[9] The men were not to fire at game, because a
single shot was the alarm for an approaching enemy. The march
was not easy. The lowlands next to the river were narrow, and
the mountains presented an obstacle. Dr. Jabez Campfield
wrote: "How hard is the soldier's lott who's least danger is in
the field of action? Fighting happens seldom, but fatigue, hunger,
cold & heat are constantly varying his distress." [10] Yet the men

marveled at the fertile plains, well-timbered land, and abundant game.

At the abandoned farm of Frederick Vanderlip the army camped the night of August 4. Sullivan's orders of that evening warned of a possible enemy attack somewhere between there and Wyalusing, which they expected to reach the following day, but no attack was forthcoming.[11] At Wyalusing, a former Moravian settlement, they remained for two days. It was not until August 8 that the army moved again, and this time General Sullivan, who was somewhat ill, went by boat, and Maxwell assumed command for the day. That night they rested at a flat called Standing Stone, with the Light Corps out three miles ahead. The army took all precautions to maintain proper security, and scouts were constantly reconnoitering ahead of the main forces. As yet they had sighted no enemy, but at Sheshequin signs were evident of recent fires.[12]

By now they were just a few miles from Tioga. On the 10th Sullivan, having resumed command, reconnoitered ahead with some of his field officers to select a suitable fording place.[13] On Wednesday morning, August 11, the army continued north, and at a place opposite what is now Milan forded to the west side of the Susquehanna. The river was rapid at this point, and the men, up to their waists in the swirling waters, found the crossing difficult. Safe on the other side, they continued and soon, after fording the Chemung, they arrived on a peninsula between that river and the Susquehanna near the point where they joined. Tioga had been reached.[14] Sullivan a few days later reported that the country over which he had traveled was ideally suited for ambuscade, but that he had met no opposition.[15]

About twelve miles beyond stood the Indian village Chemung, nestled next to the river of that name. Since Sullivan had heard that Chemung was probably the enemy's place of rendezvous, he did not wish to let part of his force go to meet Clinton until after he had attacked Chemung. At last he might challenge the enemy.[16]

That night Sullivan sent a small scouting party toward the Indian town under Captain John Cummings of the 2d New Jersey Regiment. The following afternoon, August 12, the men returned to give their report to Sullivan. Both whites and Indians were in Chemung, but the scouts could not find out whether they planned to leave or defend the village.[17] Sullivan made his plans. In his general orders he warned of the cruel, clever enemy, unrelenting in their hate and satiated only by total slaughter.[18] Except for a small force which would guard the camp, the army would march for Chemung immediately; so at nightfall they left camp, carrying just one howitzer on a light machine which Proctor had devised. They found the march exceedingly difficult, because the night was dark and the path seldom used. Toward daybreak the men, shrouded by fog, reached the village where they hoped to surprise the inhabitants. General Hand took his brigade around the town toward the path that led north. He would attack from the upper end. Poor was to enter from the east. Across the river went Lieutenant Colonel George Reid with two regiments to take position opposite the town. Sullivan, with the Jersey troops, some volunteers, and some of the artillery corps approached the lower end of Chemung ready to prevent escape or to throw reinforcements in any direction. The plans were well laid; the assault would be simultaneous. But the enemy had left the town vacant. Instead, they had taken a position a mile to the north. Hand pushed on toward them and at the top of a hill met desultory resistance; six men were killed in this action. A bayonet charge was not necessary because the enemy quickly fled.[19]

The General ordered the houses destroyed, including what he termed the "Chapel and Council House." This house intrigued Major James Norris who found within it an idol "which might well enough be Worshiped without a breach of the 2d Commandt. on account of its likeness to anything either in heaven or Earth." [20] The soldiers also burned the corn fields and gardens before returning to Tioga. Sullivan reported his loss as seven killed and thirteen wounded and questioned whether his men had inflicted any casualties because he had met practically no resistance. In fact the General was amazed that the Indians had not defended their town.[21]

The campaign had had a favorable start. One officer reported the troops in good health and high spirits, and that one month's time should see the end of the venture.[22] Another soldier wrote: "Notwithstanding the General's ill state of health, he has in every instance, exerted himself in a most surprising manner, and plainly shewn that nothing but his industry could have put this army so soon in motion. What we are to expect from his activity and enterprise some future time must unfold." [23]

Sullivan seemed enthusiastic about the success of the raid against Chemung; yet the casualties worried him. He ordered officers of regiments never to be absent from their command when there was possibility of attack. He insisted that soldiers should fire only upon direction of their officers, and he implied that some of the casualties may have been inflicted by the American troops themselves.[24]

Now that there was no danger of attack from Chemung, Sullivan ordered about 1,000 men under General Poor to leave Tioga on the 16th to join Clinton and escort his troops to camp. The army then settled down to routine camp life waiting for the arrival of Clinton before moving farther into the wilderness. On August 20 Sullivan wrote General Washington that he expected Clinton to arrive the next day and that he would move forward on the 23rd. Once again he worried about his provisions, claiming he did not believe he would have enough to carry him through the Indian Country and that he hoped a further supply might be deposited at Wyoming, which could be either forwarded to him or at least be awaiting him upon his return. Otherwise he was optimistic. He assumed the Indians would be collecting their forces around either Catherine's Town or Canadasago; nevertheless he asserted that no force could stop him once Clinton arrived.[25]

Finally on the 22d Clinton appeared at Tioga. With him were about 1,500 men, bringing the total for the two armies somewhere in the neighborhood of 4,400 fit for duty.[26] Sullivan's men greeted the approaching army by firing a thirteen-cannon salute, and Clinton's field officers dined with Sullivan. Albert Pawling had not joined forces with Clinton at Ononquaga, so that his small detachment of 200 men never took part in the campaign.[27]

Sullivan ordered Colonel William Shreve to take command of the small garrison that was to remain at Tioga, and to get the supplies up from Wyoming. The women must return to Wyoming except "such as may be applied to the use of the Hospital, or may be deem'd necessary to keep the Soldiers clean at their Return." [28] Thus, toward the end of August, General Sullivan started the major push into the Seneca country. In an apprehensive vein, Hand thought a speedy conclusion to the campaign was absolutely essential. The expedition had double the numbers needed. "I wish the savages may venture to fight us early (if at all)" he wrote, "that only can prevent our being laught at." [29]

On the day before leaving Tioga, runners came in from Brodhead saying that he had left Fort Pitt and that he hoped to make junction with Sullivan near the Genesee.[30] As events unfolded, the junction never did occur, and Brodhead's endeavors were a separate phase of the Sullivan-Clinton Campaign.[31] At noon on the 26th the army left Tioga and proceeded about four miles.[32] That same day the loyalist John Butler wrote Mason Bolton, in command at Niagara, that the approaching Americans consisted of "some of the best of the Continental Troops commanded by the most active of the Rebel Generals." [33]

Sullivan's marches were well organized. In the van was Hand's brigade in six columns, each two to three hundred yards apart. Maxwell's brigade followed Hand's left, in one column by platoons; Poor's brigade followed Hand's right in the same fashion. Clinton's brigade took up the rear, and the artillery and pack horses were in the center. Flankers were on each side and rifle men reconnoitered ahead of the army.[34] The march toward Chemung was difficult, the General reported, since the rains had swollen the river, but on the evening of the 28th they did reach the town.[35] Scouts brought information that the enemy was about five miles away, supposedly in considerable force, at or near Newtown, an Indian village a few miles below what is now the city of Elmira.[36] The scouts reported that they had heard the sound of enemy axes, which led Sullivan and his officers to believe that the adversaries were erecting works to obstruct their path.

The next morning, Sunday, August 29, Sullivan marched toward Newtown. At 11:00 A.M. a messenger came to the General from Major James Parr, who commanded Hand's advanced rifle corps, with information that there was an enemy breastwork about a mile in front of Newtown upon a rising ground and in command of the road over which Sullivan's artillery would pass. The enemy was placed in such a way that they could fire upon both the flank and front at the same time.[37] Sullivan pushed forward and found General Hand holding his troops before the enemy position, awaiting his arrival.

The location was ideally suited for an ambush. The waters of the Chemung River flow from the Elmira region in a southeasterly direction, then turn northeast before proceeding eastward toward Chemung. The switch in course from the southeast to the northeast creates a little pocket, or semicircle, which consists of a low flat. As the Americans moved into the semicircle, they faced the eastern terminus of a hogback, which ran northwestward toward an island in the river. The road along which Sullivan came crossed a stream opposite the end of the hogback, then turned to the right. Along here and on the hogback the enemy had placed works. A hill, later called Sullivan's Hill, arose about 150 rods to the enemy's rear and to Sullivan's right. Indians and Loyalists stood here, ready to fall on Sullivan's right flank as soon as his front became engaged before the works, for, in order to approach Newtown, the army would have passed the hogback to its left and moved toward the river south of this second hill.[38]

Hand's men were about four hundred yards before the enemy works. Upon his arrival, Sullivan learned that the enemy had tried to entice Hand forward by making frequent sallies, then suddenly retiring. It appeared that the enemy believed the works were still unnoticed, since they had placed a facade of shrubs before the fortifications. Poor went to Hand's rear, and Maxwell came up abreast with Poor. Sullivan took notice of another hill, about a mile due north of the Americans' position, and conjectured that an enemy force was upon one or both of the hills prepared to attack his right and rear when he attempted to assault the fortifications near the hogback.[39] One of the diarists described the enemy position in this fashion: "The main body . . . had their front secured by a large Morass & brook, their right by the River & on their left partly in the rear was a very large hill, their lines extended upwards of a Mile." [40]

The Americans did not wish to make a frontal assault upon the enemy, since they held a strong position. Instead they preferred either to surround them or bring them into open ground for action. Sullivan, therefore, held a council of war, which determined that Hand with infantry, the rifle corps, and the artillery would start the action on the front. In the meantime, Poor, supported by Clinton, was to flank them on the right, and Colonel Matthias Ogden on the left. Maxwell would be held in reserve.[41] Sullivan ordered the artillery to open the attack at about 3:00 P.M., believing he had allowed enough time for Poor and Clinton to reach the enemy's left at the foot of Sullivan's Hill.[42] The infantry and light corps prepared to advance. But the enemy, choosing to offer only token resistance, soon broke ranks and retreated from the front. One soldier in describing the effect of the howitzers and the six three-pounders, said: "But the Indians I beleive [sic] did not admire the sound so much, nor could they be prevailed upon to listen to its music, although we made use of all the eloquence we were masters of for that purpose, but they were deaf to our entreaties and turned their backs upon us in token of their detestation for us." [43]

A swamp had delayed Poor so that he had not been able to commence his attack at the same time, and, when he did attempt to storm the hill, he found opposition. Doubtless it was not until the foe was in full retreat that Sullivan learned the action had been hot for a time in Poor's sector, and that Lieutenant Colonel George Reid's regiment had borne the brunt of the enemy resistance until relieved by Colonel Henry Dearborn.[44] Sullivan thought the cannonading on the front and what he believed to be Poor's unexpected assault on the enemy left made them retreat in a hurry.[45]

The battle of Newtown was the sole conflict involving the entire army of the Sullivan-Clinton Campaign. The enemy had barely given resistance at Chemung. The rest of the campaign would see the army razing towns and burning fields. Sullivan estimated that 1,500 troops had opposed him at Newtown, much too high an estimate.[46] The two prisoners whom the Americans captured said there were only 800, but Sullivan discounted this figure. The force with the Butlers, Captain John McDonnell, and Brant consisted mainly of Indians, although there were over 250 whites.[47] The losses on both sides were not at all high.[48]

Did Sullivan miss an opportunity to crush the opposing force at Newtown? The enemy thought that Sullivan had been too hasty in firing his artillery, thus enabling Butler and his party to escape before Poor had gone around him.[49] Certainly the Indians had been thrown into confusion, and Butler admitted he could not persuade them to change front to meet Poor's threat. Butler commented that Sullivan moved with the "greatest caution & regularity." [50] It seems unfair to blame Sullivan for opening the artillery fire before Poor was in position. He figured he had allowed him enough time; the swamp had delayed him. The army pursued the fleeing enemy, but, in Sullivan's words, "fear had given them too great speed to be overtaken." [51]

The rest of Sullivan's campaign is more the story of a moving army. The many diaries tell of the soldiers' thrill at the sight of the beauties and richness of the country through which they traveled; yet relentlessly they destroyed in accordance with their orders. The Indian threat must be stilled. Before moving beyond Newtown after razing it, General Sullivan, still worried over the scantiness of his supplies, asked his army to go on half-rations, which the men readily agreed to do. The General estimated that on half-rations each man would have twenty-two pounds of flour and sixteen pounds of beef for the remainder of the march.[52] On the 30th the wounded, four pieces of heavy artillery, and the wagons went back to Tioga. The only artillery the army kept with them consisted of four brass three-pounders. Early on August 31 Sullivan moved his men toward Catherine's Town (also called French Catherine's) just south of Seneca Lake, where the army camped the night of September 1.[53]

The next morning soldiers found an old squaw hiding in the bushes and took her to Sullivan's marquee. Through an Oneida interpreter the General learned that Butler had been there two days earlier and that the Indians were demoralized. The squaws had wished for peace, but the warriors had forced them to leave. Because she led Sullivan to believe that the squaws and children were just a few miles away, he sent Colonel William Butler with a small detachment in pursuit, but with no success. The army again was on the march by the morning of September 3, after destroying Catherine's Town and leaving the old squaw with some provisions.[54] Upon reaching Seneca Lake, the General chose to proceed along the east side. The army arrived in Kendaia, "considerable of an eligant Town," on Sunday, the 5th.[55] Here they met Luke Swetland, captured at Wyoming a year earlier, who informed Sullivan that the enemy had left the town in great confusion three days before and that some Tories were saying the only safety was in flight. Evidently Butler was trying to persuade his force to make a stand at Canadasaga but was having little success. So Sullivan reported, but others said that Swetland believed resistance would be offered at Canadasaga.[56]

Canadasaga, the Seneca Castle, was at the foot of Seneca Lake, near what is now the city of Geneva. Sullivan approached the town with caution, since there was a possibility of an ambush, but found it empty when he arrived on September 7.[57] As described by Major Fogg, the entry into the town more closely resembled comic opera than anything else, although Fogg embroidered his account when he wrote it in his journal, most likely some time after the event:

Notwithstanding the occult and evasive qualities of the Savages with which our general must before this time have been acquainted he made a disposition of his troops, thinking to surround and surprise the town, after having been five hours within three miles of it. Genl. Hand's infantry and Col. De Bois' flank men were to begin the investigation on the west, while the main body encircled them from each wing. But oh! sad mishap! When our commander advanced to complete his part, to his great mortification, he found the detachments either misled by their guides or else had mistaken a field of pompions for the town. But whatever might have been the cause, the whole party from the monkey to the rat, had armed themselves with almost every species of the vegetable creation, each man with three pompions on his bayonet and staggering under the weight of a bosom filled with corn and beans, when in accents more sonorous than those of an injured husband, he broke out "You d—d unmilitary set of rascals! what, are you going to storm a town with pompions! Turn aside, open to the right and left, that men unaccostomed to plundering, and such scandalous conduct may execute the design! Ye officers, never more show your heads with military characters." In an instant the whole band was disrobed of their vegetable accoutrements and armour, and pompions, squashes, melons and mandrakes rolled down the hill like hail-stones in a tempest.[58]

There was some discussion in council as to the expediency of proceeding farther, because of shortage of provisions, but Sullivan was determined to lay waste the Seneca country and wished the army to continue to the Genesee Castle.[59] There seemed little chance of meeting the enemy in battle, since Butler had not been able to cajole the Indians into making a stand at Canadasaga.[60] Sullivan's orders of the afternoon of the 8th announced that they would continue the following morning. Genesee Castle was thought to be about eighty miles beyond, and already the provisions were short; the men ate meat twice in three days and bread once in four or five days. The diet consisted mainly of corn and beans, which were plentiful.[61]

Toward the west they moved and reached Honeoye on the 11th. Here, in order to gain speed, he left a small garrison and those who were slowing the march.[62] The night of the 12th the army camped outside of Kanaghsaws, a town at the head of Conesus Lake. That same night Sullivan sent out a scouting party under Lieutenant Thomas Boyd to reconnoiter Genesee Castle, Little Beard's Town, so that if possible a surprise attack might be planned. That Sullivan thought he could effect a surprise attack was certainly naive, for his army was under constant surveillance, the enemy keeping just a day or two before him. Sullivan suggested that Boyd take only three or four riflemen, a guide, and an Oneida, but Boyd, however, chose to take a larger scouting party.[63]

Runners came in from Lieutenant Boyd the following morning, reporting that he had reached a town, which later turned out to be Gathtsegwarohare, south of Genesee Castle, only to find it deserted except for a few Indians who straggled in. Boyd's men scalped two of these Indians. The runners told Sullivan that Boyd was returning. Later in the morning some more of Boyd's party hastened into camp with alarming news. On the way back Boyd had first decided to wait for the army to come up to him. Two men, sent by Boyd to tell Sullivan about this, discovered a small party of Indians and therefore returned to Boyd. Against the advice of his Indian guide he chose to give chase, only to find too late that he had led his party into an ambush which had been awaiting Sullivan's army. Perhaps this saved Sullivan considerable embarrassment, but Boyd's men found themselves faced by overwhelming odds. Those who had returned to camp had broken through the enemy on the flanks, but most of the party failed to return.[64]

Sullivan immediately sent Hand forward with light troops to speed to Boyd's assistance, but they were too late to save the men.[65] The army proceeded to Gathtsegwarohare where they camped for the night. Sullivan thought Genesee Castle was within just a mile or so, but reconnoitering soon showed that the town was a few miles ahead and on the other side of the Genesee River. On the 14th the army crossed the river and moved into the town. Here they found the mutilated bodies of Boyd and Michael Parker. Sullivan reported: "They [the Indians] had whiped them in the most cruel manner, pulled out M[r] Boid's nails, cut off his nose, plucked out one of his eyes, cut out his tongue, stabed him with spears in sundry places, & inflicted other tortures which decency will not permit me to mention; lastly cut off his head & left his body on the ground with that of his unfortunate companion, who appeared to have experienced nearly the same savage barbarity." [66]

Early on the 15th the army razed the village and burned the corn, possibly 15,000 bushels in all being destroyed.[67] The same day a white woman, who had been captured at Wyoming, came into the camp with her child and reported not only that the enemy had fled to Niagara, but also that the Indians, in great distress, were angry at Butler.[68] Sullivan determined the time had come to return, since there supposedly were no further villages in the area, and he had not as yet destroyed the Cayuga country. Also his supplies were low. There is no indication that he considered pushing on toward Niagara, since Niagara never had been considered as a primary goal.[69] The General informed his army that they had accomplished their mission, and in the afternoon after completing the destruction of Genesee Castle, Sullivan turned toward Tioga.[70] Stragglers, he said, were to be lashed on the spot.[71]

Behind them the retiring army left Little Beard's Town in

flames. On the 18th the troops camped at Canandaigua, where they were met by Oneida warriors whose assistance Sullivan had sought earlier.[72] The Oneidas asked Sullivan not to harm the Cayugas, whom they claimed were friendly to the American cause. Also they feared that should the Cayuga towns be destroyed, the inhabitants would be thrown upon the Oneidas for support. The amazed Sullivan answered that the Cayugas had not shown signs of friendship, and that their homes and crops should not be spared.[73] He held a council on September 20 to determine what actions he should pursue toward the Cayugas. Because they had been in alliance with the Senecas and only now were seeking peace, the council decided that they should make no treaty and that they should send a detachment under William Butler to the east side of Cayuga Lake to destroy their towns.[74] The same day Sullivan ordered Colonel Peter Gansevoort to capture the lower Mohawk Castle, destroy the homes, and march on to headquarters by way of Albany with his prisoners. By no means was he to harm the Oneidas through whose country he would travel on his way to the Mohawk Castle.[75]

Although Sullivan planned to return to Tioga the way he had come, he sent out other parties in addition to Butler's and Gansevoort's to complete the destruction. Colonel William Smith went along the west side of Seneca Lake to burn Kershong, and on the next day, the 21st, Dearborn set out to destroy the villages on the west side of Cayuga Lake.[76]

By the 23rd Sullivan was at Catherine's Town, and the night of September 24th found the army at the forks, in what is now Elmira, where Newtown Creek joined the Chemung. A garrison stationed there, after being sent on from Tioga, greeted the army with thirteen salutes, which the army returned. Sullivan allowed the men one gill of whiskey and a full ration of beef.[77] The next day he ordered a *jeu de feu* in honor of Spain's entering the war against England and of the Congressional resolution which raised the subsistence of officers and soldiers. At 5:00 P.M. the men paraded. They fired their muskets, beginning on the right and running through the whole assembled army; but the General was not pleased with the way the firing went. He ordered the army to fire once more, then rode his horse from right to left indicating that the men should fire as he came opposite them. This time he was pleased, saying that it went like a "hallelujah." [78] Then the feast began. Amongst the many toasts one, in particular, has appeal: "May the Enemies of America be Metamorphised in Pack horses and sent on a Western Expedition." [79]

On the 26th Dearborn arrived in camp after razing six towns. The next day a party moved along the Chemung to burn corn, and on the 28th Butler rejoined Sullivan after he had destroyed five towns and a number of scattered houses. On the evening of September 30, Sullivan's army reached Tioga where Colonel Shreve provided the general and field officers with an elegant dinner.[80]

That night John Sullivan wrote his report to President Jay. He placed the number of towns destroyed at forty and was sure that none remained in the Indian Country except for one near Genesee Castle. In addition to many vegetables destroyed, the army had ruined about 160,000 bushels of corn. Not forty men had been lost. Had he had further supplies he would have gone on to Niagara, he told Jay; but he said that he did not consider marching there as coming within his orders. "I flatter myself," he concluded, "that the orders with which I was entrusted are fully executed, as we have not left a single settlement or field of corn . . . or is there even the appearance of an Indian on this side of Niagara." [81] On October 3 the army demolished the fort at Tioga and started for Wyoming, which they reached on October 8. Orders came for Sullivan to proceed to headquarters, and on the morning of the 10th he set out for Easton.[82]

On the whole the results of the campaign met favorable comment. Thanks poured upon General Sullivan for his efforts from the inhabitants of Northampton County and from some of the officers of his army.[83] One officer, writing earlier from

Tioga, claimed that a valuable country had been conquered. Congress on October 14 chose to tender its thanks.[84] Washington's general orders for October 17 briefly reviewed the accomplishments and said that the army had "manifested a patience perseverance and valor that do them the highest honor." [85] Major Jeremiah Fogg said: "The unbounded ambition and perseverance of our commander and army led him to the full execution contrary to our most sanguine expectations." [86] Major Fogg, however, closed his journal on a note that was disturbing to many:

The question will naturally arise, what have you to show for your exploits? Where are your prisoners? To which I reply, that the rags and emaciated bodies of our soldiers must speak for our fatigue, and when the Querist will point out a mode to tame a partridge, or the expediency of hunting wild turkeys, with light horse, I will show them our prisoners. The nests are destroyed, but the birds are still on the wing.

These birds on the wing could again cause trouble. Edward Hand feared they might seek revenge and argued that Pennsylvania's frontiers were insecure.[87] Inhabitants of Tryon County in New York petitioned Governor Clinton for protection, and in November Joseph Reed, noting that the Indians showed few signs of submission, asked that preparations be made to meet any incursions.[88] Sullivan did not escape coming under fire, for some ridiculed his excessive demands for supplies, criticized his verbal attacks upon the Board of War in front of his officers, and described his report to Congress as pompous which gave officers on Washington's staff many a laugh.[89] Sullivan's pompous ways felt the pricks of other men. Ebenezer Hazard wrote Jeremy Belknap: "I do not suppose General S's letters are 'simple narratives,' but rather pompous accounts of simple transactions." [90] Hazard thought Sullivan had embroidered in his lavish descriptions of the houses and towns destroyed. "Besides," he continued, "it is not to be expected that a *General* would tell a story in the way that you and I and other common folks would. What advantage would arise from *being a General* if, after all, he must be like other people?" On the whole Hazard praised Sullivan's accomplishments. The Indians seldom resettled on land that had been devastated; therefore the country might be considered acquired. For this reason, and because the Indians had been driven from the frontiers, the expedition had been a success, in Hazard's opinion, and he concluded that Sullivan had led his army judiciously.

Just what did the Sullivan-Clinton campaign accomplish? Possibly it broke the power of the confederacy; yet the Indians were able to carry out sporadic raids in 1780, although during the winter of 1779 many warriors had suffered.[91] Sullivan, by devastating the towns, had pushed the Indians back upon Niagara, and these refugees would increase the troubles of the British. Yet although the British still held Niagara and Detroit and still could supply the Indians for frontier skirmishes, Sullivan had carried out his orders and had done a thorough yet destructive job.[92] War, however, is destructive. After peace came, the veterans of Sullivan's army poured into the rich country over which they had marched in 1779 and opened this land for the youthful nation.

Sullivan's military career was near its end. A man who had flirted with failure throughout the war, he at least could see that his final effort had been successful. Hand might say that the victorious army was turning its "Corn Stalks into Laurels "; and James Madison might later belittle the results by writing that Sullivan's campaign "seems by its effects rather to have exasperated than to have terrified or disabled" the Indians; yet on the whole the march had not been in vain.[93] Ironically, Sullivan's most successful venture during the war led to his retirement. He had carped and criticized too often; and this time his barbed language knew no curb. Earlier in the summer he had slanted his ire against the Board of War in his general orders of July 21, and the members struck back.

Late in August the Board of War complained to Congress

that Sullivan's criticisms were unjust. Congress decided to appoint a committee to investigate the charges, but in the midst of
the deliberations Sullivan offered his resignation from the army
early in November.[94] He complained of his ill health, and, since
he did not expect a winter's campaign, he felt justified in quitting
the service. Bad health may have pushed him to resign, but the
suspicion lingers that he felt persecuted. Perhaps he was bluffing
and did not expect his bluff to be called. He wrote General
Washington: "My Health is too much impaird, to be recover'd,
but by a total release from Business, and though the Physicians
give me encouragement, that this will restore me, I am myself
convinced of the contrary, and fear, that I must content myself,
with enjoying the reflection, of having used my utmost to serve
my Country, as the only thing I shall receive, in exchange for
a Constitution sacrificed in endeavouring to promote its interest." [95]

Washington waited upon Sullivan and tried to persuade him
that he might regain his health sooner than he thought. He
hoped Sullivan would not resign but referred him to Congress.
Hence, on November 9, John Sullivan submitted his resignation
to the Continental Congress. The majority within Congress
wanted to see him out of the army and referred his resignation
to a committee rather than accept a temporary leave.[96] The
committee performed as expected and recommended on November 30 that the resignation be accepted. Elbridge Gerry
wished to amend the resolution and suggested the words, "as
General Sullivan's health will not permit his continuance in the
American army," be replaced by the words, "and that General
Sullivan have leave to retire from the service so long as he shall
judge necessary for the recovery of his health." [97] Only a small
handful of delegates, including New Hampshire's Nathaniel
Peabody, backed Gerry's resolution. The majority chose to let
him go and voted their thanks for his past services to the country.[98] Sullivan had not expected Congress would take the action
it did and had thought his retirement would be temporary, if

any were granted at all.[99] Now out of the army and free to return home, John Sullivan realized that his military career had
run its course. The end was pathetic, but his constant complaints had alienated too many people, and his few friends in
Congress could not save him the embarrassment of having his
resignation accepted permanently, thus easing him out of the
army.

The next day, December 1, Sullivan wrote Washington that
never had his devotion to his Commander-in-Chief wavered:
"My Publick & Constant Declarations have been, & I now re-
peat, that in my opinion, you are the Saviour of this Country,
And that to your fortitude, bravery, & Steady Performance, do
we owe the Independence & Freedom we Enjoy." [100] Then he
warned Washington that he still detected faction, that the opposition against Washington which had centered about Conway
had not yet been destroyed, and that Washington's critics
wished to diffuse his powers. General Washington thanked Sullivan for his sincere friendship, and for the information about
intrigue against him, and said that he relied upon the justice of
the country to back him so long as he discharged his duty faith-
fully. He closed by regretting that Sullivan was leaving the
service.[101]

Sullivan headed back to New Hampshire. On December 3,
Peabody had nominated him for the Board of War, but nothing
came of the nomination.[102] Although Sullivan had lost some favor, he still had much to look back upon, like the other ardent
patriots of the day, because he had made sacrifices for a cause
by spending weary months in the field fighting for the independence he so eagerly wanted. He suffered financial losses for
his efforts, since any remuneration he received hardly covered
his expenses in the army or at Durham.[103] Sullivan brought the
best of his abilities to his tasks, and, in spite of his many personal
failings, Washington found in him an able general. Brave, energetic, resourceful, the fiery Sullivan had brought to his post in
the army a keen desire to be of service. His failures during the

war—and they were not inconsiderable—came more from bad luck than from incompetency. He had been at his worst at Long Island and at Brandywine. He had been an able soldier at the brilliant victories of Trenton and Princeton. He had been at his best during the retreat from Canada, in organizing the offense at Rhode Island, and in conducting the campaign against the Six Nations. Yet throughout the years complete success, at times within his grasp, had eluded him.

$\mathcal{S}$*ullivan* looked forward to retirement, but he was not to enjoy it for long, because in the summer of 1780 he agreed to enter Congress. In the meantime, however, he had a few months of rest and change. It probably was toward the end of December, 1779, that he arrived in Durham, his first visit to New Hampshire since his short trip the previous March before undertaking the Indian campaign. Now safely back home, General Sullivan welcomed the adulation which came in his direction. In February, by vote of the General Court, the President of New Hampshire and the Speaker waited upon John Sullivan, who at that time was in Exeter, to congratulate him upon his return and the mending of his health. The legislators trusted that the General would support the civil rights of the people as bravely as he had opposed the enemy on the field of battle.[1] Sullivan's answer was flamboyant, in the style of the day, yet gracious. He hoped that at all times his conduct would "sufficiently testify my Zeal for the common Cause." [2]

As his health improved, Sullivan got his law practice going again, "to repair the repeated & almost inconceivable Losses" he had sustained.[3] By May he was advertising that his mills once more were operating and suited for dying silks and dressing cloths.[4] Although he seemed to be making an easy transition into the activities of his community, he could not remain in Durham for long. Against his desire, the legislature chose him as a delegate to the Continental Congress, to serve one year beginning in November. He was out of the state at the time of his selection, and the legislature adjourned before he returned. To call another session to elect someone in his place would have been prohibitively expensive; moreover, Sullivan realized that the New Hampshire Grants controversy made it essential for the state to be represented in Congress. Without enthusiasm, therefore, he accepted the assignment.[5]

The controversy over the Grants seemed to be nearing a climax. Both New York and New Hampshire had conflicting claims west of the Connecticut River, and both were reluctant to give way. Although the King in Council in 1764 had set the western bank of the Connecticut as the boundary between the two colonies, the inhabitants of the western area were unwilling to remain under New York's jurisdiction and in 1777 sought admission to the young nation as the state of Vermont. New Hampshire might have agreed to this until she learned that certain of her western towns in Cheshire and Grafton counties desired to join the new state. Certainly New Hampshire had no intention of relinquishing these frontier communities, but fortunately Vermont for a time appeared cool to the idea of incorporating the Cheshire and Grafton towns. The people in the valley on both sides of the river wished to bind themselves together, and, when some of the towns east of the Green Mountains began to look in the direction of New Hampshire's western hamlets, the New Hampshire legislature reasserted the old claims to the land west of the Connecticut. Not only did Congress in 1779 ask Vermont to abandon her jurisdiction over any people on both sides of the river who had not denied the authority of New York or New Hampshire, but it also requested Vermont to abstain from granting lands and confiscating estates until her boundaries had been determined. This Vermont failed to do, although New Hampshire and New York had passed acts allowing Congress to settle the problem of boundaries.[6]

Sullivan had a knotty problem facing him, and he had to face it alone. George Atkinson had declined election as delegate with Sullivan, and Samuel Livermore announced that he would not return to Philadelphia as agent in the Grants matter. Nathaniel Folsom, in Philadelphia as delegate, was not to stay for long. Sullivan met with the Committee of Safety on August 4 and agreed to act as agent as well as to serve as delegate. A few days later the Committee tried to get a horse for Sullivan's trip to Philadelphia and forwarded to him his credentials. These credentials Sullivan presented to Congress on Monday, September 11, and took his seat in that body for the third time.[7] His confidence in himself as he prepared once again to take on the duties of delegate reflected nothing less than arrogance. A few years later he said that he took the assignment because he thought New Hampshire would suffer if Vermont were annexed to New York. He continued:

as I was well aware of the State of New York having Special Delegates for the purpose of arguing their Claim & as I was fully sensible that those were Gentlemen of the first abilities it became necessary on my part to acquaint myself with the various grants Discoveries possessions & Claims by the first grantees & proprietors of this Country Especially north of Hudson's River & was Left alone to oppose the pretensions of New York urged with all the zeal & Eloquence that could possibly be Displayed by three of the Most Emminent Lawyers upon the Continent.[8]

What was the situation as Sullivan entered Congress? The delegates had already criticized defiant Vermont and continued to ask her not to assert authority over towns in the disputed area. They set the second Tuesday in September as the time for hearing and examining the controversy, and on the day appointed, September 12, the delegates heard a letter written on July 25 by Vermont's Governor, Thomas Chittenden.[9] He threw down the gauntlet by denying that Congress had any authority to destroy Vermont as an independent government. If Congress denied union, then Vermont would negotiate with the legislatures of the separate states "and take such other measures as self-preservation may justify." [10] No sooner had Sullivan arrived in Philadelphia than he found himself in the midst of the struggle. On the night of the 15th Peter Olcott, who, along with Bezaleel Woodward, was the agent for the Connecticut River towns, called on Sullivan, bringing with him a letter from Moses Hazen which outlined the position taken by the people of the river towns. Their first concern was to see that the river valley area remain a unit; they did not wish to be divided by the Connecticut. If Vermont should be admitted as an independent state, then the towns as far east as the line of the Mason Patent, the original New Hampshire grant, would favor joining the new state. If Vermont were not independent—and the people frankly were not expecting it—then the towns would prefer the sovereignty of New Hampshire to the sovereignty of New York. One thing was certain; they hoped for a quick decision.[11]

Both Sullivan and Folsom, who was soon to leave Congress, had taken the position that the delegates should entertain neither the question of independence nor, should independence not be granted, the question of jurisdiction. Sullivan argued that the problem ought to be determined by a commission in accordance with the proposed Articles of Confederation. Although he based his argument on the grounds that Congress did not have jurisdiction, he asserted further that the delegates had too many other important matters to ponder; they had no license to become involved in a lengthy trial.[12] He considered his instructions from the New Hampshire Committee of Safety to be quite explicit: he must argue for a commission rather than allow Congress to settle the controversy. If, however, Congress decided to intervene, he understood that he was to woo the people of the Grants so that they would prefer joining New Hampshire rather than New York. If he found that Congress would not recognize his state's claim, then he was to try to secure the independence of the Grants rather than have them come under New York. Certainly he knew that New Hampshire would not countenance any dismemberment of the state east of the Connecticut River.

Sullivan had little confidence in the strength of New Hampshire's claims to the land west of the Connecticut, and this accounts for his behavior in September. He believed that with the passage of time more and more persons in the Grants would favor New Hampshire over New York. He would appear moderate, for the New York delegates were "breathing out nothing but Death & Slaughter" against the Vermonters.[13] He would state that New Hampshire would acquiesce in any decision made by Congress, even independence for the area west of the river; although certainly he did not expect such a decision. He hoped to show that New Hampshire was flexible and agreeable, whereas New York was unbending. He wished to make it clear that the Grants supported New Hampshire and not New York, and then the delegates would "begin to See that If the Lands are adjudged to New York the Continent must be Involved in a war to Inforce the Determination of Congress which Can only be avoided by adjudging it to New Hamps^r & I am Convinced this will finally Turn the Scale in favor of New Hampshire." [14]

John Morin Scott, one of New York's delegates, thought New Hampshire's tactics were obvious; and he said that Sullivan, by advocating the selection of commissioners, was seeking delay. Any delay would be to New York's disadvantage. That state pressed for a decision, and late in September Scott thought his cause might win by the margin of one vote.[15] By then New York had presented its case to Congress. It was now Sullivan's turn to begin his argument, and he quickly gained the upper hand when Congress postponed making a decision. New York's call for a vote had been a premature move; considerable opposition suddenly arose in Congress against her claims. The New York delegates blamed Vermont's threat to make a separate peace for their failure to secure a favorable vote, although Duane said that several states seemed ready to support Vermont independence at the time.[16] No doubt the tide had turned. The confident Sullivan wrote: "The Arguments ran so much against New York that the Agents who were before pressing a Decision have never Mentioned it since & thus it rests at present." [17] No clear-cut decision had been made; obviously the delegates preferred to temporize.

Sullivan's delaying tactics later caused some criticism in the area of the Grants. One influential resident of eastern Vermont, Jacob Bayley, feared that lack of decision might mean annexation of Vermont to Canada. He thought that New Hampshire could win and maintain jurisdiction throughout the entire area, but he insisted that splitting the Grants by the Connecticut River would merely continue the confusion.[18] Peter Olcott was disappointed that Sullivan seemed indifferent to the idea of a union of the whole of the Grants, especially as Sullivan may have led Olcott to believe that he would not object to independence for the area west of the river. Rumor evidently circulated in the Grants that the Vermont legislature had bribed Sullivan with land in return for his backing independence.[19] Sullivan quite rightly raised strenuous objections to the charge that he had not acted in New Hampshire's best interests. Never had he taken a bribe, he said, and he had not behaved in any way contrary to his instructions. He had only been against New York's proposed course, which was for Congress to decide without the intervention of any commissioners.[20] Obviously Sullivan had been trying to delay the decision, since he realized that time was New Hampshire's strongest ally.

Because of criticism from home and because his own legislature pressed for action, Sullivan, against his better judgment, asked Congress to reach a conclusion in March, 1781. He was still smarting from accusations that he had not properly represented New Hampshire, accusations which gave credence to another rumor that he would be made governor of Vermont. This angered him, particularly since there were reports that the Vermonters might negotiate with the British in Canada. He would much prefer to lead troops against them, he said, should they make terms with "the most Arbitrary & unprincipled nation that Ever Disgraced human nature." [21] Although he feared New

York would be granted jurisdiction over the Grants if Congress did not give independence to Vermont, Sullivan sought a decision according to his instructions.[22] As yet none was forthcoming; but, as time went by, New Hampshire became more and more insistent. The matter had to be settled. Towns in Grafton and Cheshire counties in convention had renounced the jurisdiction of New Hampshire and had determined to join with Vermont. Meshech Weare did not know what would happen next.[23]

On June 20, 1781, he wrote Sullivan and Livermore, who had returned to Philadelphia that spring, urging a decision; the turmoil in the western portion of the state prevented New Hampshire from meeting the requisitions sought by Congress.[24] By now Sullivan's time in Philadelphia was running to a close. He no longer saw need for his services and hoped that the matter of boundary could be settled by a commission for which he had been arguing so consistently. He did not care to see Vermont gain independence but knew it must come; certainly that was preferable to New York's gaining the area.[25] Everyone seemed anxious for a decision of one sort or another. On August 3 Sullivan seconded a motion that a committee meet with representatives of the Grants area to see how they might enter the Confederation as a free and independent state.[26] The fear that Vermont might negotiate separately with the British was convincing Congress that decision, rather than delay which had been the previous policy, was necessary. Sullivan realized that the area would be granted independence, but he did not foresee the months of bickering that were to cloud the whole question of Vermont's admission to the Union.[27]

Although the problem of Vermont had been the first task to face Sullivan when he joined Congress, never was it the most important. He showed more interest in other matters, particularly domestic finance and foreign affairs. From the time he entered Congress he had played an important role in the committee assignments and floor debates which consumed the delegates' time. He was disturbed over the noticeable weakness of Con-

gress and over the factional strife which had debilitated it. As he
looked about him soon after reaching Philadelphia in September,
1780, he noticed that most of the men were new in their job.
Fortunately only a few of those who had been influenced by
factional feuds were still present; but, he reflected, "I am Sorry
to Say that in my opinion Greater wisdom than the present
members possess would be requisite to Conduct or rather to
Restore our publick affairs from that Situation into which Ignorance Treachery or Inattention have thrown them." [28] An
unhealthy pessimism prevailed. An empty treasury, poor credit,
a chaotic paper currency, failure to meet requisitions, Horatio
Gates's defeat at Camden in August, and Benedict Arnold's de-
fection—all contributed to the gloom. The prognosis was not
favorable, and, even if the Articles were adopted, Sullivan feared
they would be too weak. Disturbed because government was so
ineffective, he wrote: "Congress of Course becomes a Body
without power & the States the Several Componant parts of a
Monster with Thirteen Heads." [29]

Only by giving Congress more powers and vesting it with
authority to coerce compliance with its measures could relief
be obtained. Sullivan's army career had shown him the necessity
of a strong government and of the wisdom of real authority in
time of crisis. He was not in sympathy with the ideas of some
that a republican Congress with its powers diffused should be
supreme. Unfortunately the states were too jealous of their
sovereignty, and there was opposition to placing considerable
power in the hands of the military.[30] But Sullivan wished Congress to have authority; already he was on the course that would
lead him eventually into support of the Federal Constitution of
1787.

Authority in financial matters, he argued, was particularly
needed. In writing Meshech Weare on November 15, he noted
the failure of some states to meet requisitions and observed that
"Every Days Experience proves that many of our Distresses
arise from a want of Power in Congress to carry any of their

Measures into Execution." [31] He bemoaned the depreciation in which the country was wallowing at the time, then launched upon a discussion of his own financial troubles. He must return to New Hampshire by spring, he said, because only by managing his farms properly could he avoid poverty. Meanwhile, he needed money to enable him to stay in Philadelphia. Board was "Eight hard Dollars" a week, and this would allow him only water to drink. Liquor and firewood were extra. Forty Continental dollars a day covered the expenses for keeping his horse. "In short a thousand Continental Dollars will not purchase what five formerly did." [32] Little did Sullivan know what complications would result from this letter, for it fell into the hands of the British. Eventually this information that Sullivan was in need of funds brought him a tainted loan from the French and new overtures from the British that he desert the American cause.

Meanwhile Sullivan was spending most of his time working on the problems presented by the chaotic state of wartime finance. On November 7, 1780, he had seconded a resolution that a committee of five be appointed "to prepare and lay before Congress a plan for arranging the finances, paying the debts and oeconomizing the revenue of the United States." [33] Sullivan apparently assumed the role of chairman of this committee, an important assignment. Although he suffered from a fever that raged through the city and had to spend a few days recuperating at Schuylkill Falls, he managed to ride into Philadelphia each morning to attend committee meetings and to take his seat in Congress.

The committee knew that it had to find more money to finance the war. Sullivan opposed inflationary measures, however; he hoped for economy and wanted specie to replace paper currency which would bring an end to "Disceiving mankind." [34] What chances were there for a domestic loan? The committee considered that and other matters. [35] The members agreed that the people should lend coined silver, gold, and plate to the United States on security with interest. They also agreed that

there should be a resolution calling in the old bills and supporting the credit of the new, issued at the rate of forty of the old
for one of the new, according to the act of March 18, 1780. The
resolution should also urge the states not to emit bills of credit
save upon the advice of Congress; instead the states should redeem the new bills issued by the legislation of the previous
March. The committee would seek authority for Congress to lay
embargoes in time of war and hoped the states would lay im-
posts to help meet the military expenses. The credit of Congress
had to be established, and Sullivan, Abraham Clark, and Theodorick Bland argued that this could be accomplished only by
calling in bullion.

The committee devoted most of its time to the problem of a
domestic loan, because specie had to be obtained. How might the
central government assure the people of eventual repayment?
Sullivan argued that any specie introduced into circulation must
be on par with bills emitted by the act of March 18, 1780.
Plenty of specie was obtainable, he asserted; it was just being
hoarded since obviously paper was a far cheaper currency. The
men knew they had to have some depositing agency, with Sullivan suggesting it would be better to "Consider the whole as a
Transaction between Congress The Continental Treasurer and
Individuals." [36] Although he wished to give the task to the
Treasury, the committee finally recommended that a bank be
established. Sullivan was quite willing to have Congress take the
initiative in currency matters, because he believed it was essential
that a proper medium be established which would not be subject
to the whims of a paper currency. Depreciation had caused him
enough woe.

His scheme for getting money was simple enough. Contrib-
utors would receive notes, to be redeemed in four equal payments at six percent interest. The loaned bullion would go into
the Treasury. Only one half of the specie thus obtained could
be in circulation during any one year; that plus the original
notes would serve as a circulating medium throughout the na-

tion. A requisition upon the states would meet the expense of redeeming the notes and would serve the double purpose of withdrawing new bills of March, 1780, from circulation. Sullivan
did not wish to put all the specie in circulation, because it would
go to the countries having a favorable balance of trade. He
hoped that by controlling the specie centrally prices might drop,
thereby attracting new trade, which of course would draw
specie into the country. Obviously David Hume's economic
theories had influenced John Sullivan.[37]

On Monday, December 18, Sullivan's committee made its
report. The members of the committee recommended that the
states set up funds for redeeming the new bills of the previous
March and that they call in and cancel the bills of credit issued
prior to March 18. The report wanted the states to pass laws
granting to Congress the use of a four percent duty on imports,
to be paid in specie, and giving Congress the power to lay embargoes. In the absence of embargoes, the report urged the states
to encourage exports and to discourage use of luxuries. All efforts should be taken to avoid an unfavorable balance of trade.
The heart of the committee's report suggested a domestic loan
of six million dollars in specie, and in the main this followed
Sullivan's suggestions. The interest payments for the loaned
bullion would be met by import and export duties levied by the
states.[38]

As debate developed on this report in the winter of 1781, it
became evident that most of the suggestions would not be passed
as resolutions. Only the recommendations for an import duty for
the use of the United States seemed likely to gain approval. The
delegates preferred that a duty of five percent be levied, and a
report of the committee of the whole offered the resolution that
the states pass laws granting to Congress this duty for the use of
the United States. On February 1, 1781, Thomas Burke moved
that the resolution be reworded to read that the states would
"vest a power in Congress" to levy such a duty rather than "pass
laws granting to Congress" the use of the duties.[39] Sullivan

voted against the rewording, but he was on the losing side. The final approving vote came on February 3, but Sullivan continued to vote "No."[40] The delegates, by the passage of this resolution, had agreed to recommend to the states that they vest in Congress the power to levy a five percent duty on imports ad valorem, with some exceptions.

Sullivan gave no reason for his voting against Burke's rewording, asking the states to "vest a power" in Congress. As he wished a stronger government, his vote appears inconsistent. Probably his eye was on the commercial interests within his own state, realizing that at this time placing commercial powers in the hands of Congress might not meet with the approval of his fellow citizens of seaboard New Hampshire. Possibly his dislike of Burke influenced his vote. Conceivably he feared that passage of the message might spell the doom of all other legislation on finances at the time. He may have been trying to fight for more, because, a few days before the final vote, he had written Washington that he still hoped for a loan of specie and the establishment of a bank.[41] The impost was doomed when Rhode Island refused to approve. The committee had finished its work. Having started with grandiose schemes, the members simply requested the power to levy an import duty; but that in itself was a considerable step toward the concept of a strong central government.[42]

Sullivan still picked away at the financial plight of the young nation. In May he sat on a committee, formed upon his own motion, to regulate the uncertain public finance.[43] The most important action taken by this committee was to approve of the bank proposed by Robert Morris, a plan agreed to by Congress on May 26.[44] Sullivan had contributed much to the deliberations on finance during the months he spent in Congress, for at all times he saw the necessity of economic stability and the need for creating order out of chaos. Perhaps here he made his most worth-while contribution.

XI: WOOED BY FRIEND AND FOE

Throughout his military and congressional careers Sullivan always seemed to have plenty of trouble on his hands. He is a perplexing figure because his actions, although often meritable, at times were censurable. He wanted to do the right thing, and he yearned for success and adulation. Yet at times he did not find his goal. In the army his repeated whining and occasional mishandling of assignment offset his courage and willingness to aid the patriot cause. Likewise in Congress he marred his record by an uneven performance. He had defended New Hampshire's position in the Vermont matter with vigor, and he had sought to ease the economic malady with diligence; but devious behavior tended to nullify these energetic contributions. Evidence indicates that John Sullivan became a tool of the French to an uncalled-for extent. Also during these months in Congress the British sought to win him over once more; although here the evidence, in some ways contradictory, shows that Sullivan had no intention of compromising the patriot cause for which he had fought so ardently. Some flaw in the man's character, however, suggested to both French and British, ally and foe respectively, that he might serve their purposes. Naturally, the French wanted to be able to influence Congress, as they had much at stake. Sullivan, because he was in need of money, was fair game; the Chevalier de la Luzerne, French minister at Philadelphia, knew his man and bided his time. He did not have long to wait.

Sullivan's letter of November 15, 1780, to Weare, in which he had complained of financial distress, fell into the hands of the

British and appeared in Rivington's *Royal Gazette* in December.[1] Luzerne, who quickly saw this as an opportunity to cement his influence with Sullivan, wanted to be sure that Sullivan did not waver from the cause, a fear without any foundation. From his own pocket Luzerne advanced Sullivan a bit more than 68 guineas.[2] The money may or may not have bought Sullivan's services. Unfortunately it seems impossible to arrive at the truth with certainty, but Sullivan received the "loan" either late in 1780 or early in 1781, thereby making him obligated to the French. The Comte de Vergennes, the French Minister of Foreign Affairs, never considered it a "loan" and wrote Luzerne to continue the financial assistance so long as Sullivan remained in Congress and to consider any further "loans" as part of his expenses.[3] Because Sullivan left Congress soon after Vergennes wrote this, it is most likely that he did not receive more than the original grant from Luzerne. Sullivan would have followed the French lead anyway, even had he not been given money, although this does not excuse his action. He liked the French, knew the language, and already had become a friend of Marbois, the chargé d'affaires. Most of the New Englanders were in an anti-Gallican clique in Congress, but as early as October, before Luzerne had opened his purse, Sullivan opposed this clique which had been under the influence of Arthur Lee and Samuel Adams.[4] From the beginning of his stay in Congress Sullivan had followed the French lead, although the "loan" would have made it difficult for him to strike out on an independent course had he wished to do so.

Earlier in the fall of 1780 Sullivan had pressed for French financial help for America. Not only was he anxious to send an emissary to get a loan, but also he approached both Luzerne and Marbois, asking them to intercede with the French Court in favor of a grant of money to the American cause.[5] In addition to monetary assistance from France, America also wanted an alliance with Bourbon Spain. Insistent American demands for freedom of navigation on the Mississippi and extensive claims to the west weakened the chances of getting an alliance. Spain naturally wanted to hem America in on the coast, because a vigorous revolutionary country might serve as an eventual threat to the power of the Bourbons. Sullivan was on the committee that instructed John Jay, already in Spain, not to back down on the American position, and at this time he was not following the French, who obviously wanted the Americans to temper their demands so that they might obtain Spanish help in the war.

Although the committee's report, prepared by James Madison, turned out to be a masterly defense of American claims, the brutal facts of the situation would not allow the Americans to remain adamant on western demands.[6] Sullivan went along with the rising opinion that Congress would have to ease up on its claims. Now he was under Luzerne's influence, but also the situation had changed for the worse. Both the bleak military picture in the South and fear that the war might end on the principle of *uti possidetis*, thereby leaving the British in control of parts of the South, caused many of the delegates to realize that they needed Spain's help. Naturally they would have to give in somewhat on their claims, which is exactly what they did in a vote taken February 15, 1781. Sullivan went with the large majority; only Massachusetts, Connecticut, and North Carolina voted "No." Some of the New Englanders were against making concessions, but Sullivan, along with most of the delegates, followed the French lead.[7]

Not only did Sullivan differ from his fellow New England delegates in the field of foreign affairs but also in his attitude toward Congressional reorganization which he had been hammering at since early fall. His fiery behavior had made enemies, and he found that many opposed him for the post of Secretary at War at the time when Congress was endeavoring to establish some administrative departments. The cumbersome boards did not meet with Sullivan's approval, and he sided with the French in wishing to see the administrative functions of Congress made more efficient. Sullivan wanted to have authority placed in the hands of the few, and wrote Washington that Congress had degenerated to a state of uselessness:

I am mortified at the useless harangues which Consume our Time to no purpose. I am now Endeavoring to obtain an adjournment of Congress & for leaving a Committee to Transact the Business as the only way of having the Publick Business done with propriety and Dispatch. I fully agree . . . That Congress ought to have more power, but I also think that the old members should be in Heaven or at Home before this Takes place.[8]

He would have preferred Alexander Hamilton as Super-intendent of Finance, but he did not object to the choice of Robert Morris. He also would have liked Hamilton chosen as Secretary for Foreign Affairs; but no choice came until the end of August, and then the post went to Robert Livingston with Sullivan's full support.[9] On February 18, 1781, Ezekiel Cornell had written that Sullivan probably would be chosen as Secretary at War, but that his selection would not be unanimous.[10] The choice was postponed perhaps in order to avoid electing Sulli-van. Had he been chosen, Sullivan claimed that it would have been against his will and that he would not have accepted the post. Sullivan himself blamed the postponement on the fact that Sam Adams and others from the northern states were bent on blocking him, because he had on occasion "apostatized from the True New England Faith by sometimes voting with the South-ern states." [11]

In addition to this rift, Adams and company had most likely been displeased over Sullivan's willingness to ease American claims in the west in order to woo Spain to expand her limited war effort; the republican Sam Adams also thought Sullivan was too fond of the military.[12] When it came to managing the war, Sullivan had shown far more confidence in the abilities of the generals than in the wisdom of Congress—an attitude that must have affected the vote which postponed choosing the Secretary at War until the following October. Other reasons also delayed a vote. The Board of War would not want to lose influence, and

some questioned Sullivan's ability. For example, Thomas Rodney
wrote:

General Sulivan . . . has been in the army from the beginning of the
war, has a good Idea of Publick affairs, is of Honest Political Sentiments, desirous of supporting the credit of the States, and doing
Justice to their Servants, he is generally cool and firm with an appearance of diffidence in debate, generally keeps to the points in
question, but does not possess any great polically [sic] abilities; such
as are necessary to take into view such an Extensive Systematical
arrangement of things as is necessary in so extensive a government.[13]

On top of Sullivan's struggles in Congress to get a more effi-
ciently functioning government, he found himself in an embar-
rassing position when new overtures came from the British asking him to turn away from the American cause. Once again he
spurned their proposition, although this time with not quite the
same decisiveness as upon the first occasion when Livius had approached him. The British were well aware of Sullivan's financial plight, because some of the correspondence between him
and Weare on the state of his finances had appeared in Rivington's *Royal Gazette*.[14] This time the British had a pawn in John
Sullivan's older brother Daniel, a captive of the British. During
February a party of British had seized him at his home in New
Bristol, now Sullivan, Maine. Taken to Castine, he had refused
to swear allegiance to George III; thus the British took him as a
prisoner, first to Halifax, then to New York. Here Captain
Stephen Holland, a proscribed Loyalist from Londonderry,
New Hampshire, and now an officer of the Prince of Wales
Regiment, chose to use Daniel as a means of enticing John Sul-
livan away from the American side.[15] Holland obtained a release
for Daniel from the Jersey Hulks, and under parole the prisoner
was allowed to move about Long Island.[16]

With Sir Henry Clinton's permission, Holland sent Daniel to
Philadelphia with a letter from Holland to John Sullivan. Sometime early in May, Daniel arrived in Philadelphia, and on the
7th returned to New York. Holland had written two drafts of

the letter to Sullivan.[17] In one draft, probably the final form, he mentioned that he had Clinton's permission to approach Sullivan. In part the letter read:

Tho I have been deemed an Enemy to my Country by many, and treated as such, I am sure you neither view nor would willingly treat me in that light—You know as well as I do & much better the Character & ambitious Views of many who are now in Power in this Country you know, with all their pretensions to publick Spirit, their real ends in View are their Own private Emolument—When you look into the terms offered by Great Britain & see, as you are capable of doing clearly, the many Substantial advantages arising from a Reconciliation on such terms, you cannot but wish this Country to Accept of them before it be too late. . . . I am really at a Loss for a Reason why this Country do not eagerly catch at the terms offered. I am sure you and every cool dispassionate Friend to both Countries must needs View the matter in this light—thus I have ventured to represent and name you, my Friend, to the Commander in Chief (Clinton)—I have ventured to asure [sic] him (forgive me if I have gone too far) that you wish Reconciliation, that you will when ever a fair opportunity may present, exert yourself to effect this great Event—I have represented you as a gentleman of the first abilities & Integrity in the Government where you live—Much I think is expected from you in this matter which I in my Conscience believe to be the Cause of your Country—pray save the further Effusion of the Blood of your Countrymen Step forth & let Negotiation Originate in our Province And I sincerely wish you may have the Honour, as well as the pleasure . . . of restoring Peace & Happiness to your Country.[18]

Both Daniel and John Sullivan have left conflicting stories as to John's reaction. Daniel, who ostensibly had come to Philadelphia to negotiate his exchange, reported back to Holland that his brother wished a reconciliation. According to Daniel's account, he had told his brother that the British were willing to pay him for information on the doings of Congress. Daniel probably had taken a copy of Rivington's *Royal Gazette* which contained an intercepted letter from Weare to John Sullivan, saying all he could offer him was £200 to help alleviate his financial troubles, because on May 8 Sullivan wrote Weare that he had seen the paper and that the sum available "would pay Eight weeks Lodging for a Single person without Servant Horse Liquor wood Candle or any other Article. . . . I am willing to Submit to any Inconvenience to Serve my Country but to be an Embassador & a Beggar at the Same time would be disgraceful not to me but to my constituents." [19] No doubt Sullivan was furious over his financial status; no doubt Daniel Sullivan carried overtures to his brother; but the evidence leans toward the supposition that John Sullivan had no intention of entering negotiations with the British unless it were to mislead them.

Sullivan reported his brother's mission to Luzerne and told the French minister that he had rejected the proposals scornfully, in fact had thrown Holland's letter into the fire before his brother's face.[20] Luzerne expressed doubt whether Sullivan had been so decisive in his rejection as he had declared; certainly Daniel's account said that John Sullivan had lent a receptive ear. Perhaps so; John Sullivan may have been stalling to try to save his brother from further imprisonment, or he may have been seeking some way to bait a trap in turn for the British. Luzerne said in his account to Vergennes:

He [Sullivan] made me a very strange proposition,—to pretend to lend an ear to the overtures that had been made to him, and to send a trusty man to New York to ask of General Clinton a plan of reconciliation; adding, that he had been unwilling to use his brother's services, fearing his attachment to the cause of independence.[21]

Sullivan proposed to tell four other members of Congress about his plan, but Luzerne advised against the entire scheme. Although he had trust in Sullivan, he believed that the man would be subjecting himself to temptations if he opened negotiations with the British. Therefore Luzerne made efforts to scotch the plan by demonstrating to Sullivan that it would entail much evil. "He did not promise me, formally, to abandon it," Luzerne wrote, "but if, notwithstanding the representations which I intend to reiterate to him, he persists in it, I shall so

narrowly watch his conduct that I shall hope to discover whatever may be ambiguous in it." [22]

Probably Sullivan tried no further moves, although Holland
did send Daniel back on a second mission. This time he sought
Sullivan's help in getting permission to allow Mrs. Holland to
visit Londonderry. On June 12 Daniel arrived in Philadelphia
and gave Holland's letter to John, in which the former asked
Sullivan to "equal the great Monk." [23] Daniel Sullivan's report
of his second conversation with his brother certainly raises questions as to the latter's role. The report, which is preserved in the
Clinton papers, reads:

> He arrived at Philadelphia the 12th June, waited upon his
> brother, General Sullivan, and delivered a letter to him from Capt
> Holland; after reading it several times the General told him it was
> very well, but would not descend into particulars, as his coming to
> Philadelphia twice might give suspitions, and as soon as he had an
> answer from New Hampshire, he would inform him of everything
> in his power. That Capt. Holland might assure the person [Clinton]
> which he mentioned in his letter to him, in whose full confidence
> he was, that he would do everything in his power to serve him.
> Capt. Sullivan asked his brother, if M^{rs}. Holland's visit would be
> limited to any certain time; he said he had not the least doubt she
> might stay as long as she pleased; that Captain Holland would fol-
> low her in less than six months, and that the purchasers of Holland's
> property had thrown their money away. That it was his opinion
> that unless the French make very great exertions in America this
> summer, the Congress will be torn to pieces and the people would
> return to their allegiance; that the Congress was at present in great
> Confusion, and that he was determined to take care of Himself.
> Capt. Sullivan further says that in every part of Philadelphia the
> people are swearing they would pull the Congress house down.
>   (*Signed*) Danl. Sullivan [24]

Was Sullivan trying to protect himself in case the war should
end abruptly with a return to the former allegiance? A negative
answer seems certain. That he would wish to help Mrs. Holland
visit Londonderry to see her children is natural, particularly as
Captain Holland was looking after Daniel's well-being. Sullivan

did not waver; to have done so would have been entirely inconsistent with his character, for early in May, he had written
Washington enclosing a resolution he proposed to make which
would call for an expedition against Canada. The resolution
damned the enemy: "A peace ratified by Great Britain at this
time, should even every post in the United States be given up to
Congress, must finally end in the destruction of our liberties; for
a long continuance of peace would only serve to render a con-
quest over us more certain." [25] He seemed determined that the
war should be fought to a successful conclusion, although at
times he did wonder whether the Americans would gain victory. Concern for Daniel's safety helps explain John Sullivan's
odd behavior. Perhaps Daniel embroidered his story in order to
promote his own welfare or to dupe the enemy. Unfortunately,
the truth is elusive. Daniel died shortly thereafter just as his exchange was to take place, and apparently Holland halted his efforts to win over John Sullivan.[26]

These were hectic days for Sullivan. At the time of his worries over his brother, he had to face the prospect of a duel with
Thomas Burke, who had returned to Congress the previous December. Since Brandywine the two men had been at logger-
heads. Fortunately, however, they avoided the field of honor.
Alexander McDougall represented Sullivan in the matter and
convinced Burke that Sullivan had not had Burke in mind when
he referred to the Congressman "who Don Quixot Like pranced
at a Distance" from the fighting at Brandywine.[27] Burke then
graciously said that he had not meant any personal insult to Sullivan, and that in fact he had become impressed with Sullivan's
ability now that he had seen him in Congress. There the matter
ended, and no duel took place; but Sullivan's denial that he had
had Burke in mind when he criticized the Congressional spectator at Brandywine does not quite ring true.[28]

But all was not calm. Arduous wrangling occurred in Congress over the instructions on peace negotiations, and at this
point Sullivan certainly served Luzerne's purposes. He followed

his lead, and he conveyed information on the doings of Congress. This stretched the duties of an alliance beyond the bounds of reason, and in effect Sullivan was no less than Luzerne's agent.

Sullivan could be of great assistance to Luzerne if he were placed upon a committee considering the extent of negotiations to be made with the British. Mediation of the war by Russia and Austria was in the offing, and hence it was essential that the delegates instruct their plenipotentiary, John Adams, who was already in Europe. Naturally there must be a committee to consider the manner of conducting negotiations, the powers of the plenipotentiary, and "the confidence that ought to be reposed in the French plenipotentiaries and the king's ministers." [29] Luzerne was most anxious to control the make-up of the committee, because he wanted the Americans to recede from their territorial demands in order to shorten the war, and was hopeful of having John Adams's powers as a plenipotentiary curbed. Evidently he used his influence with President Samuel Huntington to have pro-French delegates chosen, and he succeeded, because Sullivan was one of the five members. Maryland's Daniel Carroll, the chairman, certainly had no intention of pressing the western claims, and the same could be said of John Witherspoon of New Jersey. Because John Mathews of South Carolina saw his state faced with the possibility of *uti possidetis*, obviously he would sacrifice western claims to salvage his state's plight. This left Virginia's Joseph Jones as the sole member who was ready to argue for definite western claims. Sullivan turned out to be one of the most effective voices the French had, and throughout the committee deliberations he took a strong pro-French stand.[30]

Although Luzerne did not wish to sell the Americans short, he definitely wanted to undermine Adams, who had irritated Vergennes by his independent course of action. Obviously the French were afraid that Adams might negotiate with the British on his own. Luzerne took pains to tell Sullivan and the committee that Adams should be willing to accept French guidance, and that the king would protect American interests with zeal. Although all efforts should be made to prevent settlement on the basis of *uti possidetis,* Luzerne warned that mediation did entail some attendant risks. The British had to be convinced that they could not hope to conquer the United States; thus extra exertions by the army were essential, a course of action which Sullivan constantly urged.[31]

Luzerne's wooing of Sullivan now showed tangible results. The French minister kept a close eye upon the committee and claimed that their report, containing instructions for John Adams, was written under his influence. He said that Carroll stayed behind after a meeting to write the report, but the document is in Sullivan's handwriting. Perhaps both Americans stayed behind, with Sullivan acting as amanuensis. The instructions were brief and gratified Luzerne's wishes. Earlier instructions were no longer binding but might serve as a guide; independence obviously was to be the *sine qua non* of any negotiation; no recommendation was offered on boundaries; Adams was to "conform" to the "advice and opinion" of the French negotiator; and, should no treaty be possible, Adams might agree to a truce.[32]

These instructions, entered in the Journal for June 8, came upon the floor for discussion and debate at an earlier day. On the 6th, a resolution written by Madison of Virginia, proposed that no treaty should be acceded to which did not "secure the independence and sovereignty of the thirteen states." [33] The instructions written by Sullivan had mentioned just the United States, not the thirteen states. Madison wished to be sure to spike any attempt at *uti possidetis.* This resolution passed, and thus the French could find Congress as intractable as John Adams after all! [34]

New Jersey's John Witherspoon then offered an additional resolution, based on Sullivan's written report, that, although the earlier instructions showed the "desires and expectations of Congress," still the minister, when considering "disputed boundaries, and other particulars," must use his own "judgment and prudence." The second portion of the resolution obliged the minister to make "candid and confidential communications" in all matters with the French.[35] Luzerne's influence entered here, because he was trying to convince the opposition that it was senseless to insist upon a definite western boundary, particularly since the enemy was occupying such an extensive part of the southern colonies as well as New York City. On June 8 the way was cleared for a vote on Witherspoon's original motion. The first part, allowing the minister to use his own "judgment and prudence," had the approval of all but Virginia. The second part, instructing the American minister to confide in the French, had the approval of all but Massachusetts. On both votes Sullivan followed the French lead. The French had won the first encounter.[36]

Sullivan had been of considerable help to the French, but then the vast majority of Congress had gone along the same road. Not satisfied with his victory, Luzerne pushed for even more. He strengthened his victory when a resolution, passed June 11, instructed Adams "ultimately to govern yourself by their [French] advice and opinion." [37] He capped his victory when Congress decided to enlarge the peace mission, although on June 9 such a proposal had failed.[38] Sullivan had voted against the idea of enlarging the mission at the time of the first vote. When Congress did change its mind, at first it decided to send two men, then four. The delegates chose John Jay immediately; then disagreement arose. Sullivan pressed for the choice of Benjamin Franklin but found the suggestion met with disfavor, particularly from the friends of Arthur Lee. Sullivan and his group objected to the candidacies of Jefferson and Henry Laurens. Again Sullivan argued for the acceptance of Benjamin Franklin, but, unable to win his case, he then suggested that all three men be chosen. He insisted that they be voted on together and not separately, since he feared that Franklin would lose out if that were the case. The "package deal" succeeded, and the personnel of the mission was complete.[39]

The French had gained the day and clearly demonstrated that they had a loud voice in determining American diplomatic policy.[40] Sullivan never apologized for his performance over the instructions; in fact, he took pride in it. He realized the exigencies of the time, saw that perhaps the war might take a turn for the worse, and had little faith in Congress. "I acknowledge and glory in the confession," he wrote "that I was one of those who objected to fettering our ministers, and positively to dictate orders of peace, to five gentlemen, who were, in my opinion, more than equal in the business of negotiation, to all the members then on the floor of Congress." [41] Sullivan seemed to have forgotten that he had been unwilling to fetter even one negotiator. Certainly he had helped break down the faction that had feared French ascendancy. Luzerne commented upon Sullivan's role when he wrote:

I have always found him disposed to be very confiding, and it is to him that I always attribute the rupture of the league formed by the Eastern States; a league which, by false ideas of popularity, of liberty, and by an excessive jealousy of the Army and of the General-in-Chief, has for so long a time delayed the most urgent measures, and which on numerous occasions has shown itself equally jealous of our advantages and of our influence.[42]

Luzerne attributed his success largely to the rupture of the eastern league and to the absence of Samuel Adams from Congress, although perhaps John Witherspoon of New Jersey was the key factor in winning the day for Luzerne. Representing a "landless" state and therefore having no western claims, Witherspoon had led the floor fight to prevent instructions which demanded specific boundaries. Sullivan, therefore, had not been the sole reason or even the major reason for the French diplomatic victory, because the majority of Congress was in agreement; but Luzerne never would have gained the upper hand had it ever been apparent to the delegates that France would betray the best interests of her American ally during such trying times.[43]

Sullivan's performance leaves something to be desired. He let Luzerne influence him, and he appears to have compromised himself. Sullivan needed money and indulged in self-pity, claiming that he had drained his resources while supporting his family and himself throughout his military service. Luzerne advanced him money without expecting repayment, and Sullivan accepted the money probably with no intention of repaying it. He was ethically obtuse, for a public servant should answer only his own conscience and the needs of those whom he serves. Some of his fellow delegates, it is true, had interests in various land schemes and still took part in debate over the disposal of land. But it is also true that some delegates faced the same financial pressures as Sullivan, and yet did not take money. By accepting Luzerne's offer of money, John Sullivan made a grievous error. Yet his actions, although supporting the French, were always in agreement with his inclinations. He had faith in the French, and he never cared for the anti-Gallican faction in Congress; but never had he wished to see a peace brought about unless the United States would negotiate upon equal terms.[44]

Sullivan's time on the national scene was drawing to a close. Unfortunately, his acceptance of the "loan" and his constant wails over the lack of personal funds make him unattractive and tend to tarnish the value of the contributions he did make through his energy and enthusiasm. During the months he was in Philadelphia he had threatened to quit time and time again unless financial help were forthcoming. Although he had reason to clamor for money, his cries became almost too insistent. Luzerne commented sarcastically that in the past Sullivan often had exhorted the good men of New Hampshire to serve their nation and to ask for nothing in return but the honor of serving.[45] The previous November Sullivan had sought compensation for the depreciation of the bills paid him while in the army, but he got no satisfaction. Late in July Congress recommended that the Superintendent of Finance pay him $1500, but in early August voted down the suggestion that New Hampshire reimburse him for depreciation of his war pay. Obviously he was miffed and in his rather overbearing manner did not hide his displeasure.[46]

John Sullivan was in no happy frame of mind as he came to the end of his Congressional career. He stayed a few days longer than he had expected to so that he might vote for Robert Livingston as Secretary for Foreign Affairs, much to Luzerne's pleasure, because Arthur Lee, a favorite of the eastern alliance, had been a major contender.[47] Now his job was over. On August 11 John Sullivan left Congress to start back home. Since September, 1774, he had been either in Congress or in the army. Now he was returning to New Hampshire and would exert his talents in his own state as the young nation faced the task of bringing the war to a halt and of solving the new problems which the peace would bring.

*S*ullivan, who was just a few months past his forty-first birth-day, had accomplished far more than many men would in a lifetime. Behind him stood his military and congressional ex-periences. Looming ahead were new challenges, and the next nine years found him active in the political affairs of New Hampshire. He had the abilities and the techniques of a poli-tician: persuasive talents, the knack of leadership, popularity, and the courage to face a crisis unflinchingly. His abilities suited New Hampshire, for not only was he the military hero returning home but also the solon looking for respite after months in Congress, although he had led Luzerne to believe he might return to Philadelphia by the end of the year.[1] Sullivan may have told Luzerne to expect his return so that the French-man would not press for repayment of the "loan"; perhaps he genuinely wished to return, but that seems unlikely. Although he was leaving the national scene, he had no intention of quitting public life and told Luzerne that he expected to work at getting a permanent form of government for New Hampshire and at settling the turmoil in the western part of the state.

To establish a permanent government was a pressing prob-lem, for the temporary plan, adopted in 1776, obviously needed revision, and an attempt had failed in 1779. During the fall of 1781 Sullivan served on a town committee in Durham which studied the Constitution offered by the Convention that had come into session the previous June. The Convention did not look upon this plan as final; instead the members expected the towns to offer amendments.[2] Little did they know that they would have to wait until October, 1783, before gaining approval of a plan for government, mainly because of the people's apathy and lack of interest. The Convention was offering, on the whole, a conscious copy of the Massachusetts Constitution of 1781.[3] An element within New Hampshire was striving valiantly for more effective government but found that many were reluctant to hand over power. William Plumer, somewhat jaundiced in his views about the popular wisdom, commented: "The prejudices which the Revolution had engendered against the arbitrary government of Great Britain, made the people jealous of giving to their own officers so much power as was necessary to establish an efficient government."[4]

Some sectionalism within the state made it more difficult to get agreement. Portsmouth and the Piscataqua towns of Dover, Durham, Newmarket, and Exeter controlled seaboard New Hampshire. Aside from the Piscataqua, two other rivers determined the state's sectional pattern: the Merrimack and the Connecticut. Both flowed out of New Hampshire, so that the inhabitants of their valleys looked to other areas rather than to their own seaboard. During colonial days the people of the central and western portions of New Hampshire resented control by the tidewater region and were particularly annoyed that the colony was not divided into counties. The division finally came in 1771 when Rockingham, Strafford, Hillsborough, Cheshire, and Grafton counties were established, although Strafford and Grafton remained attached to Rockingham until 1773. Rockingham, the most populous county, contained the area in the vicinity of Portsmouth and Exeter. Strafford, Sullivan's own county, was to the north, extending as far as Wolfeborough near Lake Winnipesaukee. Hillsborough County, which was separated from Rockingham by the Merrimack River, was the central area of New Hampshire. To the west, in the valley of the Connecticut River, were Cheshire and Grafton counties, the latter reaching to the northernmost boundary. Since the

French and Indian Wars the interior sections had been filling with settlers from Massachusetts and Connecticut. What trade the settlers pursued followed mainly the route of the rivers; and thus these people, rather than have intercourse with Portsmouth, found themselves more closely connected with Newburyport, Salem, Boston, and Hartford.

Although sectionalism might have made agreement on a plan of government more difficult to arrive at, the difference of opinion was not the result of a clash between conservative and radical elements in New Hampshire for control. Of all the states, the northernmost perhaps had the most homogeneous population. With access to the sea limited to a small area, a mercantile class had emerged just along the coast, notably in Portsmouth. The vast majority of the New Hampshire freemen lived on the soil and worked their own farms. Sullivan and the men in the Convention of 1781 were no more conservative than the men who had drawn up the plan which met defeat in 1779. Although this proposed Constitution had failed to provide for a stronger executive, the leaders probably wished one.[5]

John Sullivan, when he had written Meshech Weare from Boston late in 1775, had warned against a state government that did not have all its branches controlled directly by the people.[6] By now Sullivan undoubtedly saw that effective government might entail some checks, although he was always too much of a politician to by-pass the people. The Durham committee of which he was a member held to republican principles when the members proposed that a two thirds' vote override the governor's veto instead of a three fourths' vote as the latter "approaches near yielding to the Governors negative." [7] Furthermore, the committee saw no reason for limiting the number of years a person might hold office, arguing that an annual election was a sufficient safeguard.

Durham accepted the committee's recommendations, and the Convention, as expected, had to continue its deliberations.[8] During the summer of 1782, Sullivan sat in the Convention which met for at least one session, possibly two, and for some of the time he served as Secretary pro tem.[9] The new draft which this Convention offered tried to meet the objections presented by the towns and in general reduced qualifications for voting and holding office.[10] But no acceptance was forthcoming. Sullivan did not attend the later sessions, and approval did not come until the fall of 1783, after the executive powers had been clipped somewhat. The executive lacked the right of veto and was given the name president rather than governor, an unpopular term still reminding the people of the prewar executives. The Convention may have curbed the president's powers out of conviction, or possibly out of desperation in order to get some plan accepted.[11] Durham thought the executive should have more power, and certainly Sullivan must have thought the Convention went too far in curbing the president's effectiveness.

While the argument over the Constitution continued during 1782 and 1783, John Sullivan assumed the duties of Attorney-General, late in September, 1782, although he had been reluctant to accept the post. Throughout the summer he had refused the appointment because he was engaged in some legal matters against the state, and only after the Superior Court excused him from acting in cases which had involved him, did he accept. He wished to make it quite clear that he would not initiate action to confiscate estates of Loyalists whom he had represented on previous occasions. At this time he was attorney for Mrs. George Boyd, whose husband was an absentee, and he did not wish to act against her interests. Earlier in March he had accepted a chariot from her which supposedly was partial payment for his services, but later the "gift" would be used against him in the state presidential political struggles.[12]

As Attorney-General, Sullivan had to represent the state in any action before the Superior Court of Judicature, which rode circuit and held sessions in each of the five counties. From 1782 until 1786 Sullivan held this office, and during these years the Court did not have to face too many cases.[13] Sullivan found that he was most active in Cheshire County, a western part of the state, which was in a state of confusion as poor communications between the frontier and the seacoast had led to a strained relationship. The people of the two western counties believed that the other areas of the state had neglected them. Stirred up by "envious and prejudiced persons," the westerners looked upon their liberties and privileges as having been infringed.[14] Vermont still persisted in claiming certain towns east of the Connecticut River, and this disagreement over the boundary could lead to friction, for although Vermont was willing to submit the issue to an impartial tribunal, she had every intention of defending her stand should New Hampshire resort to coercive measures.[15]

On January 10, 1782, the New Hampshire House of Representatives voted to send troops under Sullivan's command to the western part of the state. Whether to send the troops or not was left in the hands of the Committee of Safety; but the army never marched, because the legislature offered to pardon those who would return to New Hampshire's jurisdiction.[16] In February, Vermont relinquished jurisdiction east of the river; yet trouble continued since some people were reluctant to accept New Hampshire's control. For a time they tried to prevent the courts from sitting. Their efforts finally came to a halt in 1784, although peace had been largely restored before then.[17]

In 1782, however, the people in Keene of Cheshire County were by no means friendly toward the government of New Hampshire; feeling had run so high that a group of persons had prevented the Inferior Court from meeting. When Attorney-General Sullivan and the justices of the Superior Court approached Keene in October, 1782, they learned that a group intended to keep the Superior Court from holding its session. The threat of trouble, however, failed to prevent the Attorney-General and justices from moving into the town and entering the court house. A mob followed them in and petitioned that the court postpone its session. The people of Keene, many of whom were in debt, had a practical reason for desiring a postponement, namely, to prevent the civil cases from coming to trial. Sullivan donned his military uniform on this occasion, perhaps hoping that he might cow the mob; but the next day he was in citizen's garb and announced that the court would not hear the civil cases of those who were not prepared for trial. In order to maintain the dignity and respect of the Court, however, three persons who had raided the Inferior Court the previous month and one person who had incited riot, were brought to trial. Wisdom prevailed; the men pled guilty, threw themselves on the mercy of the Court, and gained pardon. The only other case involving Sullivan was a jury acquittal of a person charged with having stolen a mare.[18]

In general, Sullivan's work while riding circuit with the Court was rather routine. The criminal cases mainly involved theft of cattle. In 1785, however, there was a series of prosecutions for passing counterfeit money. Counterfeiting was a serious offense in the eyes of the Court and the Attorney-General, and one forger had his ear cropped, received a £300 fine, and had to stand in the pillory.[19] Only once did Sullivan have to prosecute a murder charge, and in that case the defendant was acquitted of having smothered her illegitimate child.[20]

His performance as Attorney-General came under attack in the New Hampshire *Gazette* in the summer of 1783 because some believed he was not pressing the sale of confiscated Loyalist estates. The legislature had done its duty, said "Cincinnatus," the author of the letter; but he charged that the executive and judiciary were remiss, thereby tarring the Attorney-General.[21] Sullivan struck back and defended himself in the *Gazette's* columns. His assailant, Sullivan said, merely wanted to serve as trustee for George Boyd's estate, and hence was attacking him because he, Sullivan, represented Mrs. Boyd and was trying to protect her from "poverty and distress." [22] He saw no cause to take action for two obvious reasons: the grand juries had made no moves, and the preliminary articles of the Peace Treaty recommended that confiscated estates be restored. To him his course of action had been obvious. "If the Grand Juries had found bills against any estates I should undoubtedly have drawn them," he wrote, "but for me to have filed information of my own head, and put the state to the expense of prosecutions, when there was not a possibility that the public would reap even the least advantage therefrom, must have excited the astonishment of all mankind, and justly brought upon me the indignation of an 'injured people.'"[23] There Sullivan chose to let the matter lie although later on, when he became more involved in New Hampshire politics, the charge was thrown at him that he had been remiss in pressing for confiscation. Not until 1786 did New Hampshire remove the barriers lying in the way of those absentees who wished to return to the state, but prior to that a number of towns had gone on record opposing their reentry.[24] The wounds of war took a long time to heal.

Probably the most arduous assignment Sullivan had as Attorney-General was the occasion when he went to Annapolis to represent his state's interests before the Continental Congress. A dispute had arisen as to court jurisdiction. Did a Court of Appeals established by Congress to determine maritime cases have precedence over the judiciary of New Hampshire? Briefly, that was the controversy. During the war John Penhallow and others had captured the Brig "Lusanna," which they took to Portsmouth to have condemned by the Maritime Court of New Hampshire. Other claimants appealed to both the Superior Court of New Hampshire and to Congress for a reversal, but failed to gain their point. In May, 1780, Congress established a Court of Appeals with jurisdiction over appeals in cases of capture, and in September, 1783, this court decided in favor of the claimants against John Penhallow, an action which reversed the earlier decisions of the New Hampshire Court.[25]

The New Hampshire House of Representatives was furious and had no intention of taking this matter lying down. The representatives wished Congress to enforce a remonstrance against the decree of the Court of Appeals and to assert the exclusive jurisdiction of New Hampshire's courts.[26] The remonstrance stated that the action of the Court of Appeals was "not more injurious to the individuals immediately concerned (Penhallow et al) than the Exercise of such a Jusisdiction [sic] by that Court is derogatory to the dignity, & Subversive of the Sovereignty & Independency of this State." [27]

John Sullivan left for Annapolis early in December, 1783, to argue before Congress in behalf of both New Hampshire and John Penhallow. He argued with considerable conviction although he was unable to carry the day.[28] In a series of questions which he submitted to Congress, Sullivan sought to show that Congress did not have the authority to establish a court which could overrule the decisions of the courts of common law. The arbitrary procedure of admiralty courts had been one of the reasons for the war with Great Britain, and, if Congress sanctioned similar action, she was supporting an unwarrantable abuse. He continued that, if Congress were able to vest herself prior to confederation with power to set up courts having jurisdiction over maritime cases, why could Congress then not have levied an import, raised money by taxation, "and in fine not only have taken all the powers given by the Confederation into their own hands prior to its ratification but even now assume all other powers which they think necessary though not mentioned as the Articles of Union? " [29] Here Sullivan's duties as Attorney-General were moving him to argue, possibly against his better judgment, against the authority of a central government. A Congressional committee reported that "neither Congress nor any persons deriving authority from them" had jurisdiction. To the committee the matter was strictly a local problem, since the seizure had been made by New Hampshire men, had been submitted to New Hampshire jurisdiction, with any right of appeal to Congress denied by the state. Enough votes could not be mustered, however, to pass the committee's opinion in the form of a resolution, offered March 30, 1784.[30]

Sullivan had already left Annapolis in January, but before

he departed he made another effort to get compensation for the depreciation of his war pay. All Congress did for him, however, was to refer his request to the Superintendent of Finance.[31] This Annapolis trip had been a difficult assignment, but usually Sullivan's chores as Attorney-General seldom involved more than cursory attention except when riding circuit with the Superior Court. Most of the time throughout the first half of the decade of the 1780s he busied himself with his mills or in his law practice, which was not one of much interest or consequence. The law was not Sullivan's chief love, for in politics he found a more alluring mistress.

XIII: THE STATE POLITICIAN

Perhaps more than any other man in New Hampshire during those days following the revolution John Sullivan understood the nature of politics and the attributes needed for success. He knew he must maintain popularity. In striving for success, Sullivan may have made just one blunder; he took on a legal case which pitted him against some of the more powerful men of the state. He chose to represent the heirs of Samuel Allen in their dispute with the Masonian Proprietors, whom he had represented before the war. John Mason had been the original grantee of New Hampshire, but his heirs sold his claims to Allen. Allen's heirs, in turn, never pushed their claims, and, because certain legal complications of entail beclouded their title, one of John Mason's descendants reasserted the Masonian claim with apparent success. In 1746 he sold his patent to some New Hampshire men who became known as the Masonian proprietors.[1] The Masonian claims appeared to have been well established in law until the Allen heirs, who mainly lived outside the state, sought to press their dormant title. The legislature undertook to settle the dispute, and it was not until 1790 that the matter was settled and then in favor of the Masonian interests.[2]

Throughout the many months that this legal embroilment lasted, Sullivan found himself pitted against Portsmouth leaders like John and Woodbury Langdon, George Atkinson, William Whipple, and John Pierce. He had not used good judgment when he chose to support Allen's heirs. Not only did he antagonize some of the leading figures of the state, but also many landholders feared that the claim to their holdings might be questionable should the Mason Proprietors, who had granted vast acreage of land, lose in the dispute, even though Sullivan had made it quite clear that he was testing the issue only in waste or unimproved lands.[3]

Aside from his advocacy of the Allen heirs, Sullivan played his hand with care. He certainly had no intention of making the error he had committed in his younger days when he had let the people of Durham rise up against him. He had to be popular, and he strove to please his fellow townsmen. Each morning at eleven the men of Durham gathered at his home for conversation and a drink of punch. By nature he was generous and desired to please, but he also hoped for plaudits and flattery.[4] His gregarious ways led him to take an active role in both the newly formed Society of the Cincinnati and in Freemasonry. By stressing his war service and by gaining the support of fellow veterans, Sullivan sought to further his career. The Cincinnati, therefore, naturally had appeal to him, and he was president of the chapter in New Hampshire until 1792.[5] He had become a Mason in 1767, and was raised to Grand Master of the New Hampshire Lodge in 1789, a position which he resigned in 1790.[6]

His popularity assured, Sullivan also sought advancement by increasing his general fund of knowledge. Though by no means intellectually inclined, Sullivan was not mentally lazy. In William Plumer's words, "he acquired an extensive knowledge of men and things, and a considerable knowledge of books."[7] Jeremy Belknap, a contemporary and New Hampshire's able historian, wrote that Sullivan was "a friend to literature, as men who have emerged from nothing through the force of their own genius commonly are."[8] Sullivan had a library of moderate size, consisting mainly of legal volumes, but he did have Rollin's *Ancient History* and Montesquieu's *The Spirit of Laws* as well as volumes of English and French belles-lettres.[9] The men of New Hampshire at that time did not have extensive libraries, and Sullivan's probably was as good as any.

He was a man of varied interests. He undertook some agricultural experimentation on his Durham farm, and he even raised bees. His success allowed him to employ several people, including a Negro coachman, Stephen Noble.[10] Sullivan always found some project to keep him occupied. Perhaps the most unusual task that he undertook during these years was his search for the carcass of a moose and the horns of other animals, to send to Thomas Jefferson in Paris. Jefferson wished to impress the French naturalist Buffon with the wonders of American natural history. Sullivan was so eager to please the Virginian that he undertook the task as though he were conducting a military campaign, at least so thought Jefferson. Upon hearing that Sullivan had started to gather the specimens, Jefferson asked not only that the bones of the legs, thighs, and head of the moose be left in the skin, but also that the hair be kept on the skin, if possible. Sullivan made arrangements to send a hunting party out from Lebanon. This party killed a moose in Vermont and sent the carcass on to Sullivan in Durham from where he reported to Jefferson that "Every Engine was set at work" to preserve the bones and skin.[11] Finally the specimens were ready, and in 1787 the moose and the antlers of an elk, a deer, a caribou, and a spiked-horn buck began the trip to France.

The blow struck for science was pleasing to Sullivan but not to Thomas Jefferson, for the expenses, over £46 sterling, were considerable and far more than he had intended to pay. Sullivan complicated the matter by drawing a draft payable on Jefferson in favor of John Adams's son-in-law, supposedly in England at the time, because Sullivan wanted payment in pounds and not francs, which were then selling at a loss. The only compensation Jefferson got was to poke some fun at Sullivan's efforts when he wrote: "The troops he employed sallied forth . . . in the month of March—much snow—a herd attacked—one killed—in the wilderness—a road to cut 20 miles—to be drawn by hand from the frontiers to his house—bones to be cleaned &c. &c. &c." [12] In spite of all these efforts, the skin arrived minus its hair.

Jefferson had had enough; he thanked Sullivan for his efforts but wished no further specimens unless obtained without expense.[13]

Sullivan's one venture into science serves as an amusing interlude, but he preferred to be a politician, not a naturalist. In June, 1784, when New Hampshire's permanent form of government had gone into effect, Meshech Weare continued as President, but it was to be his final term. Soon it became obvious that Weare, who had the respect of the people, no longer desired to serve, and so political rivalries developed between those who sought to succeed him. Sullivan entered the lists. Although there was no party division at this early date in the history of American politics, there were factions which found their basis in personal animosity rather than in genuine political or economic differences of opinion. William Plumer noticed that a factional split was appearing now that Weare was too old to run for re-election.[14]

Sullivan entered the contest for the presidency of the state as early as February, 1785, when he wrote John Wendell of Portsmouth that, although he did not seek the office, he would not refuse it if chosen.[15] John Wendell assumed the name "Agricola" and wrote the opening salvo of Sullivan's campaign in the *Gazette*. Agricola claimed that no one was better suited for the job of president than John Sullivan and tried to prove this by posing a series of questions, the name "Sullivan" being the obvious answer to each. "Who first struck against Fort William and Mary?" opened the way. The two concluding questions in the series were suggested by Sullivan himself. He thought it would be a good idea to ask who saved the army from annihilation in Canada, and who saved the army in Rhode Island after the French had abandoned them.[16] Sullivan, feigning a ridiculous modesty, wrote Wendell that suggesting the questions embarrassed him: "I confess Sir that however Just the Queries I felt a blush at Suggesting them & think my Ink now begins to assume the *Rouge* for having so far transgress⁴ as to write a single word in my own favor." [17]

During the campaign Sullivan found himself under fire from the supporters of the other candidates, particularly those of John Langdon. Old charges against him were revived: Sullivan had sought remuneration from Congress for his part in the raid on Fort William and Mary; he had not pressed for fishery rights while he was serving in Congress at the time the instructions for the peace negotiators were drawn up; and he had accepted bribes for not confiscating a Loyalist estate, presumably George Boyd's.[18] Sullivan answered these charges effectively in the *Gazette*.[19] His efforts, however, were not enough, for as the contest developed, Sullivan came in a poor third behind George Atkinson and John Langdon. Because Atkinson's margin was not sufficient, the election went to the Senate and that body selected Langdon.[20] What irked Sullivan the most, however, was the paltry nine votes given him in Portsmouth.[21]

His first excursion into the political arena as an active candidate had not been successful, but time would change that. Meanwhile he had been devoting attention to the militia, for in addition to his duties as Attorney-General, Sullivan had been given command of the militia.[22] Early in January, 1785, while addressing the freemen of New Hampshire, he had discussed a topic which has always perplexed a republic: namely, the role of the military in a democratic society. "We often please ourselves by observing, that this country is calculated for freedom and commerce, not for war—I sincerely join in that opinion," he wrote, "and most ardently wish it may ever remain such; but I have long since been convinced, that the only way to keep peace is to be prepared for the worst events—If we mean to keep our neighbours sword in the scabbard, we must whet our own." [23]

Continuing, Sullivan argued that a standing army was even more dangerous to the liberties of a country than a foreign army, certainly an odd statement, but one which enabled him to urge the maintenance of a well-regulated militia. The troops must be properly equipped, he asserted, and he wished the uniforms to be of home manufacture. The unfavorable balance of trade was draining the circulating cash, and he argued that the use of home-manufactured goods, even if more expensive, in the long run would benefit the domestic economy. Sullivan concluded his plea for a strong militia by stating that war might be in the offing, since the British had refused to leave the frontier posts.[24] He always took his duties with the militia seriously, and urged "Gentlemen of Family, Fortune and Education" to join the Light Horse, since he realized that the ordinary tasks of the foot soldier might hold little allure. He left no stone unturned.[25]

June, 1785, arrived and the new officers assumed their positions. Sullivan became Speaker of the House, and also was one of the five Councillors selected to advise the president.[26] The legislature had the usual problems which accompany a postwar period, mainly those of finance and trade, but there were other problems typical of those days, such as the need of encouraging domestic manufactures and determining the status of the Loyalists. For some time money had been scarce in New Hampshire and was hard to collect. The treasurer reported that he had none, and that the collectors could not get the taxes from the people. British trade restrictions in the West Indies were irksome, and often there was pressure to grant Congress powers to regulate both external and internal trade.[27] But the picture was by no means gloomy. John Wheelock, placed on the frontier at Dartmouth, had written in a sanguine way about the conditions in 1784. Education was thriving, and resources were abundant. No longer dependent on outside sources, Americans began to look to themselves in the middle 1780s, and even began "to act for themselves as philosophers." [28] One observer noted that "Men of right principles" were regaining the ground they had lost and once again were "a leading influence in public affairs." [29] Out of the confusion attendant upon war and its aftermath stability was emerging.

Sullivan threw himself into the legislative chores and took a constructive stand on the measures under debate. The legislature accepted his recommendations for regulating and disciplining the militia, for in this field he had experience and no one chose to contradict his views.[30] He took the conservative stand on debtor legislation when he voted with the minority against allowing a debtor to offer real or personal estate in satisfying a debt. He had the creditor point of view and wished to maintain specie payment for debts, although later he switched his stand for political reasons. This tender legislation, which became law on November 8, 1785, did not force the creditor to accept payment in real or personal estate unless he chose to do so. The debt remained, with six percent annual interest until satisfied, and thus the creditors had not completely lost the argument.[31] Sullivan believed that authority to regulate trade and commerce should be in the hands of Congress, and on the whole he disapproved of legislation which retaliated against British shipping restrictions. As far as he was concerned, British ships could carry American produce from American ports, because this would help relieve the scarcity of cash.[32] The tender act, which he had not approved of in November, came up for repeal in February, 1786. Now Sullivan supported the legislation and voted against repeal.[33] But the time had arrived for voting for President, and quite obviously Sullivan did not want to take an unpopular step, particularly when so few people favored repeal.

While Sullivan was becoming more and more entangled in politics, he got himself involved in a personal feud with the Langdons. The crisis came in the early months of 1786 with the result that Sullivan became so irate he declined reappointment as Attorney-General and resigned command of the militia. Sullivan always suspected that Woodbury Langdon and John Pickering had been behind the newspaper attacks on him the previous spring. Therefore the political rivalry between Sullivan and John Langdon sharpened, although they remained on friendly terms, and Sullivan's brother James married the Langdons' sister Martha, in December, 1786.

On February 25, 1786, Sullivan had not attended a meeting of the Council, and on that day President John Langdon and the Council appointed Woodbury Langdon a justice of the Superior Court. The nomination had been made on the 13th, but Sullivan evidently had opposed it.[34] Jeremy Belknap wrote that Woodbury's appointment so infuriated Sullivan that he resigned his offices, although Sullivan said the fact that his back military pay still remained unsettled made his resignation necessary.[35] But Belknap's words are convincing:

You will see, by our papers, that our Major General has resigned his offices. The big fellows cannot agree. J.L. has got his brother, W.L., made a judge. . . . S., though one of the council of appointment, was not present when it was done: they took advantage of his absence to do it. This nettled him, and brought on the resignation. I suppose he expects to be the biggest of all next year, and there will be a pull for it between him and J.L.[36]

The astute Belknap saw the situation correctly. Sullivan had his eye on the President's chair, and therefore had decided to pursue an independent course. March was the month for voting in town meeting for President, although the victor did not take office until June. This time John Sullivan met with success when he received 4,309 votes, and John Langdon 3,600.[37] Sullivan swept Strafford County, his home area, and ran way ahead in Cheshire and Grafton where his was a familiar name.[38]

Sullivan assumed the helm of government during an unsettled period when there was an increased demand for paper money and debtor relief. William Plumer, who had many biased comments to make about the contemporary scene, remarked when Sullivan became President:

General Sullivan is elected President by a majority of 51 votes. John Langdon is speaker of the House. They have changed places. There is much animosity between them; Mr. Langdon appears mortified. There are 45 Representatives who were not members of the House last year. The change is not for the better. If men are born legislators you may expect good laws; but if talents and extensive information are requisite to form the statesman, you will in vain look for them in the General Court. Our government is feeble, and some of our laws are better calculated to aid vice than to reward virtue. But we shall have no paper money this session, though much I fear the next.[39]

In his message delivered on the 10th, President Sullivan noted that this was a time of an embarrassed trade and a disarranged currency. He favored the promotion of agriculture and manufactures, hoped to curtail the use of foreign luxuries, and desired to see free exportation of goods. He asked that roads be improved, sought compliance with Congressional requisitions, hoped for a well-regulated militia, and asked for revisions of import duties.[40]

Nothing unusual appeared in this message, which was a rather matter-of-fact recital of the pressing issues which faced the states in those years. Sullivan saw how essential it was to have the economy on an even keel and to have nascent industries encouraged. Like the other leaders of the day, he also saw the necessity of supporting Congress. He was doing all in his power to increase New Hampshire's manufactures. His mills were operating, although they had been damaged by a flood the previous autumn, and his constant prodding for use of homespun regimentals met with success.[41] He had also encouraged foreign artisans who came to New Hampshire for their start in the New World.[42]

The money crisis faced Sullivan during the summer and fall of 1786, for an increasing voice made itself heard in demand of paper money. Jeremy Belknap quite prophetically had noted the previous March: "We want some imminent common danger pressing hard upon us, to make us feel our need of union."[43] Just that was about to appear, for the money riots of New Hampshire, and more particularly, Shays's Rebellion in Massachusetts, were an "imminent common danger" that helped create a feeling for the need of union.

Money was scarce in New Hampshire. The tax burden was considerable, people were not paying taxes, the merchants were feeling a pinch, and business was dull.[44] On September 1, 1781, the Assembly had made gold and silver legal tender, and since January, 1782, New Hampshire had been trying to liquidate the paper currency by issuing new notes covering principal and interest, the value of which was determined by a scale of depreciation.[45] In February, 1785, the legislature tried to alleviate the situation by issuing certificates equal to fifteen percent of the principal of the old notes annually and the interest. These certificates could be offered as taxes and were to be equal with gold and silver. Depreciation continued, however, and the system did not satisfy the people.[46] Some strove to surmount the difficulties, and one sermon claimed, "The scarcity of money, is the only thing that will save this people—this alone can produce industry and economy, without which no people can be virtuous and happy." [47] Already the drive for paper money was moving rapidly and by 1785 had reached serious proportions. This drive was no radical movement, but instead an attempt, perhaps ill conceived, on the part of numerous respectable persons to obtain a circulating medium. Internal extravagance and importation of luxury items caused part of the shortage, a judgment borne out by the constant demand for developing domestic manufactures.[48] The entire economy was affected, and the debtor was not the only person hit. The treasurer claimed he had no money, and so did the tax collectors, for people would not or could not pay their taxes.[49] In the late summer of 1785 the *Gazette* had written of the shortage: "The distress that prevails throughout this State for want of a CIRCULATING MEDIUM is hardly conceivable:—Complaints are equally heard from the seats of affluence as well as indigence; and all the consolation we have is—A CERTAIN PROSPECT OF THE EVIL'S INCREASING." [50]

The harassed President saw that petitions had been pouring in from the towns asking for emission of paper money. Nor was this their sole wish. Some asked for disallowing of the Allen claims, free trade, closing of the Inferior Courts, and curbing of activities of lawyers even to the extent of limiting each county to just two lawyers. At least forty-one towns petitioned between 1784 and late September, 1786, for paper and redress of other grievances: sixteen in Rockingham County, six in Strafford, ten in Hillsborough, five in Cheshire, and four in Grafton.[51]

During the summer Sullivan sent letters to other states requesting information on paper money legislation within those states, and answers kept coming back to him as the summer drew to a close.[52] In June the feeling in the legislature had been to avoid issuing paper; throughout the summer, however, a number of conventions met in various towns, and in turn these conventions sent on demands to the legislature.[53] Once more the revolutionary apparatus of conventions was in use, although these were not desperate people, but rather citizens simply seeking a united front so that the legislature and President Sullivan might listen to their requests. One man, Jonathan Moulton, emerges as a manipulator behind the scenes. He controlled the convention that met in Rochester in Strafford County early in September. A controversial figure in New Hampshire history, Moulton gained the enmity of many, and unfortunately for him those who commented on his personality loathed him. Yet the picture of a rather unscrupulous, grasping person somehow strikes home. Belknap said he stirred up all "bankrupts, hawkers, debtors, peddlars, jockeys, cheats, etc., etc., to clamor for paper money." [54] Plumer, who never was impartial and who distrusted the paper money forces, was not charitable in his estimate. He said that there were many instances of Moulton's "fraud and deceit, injustice and oppression." [55] Although Moulton had built up some wealth and owned vast tracts of land, still he was for paper money because of his taxes, his debts, and the suits that threatened him with imprisonment.

By September the legislature was beginning to give in to public pressure. The towns kept hammering away with petitions, and the conventions evidently had their effect. On Friday, September 8, the legislature chose to consider the grievances of the various towns and conventions. That afternoon both houses met as committee of the whole, and appointed a committee, of which Sullivan was a member, to examine the possibilities of issuing paper money. The next day that committee chose a subcommittee, which also included Sullivan, to submit a plan. A report came back on the 13th, and a plan was submitted to the towns for approval or rejection.[56] This plan, which went out over Sullivan's signature, recommended that £50,000 be emitted in bills of credit, £10,000 of which would be used by the state "to discharge the specie orders on the treasury, and for defraying the expense of government." The other £40,000 was to be loaned, in amounts of no more than £150 nor less than £50, secured by land at double value of the loan and payable in six years at six percent interest.[57] This was a moderate plan and might have been successful, but it was being left to the voters in town meeting to make the decision. The General Court, perhaps wisely for political reasons, chose to dodge the issue. Time alone would tell whether the action of the legislative body would appease the members of the conventions.

The wait was not for long. The General Court, meeting in Exeter, heard on the morning of September 20 that an armed mob was marching upon the town under orders from the Rockingham County convention. Apparently the conventioneers planned to take matters into their own hands. By midafternoon they were in the town and sent a message to the General Court. The message was brief; the Court must meet demands for paper money as set forth in the petition from the convention. Perhaps 200 men in all were in the mob that sought to intimidate the legislators at Exeter. Some were on horse; about fifty had muskets, while the others wielded bludgeons. They paraded about the town with drum accompaniment, and then took up position before the Meeting House where the General Court was sitting. The ubiquitous Plumer listed the towns from which the men had come: Londonderry, Hampstead, Hawke, Sandown, Bedford, Goffstown, Raymond. "They made a miserable appearance—dirty, ragged fellows—many of them were young and most of them ignorant." [58] The leader was Joseph French of Hampstead.

The House chose to appoint a committee to join with one from the Senate to consider the matter of the petition, but the Senate would not agree to that proposal. Then both Houses met together. Sullivan, a Senator ex-officio, rose to speak and told the assembled General Court that the Senate did not approve of the original petition from the convention. But even if the petition were just, should the General Court consider it because perhaps thirty towns out of about two hundred were pressing for action? To him the answer was obvious. Continuing, Sullivan argued that, even if the entire state were behind the petition, still the General Court should not comply so long as it was surrounded by an armed force. To yield to the demands of a mob would be to sacrifice one's duty. He concluded by stating that "no consideration of personal danger should ever compel him to betray his trust." [59]

When Sullivan's inflexible position became known, the insurgents surrounded the Meeting House, and those with muskets moved forward. The legislators, who took no notice, continued with their business, while the uninvited guests peered in through the doors and windows. They allowed no one to enter or to leave. Plumer, who approached the mob to seek further information, described them:

Some were clamouring against the Court for passing a law authorizing the return of the Refugees, declaring that those who voted for it ought to be punished with death. Some demanded paper money; others, an equal distribution of property. Some the annihilation of debts, freedom from taxes, the abolition of lawyers, the destruction of the Inferior Courts, the reduction of salaries, and all of them exclaimed against law and government. I reasoned with several of them upon the unreasonableness of their demands and the impropriety of their conduct; but the answer I received was the bayonet pointed to my breast.[60]

The fact that Plumer's dignity had been ruffled may have led him into excessive condemnation of the rioters. He had no use for paper, was unduly alarmed, and surely exaggerated their demands, but still they maintained a siege. Toward sunset Sullivan and the General Court tried to leave the building, only to find that the insurgent group refused to let them go through their lines. Sullivan, remonstrating with them, warned them of the possible consequences of their actions, and asserted that the people of the state would support him and the government; but the rioters assured him the opposite would be the case. The legislators retired inside to await developments. There they sat until evening when they heard cheers for the government coming from the outside. The people of Exeter, disapproving the role taken by the insurgents, chose to support the lawmakers. With the clamor in favor of the government increasing, the rioters became afraid, and some began to run. This time the General Court did come out, along with Sullivan, who assured the mob he would see that no blood was shed. Then he retired to his lodgings while the rioters camped on the outskirts of the town. The General Court immediately authorized the President to call out the militia, and that night Sullivan sent the necessary orders for them to proceed to Exeter the next day.

The militia responded to the call, and by morning, according to Plumer, 2,000 men were under arms, although this does seem a high figure. The opposition collapsed, and the ringleaders were taken into custody. About forty prisoners in all were rounded up. Sullivan, now completely in control, rode between the lines of the militia drawn up at either side of the road. He bowed to them. Then the prisoners had to walk between the lines twice so that they might realize how staunch was the government's defense.[61] The challenge to authority had been a complete fiasco. The prisoners, with a few exceptions, were released while the leaders were examined by both houses. Joseph French, who was most contrite, with some success placed the blame for the riot on Jonathan Moulton and was set at liberty.[62]

Each house voted its thanks to Sullivan "for his firm, zealous and decisive exertions," and voted that the President was fully empowered to call forth the militia whenever orderly govern-ment was challenged.[63] Then each chamber voted to turn over five ringleaders for trial by the Superior Court. After that the legislators adjourned to meet next at Portsmouth in December.

Why did New Hampshire have an easier time with the paper money rioters than Massachusetts? Shays and his followers had a much stronger grasp on the situation in Massachusetts and managed to create considerable havoc. The rioters in both states were not violent mobs; they were trying to gain what they con-sidered a legitimate redress of bitter and ever-present grievances. The ease with which Sullivan subdued the insurgents in New Hampshire shows that they were not desperate persons intent on a showdown regardless of consequences. Jeremy Belknap ob-served that the insurrection in New Hampshire was a direct challenge to the head of the government, and that therefore the force of the state rose in his defense, whereas the challenge in Massachusetts was aimed at the judiciary, which in itself had no means to oppose the Shaysites.[64] Law and order had gained the upper hand in New Hampshire, thanks to John Sullivan.

XIV: BATTLE FOR THE CONSTITUTION

OCTOBER, 1786–JUNE, 1788

The money riots put John Sullivan into the limelight as a defender of the peace, for he had not given in to the demands of the mob. Paper money had no appeal to Sullivan. Conservative people said that these ills of the day called for more effective federal organization. The Continental Congress seemed incapable of handling the intricacies of government and lacked the power to drive ahead with a consistent program. Something had to be done, and John Sullivan was one of the leaders in New Hampshire who charted the course toward better national government. He was in a position where he could be instrumental, for on the whole his actions in the money riots brought him praise. "Gen. Sullivan has behaved nobly," David Humphreys wrote Washington, "& put a period to a very considerable insurrection, without the effusion of blood." [1]

Now very much in control of the situation, late in October, 1786, Sullivan began a tour of the state, ostensibly to review the militia, but also to prove that government was in control and to allay the fears of those who were apprehensive about the troubled times. Not least of all, he wanted to show himself to the people and to make a good impression. Jeremy Belknap commented favorably on Sullivan's actions: "The General is now gone a month's tour (as far as the upper Cohass) to review the militia. We could not have had a better *military* governour, and certainly one of this character is necessary at this day. Massachusetts suffers for want of a militia, and a little more *spunk* in her Executive."[2] The dyspeptic Plumer was not so pleased with New Hampshire's militaristic President. He wrote:

I never knew a mortal so greedy of flattery; he swallows the grossest. Like his brother, James, of Boston, he wants what really renders man estimable, *integrity*. From my acquaintance with him I am confident his knowledge as a lawyer, and his talents as a man, are rated too high. His bold, unqualified declarations often supplies the want of knowledge.[3]

Although Plumer's words were not flattering, they were to the point. Sullivan was fond of pomp and circumstance, and it is not difficult to imagine him as he strutted through New Hampshire to keep his name before the good people of his native state. The trip was a great success. "The inhabitants of the several towns received him with the greatest marks of respect, and announced his arrival by the discharge of cannon, ringing of bells, and firing of musquets."[4] Londonderry greeted him with a flowery address in which the town expressed shame that some of its citizens had taken part in the recent riots.[5] On November 18 he returned home, and one citizen, in commenting favorably on his travels, said his "exertions to establish & confirm government, & reviving military discipline" merited honor.[6]

Sullivan reported to the General Court, upon its reconvening in December, that most people seemed determined to support the government against any form of sedition. He found pleasing that articles previously imported were now being manufactured at home, and he hoped that measures might be taken to encourage production of items like glass and steel. He wanted a revenue from imports, particularly on foreign manufactures.[7]

The most pressing matter, though, concerned the rioters whom Sullivan earlier had ordered court-martialed.[8] The trials came in December, and some were pardoned, others broken. The court-martial proceedings brought Sullivan criticism, because certain members of the legislature thought a military trial of civil offenders was illegal and unconstitutional. John Langdon found this an occasion to question whether Sullivan had stretched his powers—a comment which meant that the presidential campaign for the ensuing year was under way. Evidently the General Court, however, had authorized the court-martial, and on January 5, 1787, both houses agreed to accept the findings of the court with two exceptions.[9] But Sullivan's militaristic ways would be used against him as the political campaign picked up.

At this juncture, however, Sullivan was riding the crest of a wave. The towns did not care for the General Court's plan for paper money, and so none was forthcoming.[10] President Sullivan was exultant. The *New Hampshire Spy*, established the previous fall in Portsmouth by George Osborne as a paper friendly to Sullivan, delighted in poking fun at the defeat of paper money.[11] Compliments came from Eleazar Wheelock, and from Jedediah Huntington in Connecticut came word that Sullivan's suppression of the riots had delighted many.[12] Now that New Hampshire was finished with its own money crisis, Sullivan wrote Governor Bowdoin of Massachusetts that he would try to help in seizing the Shays rioters who had come into New Hampshire. Once more Sullivan made it quite definite that he opposed any attempt to subvert government, and that he would do all in his power to defend what he considered to be the constitutional process.[13]

Throughout the years Sullivan himself had been carrying on a one-man riot in financial matters, for he never ceased trying to get payment for depreciation of his war pay. As 1787 opened, he seemed to be making some progress in the struggle. Congress took the position that he had resigned from the service, whereas Sullivan argued that he would have been perfectly willing to accept leave. Therefore he claimed it was the wish of Congress, and not his, that brought about his retirement from the army.[14] His badgering brought results. On August 31, 1786, Congress suggested that New Hampshire pay Sullivan $4,300 for war expenses and charge it to the United States.[15] On January 9, 1787, both houses voted him the money plus certificates for interest since January 1, 1780.[16] But receiving payment was another matter. He had difficulty collecting, although it remains uncertain whether this was for his war expenses or other money owed him by the state. He tried to get the import collector to meet his demands but had no success. Nor did the state treasurer, John Taylor Gilman, have any money on hand, because he had been unable to collect the specie tax for 1786. Public servants often found that they were donating their services in those years.[17]

The payment voted to Sullivan had its political repercussions. As March approached, once more it was time to vote for President. The *New Hampshire Mercury* opened the campaign that February when it carried an article criticizing the payment. Back interest was but a gratuity, the writer claimed.[18] The attacks against Sullivan continued. A handbill was circulating about the state challenging the wisdom of having a military man at head of government, attacking Sullivan's abilities, falsely stating that he had not been born in New Hampshire, hinting that since he was a lawyer he would fill offices with lawyers, and calling the recent grant of money an unfair tax upon the people. The charges were flimsy and barely merited the answer that appeared in the *New Hampshire Spy*.[19] The votes had Langdon ahead of Sullivan, but, since Langdon did not have a majority, the decision went to the Senate, which on June 12 selected Sullivan to continue as President, probably because of his firm stand during the riots.[20]

In his message to the Senate and House, President Sullivan called attention to the convention that was meeting in Philadelphia to revise the Articles of Confederation, and expressed the hope that New Hampshire would be represented. The previous summer Sullivan had tried to get four men to attend the Annapolis Convention, but had had no luck.[21] He had shown interest in the Philadelphia Convention from the very beginning, and on March 3, 1787, had sent to the Continental Congress a resolution passed by the legislature in January stating that any two of New Hampshire's delegates to the Congress might meet in a convention. He also sent it to various states hoping to exert what influence he could on the side of the convention.[22] At that time New Hampshire was not represented in Congress, so that on June 27 the General Court chose John Langdon, John Pickering, Nicholas Gilman, and Benjamin West, all four or any two of them to represent New Hampshire at the convention.[23] Langdon was willing to underwrite the expenses, and Gilman and he left for Philadelphia in July. Although they were late, New Hampshire finally was represented. The rivals, John Sullivan and John Langdon, were at last in agreement. Both realized that the government had to be strengthened, and their agreement was an important factor in bringing about New Hampshire's ratification of the United States Constitution the following June.

On September 18, 1787, Nicholas Gilman wrote Sullivan that the convention had completed its work, and on the 28th Charles Thomson transmitted a copy of the Constitution asking that it be placed before the legislature.[24] Sullivan approved of the Constitution and planned to exert his influence to obtain its ratification. He thought this would not be too difficult a task. He was optimistic in his outlook: business was improving, the militia was orderly, money was available. He wrote Gilman: "Government is so well Established that the voice of Rebellion cannot be heard . . . & I doubt not with the blessings of our new plan of Government we shall soon be a happy people." [25]

Already the lines were being drawn for the struggle over the Constitution. No longer would people use the epithets "Whig" or "Tory." Now the names "federal" and "antifederal" came to the fore, and, according to one person, "the latter [antifederal] so opprobious a name as only fit for a daemon." [26] Jeremiah Libbey of Portsmouth reported that the Constitution was generally liked throughout the state, and expressed surprise that Sullivan had not as yet called the General Court together so that delegates might be summoned for a ratifying convention. One cynical observer, according to Libbey, saw no hope that the Court would agree since ratification would mean the end of tender laws and the deathblow to any chances for paper money.[27] John Langdon wrote from Portsmouth that he had not heard a single objection to the plan, whereas Plumer wrote from his home in Epping that many opposed it as being "a grant of too much power." [28]

Sullivan finally called the General Court together and, in his message of December 5, stated that the Constitution, although not perfect, seemed to be about the best that could be devised. He trusted that the General Court would call delegates to a ratifying convention. Everyone seemed quite sanguine, and reports were abroad that New Hampshire surely would ratify before long.[29] On December 11 and 12 the Court, although not a legal quorum, considered the matter, and agreed to call a convention to meet on the second Wednesday in February.[30]

The turmoil of war and immediate postwar adjustment had run its course. It was time now to look for consolidation and effective government. Sullivan was in the van of this movement that sought to bring about a more secure and staunch union of the American states. He was one of the many who had taken an active part in the revolutionary war and who then had returned to their states to assume roles of leadership. These men had seen that the complexities of the postwar years necessitated firmer government. Sullivan's war years, his months in Congress, and his duties as President of New Hampshire, during which time he sought more interstate cooperation, all led him quite easily to a nationalist point of view. Many worthy persons criticized the proposed Constitution as being too large a grant of power, but those persons generally were parochial in their outlook. Sullivan himself had traveled as far south as Annapolis, had seen many parts of the eastern states during the war, and had been in all areas of his own state. That in itself was an antidote to parochialism. Motivation at times is almost impossible to gauge; but it does not seem unreasonable to assert that Sullivan's support for the Constitution came more from psychological factors than from economic motives. His love of law and order, as seen in his delight in things military, would place him on the side of ratification. He saw in the Constitution something stable, a device that would have scotched, for example, the conditions leading to a paper money riot. Here was the military man who preferred order and who saw the Constitution as the means of salvation. The times had changed and those who sought stability were the favorites. "Probus," writing in the *Freeman's Oracle*, indicated this change when he asked that men of judgment and patriotism be sent to the ratifying convention. He then continued:

By *patriotism*, however, I would not be understood to mean *whiggism*, because I apprehend them to be very different things. A stanch whig may be a wretched patriot: and one who during the contest between the United States and Great-Britain was denominated as a *Tory* may now be a firm friend to the liberties and happiness of America . . . but the glorious title of PATRIOT is confined to him who generously stretches his views to the utmost limits of the United States; grasps the common interests of the large society with which he is politically connected.[31]

Henry Knox wrote to Sullivan that New Hampshire must hurry and ratify; otherwise "we shall be involved in all the horrors of anarchy and seperate [sic] interests." [32] Knox was to be disappointed, because New Hampshire, although she finally ratified, did not hurry. The delegates assembled at Exeter on February 13. The next day about 100 members were present, and proceeded to choose Sullivan as president of the convention, having first selected John Calfe as secretary.[33] They decided to hold future sessions in the Meeting House rather than in the Court House.

Many of the first figures of New Hampshire attended the convention. Both Sullivan and Langdon were present, and their being on the same side gave real cause for hope. Others supporting ratification were Samuel Livermore, Dr. Josiah Bartlett of

Kingston, Portsmouth's John Pickering, and the Reverend
Samuel Langdon of Hampton Falls. The most influential spokes-
man for the opposition was Joshua Atherton, a lawyer from
Amherst. During the war he had been pro-British but had never
committed an overt act against the American cause. Evidently
he was a man who temperamentally opposed change. Successful as a lawyer, he was courteous, urbane, and hospitable, and
was a formidable opponent.

Unfortunately, little information remains about the debates
in the convention. Sullivan entered the debates on the judiciary,
but on the whole the record remains silent, and the Journal of
the convention is merely a skeleton.[34] The men discussed the
Constitution paragraph by paragraph. They reached discussion
of the judiciary on the 19th and spent part of that day and part
of the 20th arguing on that article of the Constitution. At this
time Sullivan and Atherton met head on in debate, although it is
likely Sullivan had already taken an active role in the deliberations. Atherton objected to Article III, Section 2, which described the judicial power, for he feared the statement that federal judicial power extended to disputes between citizens of different states. A revenue officer could haul a citizen of New
Hampshire before a federal court and obtain payment, he
claimed since obviously the court would be interested to "increase the revenues of continent . . . and . . . always decide in
favour of an unprincipled collector of excise." [35] Livermore rose
to answer by saying that the federal courts would have appel-
late jurisdiction in such a case but not original jurisdiction. He
believed that Atherton's fears were unjustified and went on to
claim that John Langdon, who had been at the Convention, interpreted the section in the same way. Atherton appeared content with such an explanation, but thought it would be too expensive for citizens if they had to be hauled before federal
courts in disputes with other private citizens.

At this point Sullivan entered the fray. He defended the
judicial article as being the best in the Constitution, and saw

every reason for giving the federal judiciary original jurisdiction in the cases described in the Constitution. He saw no reason why suits between citizens of different states should not come before the federal courts. Too often judges had shown bias when trying cases involving citizens of their own state and citizens of another state. In the only speech that survives from the Convention, he went on to say:

It should seem singular, that gentlemen, who consider the British constitution as perfect, who supported our situation, when subject to the British king, was as eligible as that of any people could be, complain of this regulation as a hardship, and destructive of the rights of the people. They quietly suffered an appeal to Great-Britain in all causes of consequence; they then boasted of their liberties, boasted of the liberty of appealing to judges ignorant of our situation and prejudiced against the name of an American. And will these gentlemen object to this provision in the constitution. Could they be content under the former bondage, and will then now refuse a constitution, because an unprejudiced American court are to be their judges in certain causes under such limitations and regulations as the representatives in Congress shall provide.[36]

Colonel Benjamin Stone, who had been implicated in the paper-money riots, doubted that "our situation would be much happier by changing one set of tyrants for another—British for American tyrants." John Pickering sought to allay Stone's fears by showing that a contrast existed between the judicial power of king and council which "reminded us of our humiliating dependence upon (a) foreign, distant and haughty nation" and a federal judiciary whose power "was secured from excess and oppression." [37]

In the afternoon of February 20 the convention discussed the fourth, fifth, and sixth articles. That part of Article VI which stated that no religious test would be required as a qualification for any office under the United States caused considerable debate, a debate which carried over to the following morning. Deacon Stone of Claremont sought a religious test; the

Reverend Samuel Langdon argued that religion must stand on its own feet, and that one should not call upon the civil arm to support it.[38] Sullivan offered a somewhat acid comment on the argument for a religious test when he wrote Belknap: "The want of a religious test was used here . . . but even if that was given up in all other cases The president at Least ought to be compelled to Submit to it for otherwise says one 'a Turk, a Jew, a Roman Catholic, and what is worse than all a universalist may be president of the United States.' " Sullivan continued, "If time would permit I could give you many other Specimens of original Genius in the members of our Convention." [39]

Those in favor of the Constitution soon realized that they could not muster enough votes to secure ratification. Jeremiah Libbey, who kept his friend Belknap up to date, castigated the opponents in a letter: "They, the Antifederalist, except two or three of their leaders, are as dumb & obstinate as ———. They will not say a word on the subject, even in private conversation." [40] According to Libbey, the important opponents of the Constitution in the convention were Atherton and Joseph Badger of Gilmantown and, on the outside, Nathaniel Peabody. Libbey, who was at the convention during the debate on the judiciary, was somewhat more optimistic about ratification. He had hopes that Atherton would talk so much that he would do more damage to his cause than good, and reported that there was talk of an adjournment without a vote.[41]

An adjournment did occur on February 22. Those wishing ratification knew they could not possibly win. A number of delegates had come to the convention instructed to vote against ratification; but during the debate they had been convinced that they should support the Constitution, and now sought an opportunity to obtain new instructions from their town meetings. Langdon estimated that perhaps a majority of four was against the document. He claimed that at the time of selecting delegates in one of the counties false rumors had abounded to the effect that Massachusetts had not ratified, and that as a result, many persons came from this county instructed to vote against the plan of government.[42]

Jeremiah Libbey estimated that there were forty-five for the Constitution and eleven who wished to support it but whose instructions required a negative vote. That seems to be a likely estimate. On the 22d Langdon moved that the convention adjourn to some future day, but no vote came for adjournment until some of the delegates had had time to make further general observations. Evidently Atherton was the principal speaker and inveighed against the Constitution at length, with tradition saying he attacked the tacit recognition of slavery, but, in spite of his strenuous objections, the vote for postponement came up and carried 56 to 51. The convention was adjourned until the third Wednesday in June.[43]

Sullivan took time to give Belknap some of the details of the convention. He estimated the strength of the opposition at seventy, probably too high a figure. Then he went on to describe the nature of the opposition; some were short-sighted, some longed for the "onions of Egypt," many were in debt. He said that about thirty who had been instructed to oppose the Constitution changed their minds, again a rather high estimate. He gave much credit to the Reverend Samuel Langdon for changing their opinion, probably referring to the debate over the religious test.[44] In a letter to Nicholas Gilman, Sullivan said not even a pen of a Clarendon and the pencil of a Hogarth could describe the events in the convention. He pictured the opponents as "a motley mixture of Ancient Toreys, friends to paper money, Tender Laws, Insurrection &c.; persons in Debt, distress, & poverty, either real or Imaginary; men of blind piety, Hypocrites, & Bankrupts; together with Many honest men bound by Instructions to vote against the Constitution at all Events." [45] But Sullivan, always optimistic, predicted ratification at the next session of the convention by a vote of three to one.[46]

The newspapers also believed New Hampshire would adopt the Constitution at the June convention. They argued that, if the delegates had been unfettered with instructions, ratification would have occurred in February. One paper reported the rumor that Nathaniel Peabody had come out in favor of the document, and then later reported that the persons in the more remote areas of New Hampshire had been misinformed about the Constitution by "factious demagogues and popularity-seekers, who had rode through the back parts of the State, inflaming and prejudicing the people's minds against it." [47] But now the delegates would tell their constituents the true nature of the document, for although ratification was expected eventually, still the failure to approve in February had given encouragement to the Anti-Federalists.[48]

Sullivan had his eye on both the next session of the convention and the coming presidential election. Toward the end of February he proclaimed a fast for April 10 so that the "Father of mercies" might "Grant to the Members of our Convention, that Wisdom, which is necessary to direct, and lead them into those measures which may promote the Interest and Happiness of the United States." [49] He had hopes for reelection, and believed he merited it as he thought he had been instrumental in strengthening the credit of the state.[50] Politically he considered himself in a sound position, but his personal affairs had been receiving setbacks. During the previous autumn fire had destroyed some of his mills, and later a ship carrying beef, which he was sending to Bermuda, blew ashore. These reverses caused him to press more than usual for payment of debts owed him, although this was not surprising as he always had been fairly rigid in demanding his debtors to pay up.[51]

As the votes for president came in, however, it was apparent that John Langdon had won at the polls, with 4,421 votes to Sullivan's 3,664.[52] Sullivan maintained his strength in Strafford County and managed to hold an advantage in both Cheshire and Grafton. This election, as did all the elections of the decade, hinged upon personalities, not issues, for after all both Sullivan and Langdon were ardent supporters of ratification of the Constitution. The rivals, therefore, changed places, and now it was Langdon's turn to assume the President's chair. Durham sent Sullivan to the House of Representatives, but he declined to be Speaker.[53] President Langdon's remarks in his message to the General Court must have irked Sullivan, for the President referred to the "deranged State of our finances" and "the almost annihilation of our commerce." Sullivan was one of a minority who voted not to accept the House's courteous reply to John Langdon.[54] Sullivan did not have time to remain miffed at his rival, however, because the hour approached for the second session of the ratifying convention. Sullivan and others wishing acceptance of the document had their work cut out for them, as the opponents had been trying desperately ever since the first session to line up enough votes to block ratification of the Constitution in the form presented to the states. From New York, John Lamb, a leading Anti-Federalist, had been corresponding with both Atherton and Nathaniel Peabody, urging amendments. He admitted changes had to be made in the Articles but believed that the Constitution contained "principles dangerous to publick Liberty and Safety." [55]

The friends of the Constitution found their task complicated, because so little information on the merits of the Constitution had circulated throughout the state. For example, the valuable papers by "Publius" were scarcely known, and hardly a soul had read the debates of the Massachusetts and Pennsylvania conventions. In spite of this lack of information, however, those favoring ratification were optimistic.[56]

The second session convened in Concord on June 18, 1788, and was short, perhaps mainly because of the hope that New Hampshire might have the honor of being the ninth state to ratify.[57] The opponents apparently saw they could not block approval, so they strove to have amendments accepted as the *sine qua non* of ratification. That seemed to be Atherton's strategy, for on June 11 he had written John Lamb: "To ratify, and then propose Amendments is to surrender our all, and then ask our new Masters if they will be so gracious as to return to us, some, or any part, of our most important Rights and priveleges [sic]."[58] Up to that point Atherton thought his side had the majority. "This the candid consolidarians confess," he told Lamb. "But I need not inform you how many Arts are made use of to increase their Party."

On the 20th Sullivan was one of a committee appointed to propose amendments to the Constitution. That afternoon the committee reported twelve amendments, of which nine had been recommended by the Massachusetts convention and may have been sent on by James Sullivan to his brother. The other three asked that there be no standing army in time of peace and no quartering, that Congress make no laws "touching religion," and that no person be disarmed by Congress unless he had been in actual rebellion.[59] That same day Atherton moved that the Constitution be ratified with the amendments, but that it have no effect in New Hampshire without these amendments. After debate Livermore asked for the postponing of Atherton's motion and offered a motion of his own that would merely recommend the amendments to Congress should New Hampshire ratify. Debate ensued, and the convention adjourned to the next day without any decision. The next morning, June 21, marked the climax. Livermore's motion passed. Then Atherton moved that the convention adjourn to some future day. This failed. The backers of the Constitution realized they had the necessary strength, and Livermore, seconded by John Langdon, moved that the main question be put: adoption of the Constitution.[60]

The convention's bare journal, which recorded the vote, fails to recapture the intensity of the moment. These men realized the significance of the choice which faced them. Either they must choose the nationalist aims of a strengthened central government and loss of some local sovereignty, or else they must still cling to the position that liberty was best secured by state autonomy, or in effect, parochialism. Those who had connections with other areas of the United States and who had taken part on the national scene, such as Sullivan and John Langdon, chose to accept the Constitution, and were able to pull some votes with them. Those who came from more isolated areas, or who enjoyed importance at the local level, such as Joshua Atherton, preferred the old system. The roll was called.

Rockingham County delegates were polled first. They voted 24 to 13 for the Constitution. Dr. Ezra Green of Dover was the first Strafford man to record his vote, a "Yea." Thus the vote stood 25 to 13 by the time Sullivan's name was called. He voted "Yea." Strafford County was for ratification by just one vote, 7 to 6. Hillsborough County offered the most opposition and went against ratification by a vote of 16 to 6. By the time Cheshire County was polled the vote stood 37 to 35 for ratification. Cheshire was close, 11 to 10 against ratification, so that the vote was 47 to 46 as the Grafton votes were called. Judge Livermore was polled first, a "Yea." Then all of Grafton, except Colonel Joseph Hutchins of Haverhill, voted for ratification. The county vote was 10 to 1, and the final tally read 57 yeas, and 47 nays.[61]

Sullivan immediately sent two letters, one to Hancock in Massachusetts, and the other to Henry Knox in New York. In Knox's letter he noted that the time of ratification came at 1:00 P.M., for he wanted to be sure that New Hampshire got credit for being the ninth state to ratify, because the delegates knew that Virginia's convention was in session.[62] Knox's reply was jubilant and praised Sullivan. He wrote: "Your friends attribute much of the success of the cause in your state to your unremitted exertions." [63]

Atherton questioned both the tactics of the victors and the extent of their victory. He conceded that the important men of the state had wished ratification, but the means employed by them "were it not for the Depravity of the humane [*sic*] Heart, would be viewed with the warmest Sentiments of Disapprobation." [64] Atherton was convinced that the great majority of the New Hampshire people opposed the Constitution. Tobias Lear said the majority in the convention had included three fourths of the property interests present. He smeared the opponents as being debtors and those wishing to keep the tender laws and hoping eventually to get paper currency.[65] Fortunately the opposition was conciliatory. Superior talents and better organization had won the day for ratification. The victors were exuberant, and on Sunday public thanks were offered in the churches. On Monday the celebrations began.[66]

The prestige of men like Sullivan and other federalist leaders conquered the field. Plumer asserted that it was Pickering's eloquence that was the decisive factor.[67] Livermore was influential because of his control of the Grafton vote. The coastal areas and the region of the Connecticut River Valley supported the Constitution, whereas the interior part of the state, particularly Hillsborough County and the eastern section of Cheshire did not. One other important anti-federalist area was that portion of Strafford County that bordered on Maine.[68]

Quite obviously the commercial interests on the coast would favor ratification. The remoter areas of the interior with their parochial outlook might be expected to oppose, for the Constitution had little to offer them that was tangible; but the Connecticut River towns were overwhelming in their support. Once more personal influence was a factor, because Elisha Payne of Lebanon, Benjamin West of Charleston, and, more particularly, Samuel Livermore were men of considerable prestige. The river towns also had access to newspapers to a greater extent than the interior towns.[69] The vote of these western towns may also be explained by their having an identity separate from the rest of the state. This was the area that had thought of joining Vermont, that had bitterly contested the political control of the coastal region. Perhaps, too, the area saw that it was a buffer against British intentions, and believed that a stronger central government would be able to offer firmer support in time of challenge.[70]

Was there any connection between the demand for paper money and voting against ratification? Some, but the parallel is not so strong as might be thought.[71] Possibly the more depressed areas opposed the Constitution on economic grounds, but it would be a mistake to place too much stress upon such an interpretation, for the economic interpretation is too neat, too precise. People vote for a variety of reasons, reasons that unfortunately are either irrational or inexplicable. People often play "hunches" when they vote, and reflect fears or prejudices. Votes therefore cannot be pressed into an economic mold; an undefined psychological factor is more important. One opponent of the Constitution was tired of the epithets hurled against the Anti-Federalists. He claimed that he owed no money, disliked the tender law, and disapproved of the Shaysites. Yet he was against the Constitution as it did not sufficiently secure the liberties of the people.[72] That was the major fear held by the opponents of ratification, a fear which Sullivan and the other champions of the Constitution had tried to calm by offering amendments, although they would not go so far as to make ratification conditional upon the acceptance of them.

XV: DECLINING YEARS

The struggle for ratification marked the climax of Sullivan's postwar career, and his public life was drawing to a close. The political events during the months following ratification apparently held slight interest for him. True he once more would be President of New Hampshire, but his appointment as federal judge would draw his attention to new fields. His active judicial career, however, because of a debilitating illness, was to be of short duration only.

This time as Sullivan approached the election for President in 1789 his opponent would not be John Langdon, who had resigned the office to serve in the United States Senate. Now Sullivan ran against John Pickering, who was filling out the remainder of Langdon's term. As the results came in, Sullivan showed a slight lead and ended with 3,657 votes over Pickering's 3,488. Since this did not give him a majority, the decision went to the Senate, which decided in his favor.[1] The same pattern emerged in the voting during this election as during the previous ones involving Sullivan. He had been able to maintain his sway in Strafford, Cheshire, and Grafton Counties, and had rather wide appeal. Only in Hillsborough County had he run consistently behind in the presidential elections. His home area, Strafford, always supported him, and the frontier preferred him to the Portsmouth candidates, Langdon and Pickering, although at times the frontier areas offered their own candidates. In all the elections Sullivan had been able to poll votes in Rockingham County, except in Portsmouth, which tended to hold down his opponents' final tally.[2] Sullivan had made himself known throughout the state by his reviews of the militia and by riding circuit when he had been Attorney-General. Part of the strategy of politics called for knowing people at the "grassroots" level, and Sullivan was an expert at that.

Thus Sullivan's star still gleamed bright. On June 9, 1789, for the third and final time, he took the oath as President of New Hampshire. His message, echoing his usual tone of false modesty, protested that he had not expected the honor of being elected, for evidently his health was failing. He had little to suggest except to await federal legislation, and because of the uncertainty over what the national Congress would do, he recommended an early adjournment until December.[3] Therefore little occurred throughout the summer. He found himself honored when late in August Dartmouth College conferred upon him the degree of Doctor of Laws. The previous February, while he had been serving in the House, Sullivan supposedly had argued eloquently for a grant to Dartmouth of an eight-mile square tract in the northern part of the state. Perhaps Dartmouth felt an obligation for services rendered on the floor of the House. Sullivan was pleased and wrote John Wheelock that he was "deeply impressed with the favorable opinion the honorable Board of trustees . . . entertain of my Civil & military Conduct." [4] That very same day, September 16, he wrote Henry Knox recommending John Wheelock's brother for some federal office, hardly a coincidence.[5]

With the arrival of October word came that President Washington had appointed Sullivan a federal judge for the District of New Hampshire at a salary of $1,000, and that the Senate had approved.[6] Sullivan was a logical choice. Of the New Hampshire lawyers he was the best known on the national scene and the one personally known by Washington, who had always held a favorable opinion of Sullivan in spite of occasional moments of irritation. By appointing Sullivan a judge, Washington was recognizing him as a staunch backer of his administration.

Sullivan soon was to see Washington for the first time since he had left the service, for the President decided to visit the northeastern states. When Sullivan heard the news that Washington was coming, he was beside himself with excitement and wrote his old commander-in-chief that he would take every measure to see that he was not tired by the people "with such Acts of parade as will give pain to the great personage to whom they feel themselves so much indebted." [7] On October 31 John Sullivan and other leaders of the state met Washington at the line and then proceeded with him to Portsmouth where a thirteen-gun salute greeted the President of the United States. The eager citizens lined Congress Street with "all the crafts . . . ranged alphabetically," the bells rang, and everyone "hail'd their Deliverer welcome to the Metropolis of New Hampshire." [8] The visit was a splendid success with church services on Sunday, a trip on the water Monday, and a gala ball Tuesday night at which Washington met "a brilliant circle of more than seventy ladies." The next morning President Washington left on his return journey. The genuine warmth shown him indicates a sincerity in both the people of New Hampshire and John Sullivan that left little to be desired.

Sullivan's first action on the District Court, after it had been organized in November, 1789, was to appoint his son-in-law, Jonathan Steele, as clerk, but it was not until June, 1791, that the first case came before the court.[9] In spite of the inactivity of his court, the legislature disapproved of his holding the office of President at the same time as being a federal judge, although neither house took any definite action at that time.[10] Sullivan, however, decided to leave office as President a few days before the legal expiration of his term early in June, 1790. He gave the excuse that he had duties to perform elsewhere, but at that time there was no session of the District Court or of the Federal Circuit Court, of which he also was a member. His message on taking leave of his office does not show his usual fondness for hyperbole and self-esteem. John Sullivan knew that he had

reached the end of his political service and that now he was
leaving the center of the stage where he had stood since 1774.
A person usually assumes some degree of humility when he
beckons farewell to his past. He wrote:

Will you allow me Gentlemen at this moment of my quitting the
chair of Government in the state and probably bidding a final adieu
to all posts and Offices within the Same to entreat that you as a
body in particular and through you the citizens of the State in General would accept my most cordial thanks for the repeated marks of
Confidence which you have so repeatedly and variously honored
me with? And to assure you that in whatever department of life
providence may place me I shall retain a grateful remembrance of
the generous conduct of the people of New Hampshire.[11]

The last years of Sullivan's life were pathetic. He had been
involved in a distasteful local feud in Durham, went into debt,
and rapidly deteriorated physically into senility. His excessive
drinking in these years would help explain his physical collapse,
although he quite likely had a progressive nervous disease.[12] His
health prevented him from sitting on the bench beyond the
May, 1792, session of the District Court, even though up to
that time he had not been particularly occupied by his judicial
duties.[13] Yet Sullivan never resigned his judgeship.

The feud, which occurred in the latter part of the 1780s and
in 1790, must have left its mark on John Sullivan. Ebenezer
Thompson, Jr., the son of Sullivan's old friend who had gone
with him to the Provincial Congress back in 1774, lashed out at
Sullivan in 1788 by saying he was "running down Hill" and in
debt. Sullivan claimed these remarks hurt his reputation as he
was engaged in selling and buying foodstuff and other mer-
chandise. Before the quarrel died down, young Thompson's
wife, Martha, accused Sullivan of keeping a "Bawdy House"
and encouraging lewd practices, and said he was "totally regardless of the duties he owed to God to religion & to his country." [14] Sullivan was not too successful in his suits against the
Thompsons, and asked the General Court to set aside a £20

verdict in his favor as being inadequate, to which Thompson said Sullivan's reputation was not worth the money since he was a cheat. Further complications arose when Sullivan's three sons, his son-in-law, and another man beat up Ebenezer Thompson, Jr., and then lost in a suit for assault and battery.[15] Sullivan, hopping mad, found that there was little he could do. Accordingly he sought peace, but the savage attacks upon his character and integrity surely embittered him.[16]

The fight with young Thompson most likely had arisen from some debt owed by either Sullivan or Thompson. Although Sullivan continued to sue for payment of debts throughout these years, the total amounts collected in the last years of his life came to very little. He himself faced a financial pinch and in the early 1790s had to sell some land.[17] Obviously his debts were beginning to get the better of him, but he was not completely bankrupt. At the time of his death the inventory listed his homestead, two farms, some other lands, two mills, and a press house, with a total appraised value of $4,582.33.[18] His personal estate was small. Listed were such items as two yoke of oxen, one mare, twenty sheep, four pigs, one phaeton, three sleighs, some farm equipment, the barest household furnishings, and his modest law library.[19]

His last years had seen Sullivan merely a shell of his former self, in debt, forlorn, but fortunately surrounded by his loyal family: his wife, who remains an enigma, his sons, who had graduated from Harvard together in 1790, his daughter, wife of Jonathan Steele, who lived nearby in Durham, and his parents, both of whom outlived him, who were in Berwick. His father, although over a hundred years old, occasionally rode to Durham to see his failing son.[20] And so the years slipped by, and the man's life approached its end. He was no longer competent, and William Plumer's few words show how pitiful Sullivan had become:

His health and mental faculties soon began to decline, and he indulged too freely in the use of ardent spirits. . . . His intellectual powers were broken down—in fact he approached a state of idiocy, and was utterly incapable of holding a court, or transacting any business. . . . Early in the year 1794, he could neither feed, dress, or undress himself.[21]

John Sullivan died in his home on Friday, January 23, 1795, in his fifty-fifth year, survived by his wife who lived until 1820. His lingering illness and the premature senility which claimed the waning months of his life, aggravated or caused by his excessive drinking, had removed him from the active scene. The end was so untypical of the man. There may be truth to the story that Sullivan's creditors wished to prevent his burial until the family satisfied the debts, only to find themselves thwarted by General Joseph Cilley who, pistols in hand, protected the body on the way to the grave.[22] Winter prevented any ceremonious funeral. Only Sullivan's family and a few friends trudged through the snow to the little knoll behind his home. There, in the family plot, where the land overlooks the quiet Oyster River, John Sullivan's body was laid to rest.

In his life Sullivan had sought action and had chased success. A leader of men and a talented politician, he had found happiness only when he had been in the middle of action, either in military conflict or when pursuing the affairs of state. The quiet, domestic life held little appeal for a person of his temperament. What motivated the man? Ambition mainly, but an ambition tempered by a laudable desire to serve. Sullivan was not a "big" man as a person, for he showed conceit and at times resorted to boasting. His desire for money had led him into trouble ever since his dispute with the Durham people during the days of his early law practice. In spite of these faults and weaknesses of character, however, he had tried to do the job as he saw it. He was both a patriot and a public servant, although unfortunately he compromised himself by taking Luzerne's "loan." During the war years and his months in Congress he had to sacrifice both security and comfort in carrying out what he considered his duty.

John Sullivan was a far more complicated personality than first meets the eye. Usually he has been painted as an extrovert seeking the applause of the crowd, fond of people, generous to a fault, somewhat vain and humorless. This superficial characterization is true as far as it goes; however, beneath this exterior lurked a personality that was insecure and unsettled. His tiresome carping during the years of his war service reveals a person unsure of himself. Too often his desire to be a success either had made him pester his superiors for more troops and supplies when they were simply not needed or not available, or had caused him to brag about his own accomplishments when his efforts might have been used in less wordy endeavors. But this pestering and bragging would not have occurred had he been more sure of his own capabilities. Unfortunately Sullivan, a man who had set a high goal, nurtured an ambition that soared beyond his abilities, and the tragic last years of his life seemed to echo his frustration.

That was the man—what of the historical figure? Here was a person with a keenly developed political sense who became a leader, who succeeded in helping to bring his native province into the war, and who led it afterwards toward stability. He wanted power, he wanted to lead. In the rising troubles with Great Britain Sullivan saw his chance not only to strike a blow for a cause in which he had faith but also to seek leadership. He was in the front ranks of those who rebelled against King George and his Britain, and had he not been cursed by excessive bad luck, his military reputation would be far more secure, for he had fought hard and with courage.

Once the war was behind him, Sullivan developed his political talents. His career in Congress was a testing ground, and here undoubtedly many of his ideas became hardened or fashioned, particularly his loathing for anything that was disorganized and diffuse. At Philadelphia, and even earlier while in the army, Sullivan realized that the government under the existing arrangement would hardly suffice. With these ideas in mind he entered the political scene in his native New Hampshire, and there he sought order. He tried to appeal to those in the western part of the state who were jealous of the tidewater area, and although he disapproved of their efforts to join with Vermont, he always maintained his popularity with them. As President of New Hampshire he had to quell the money riots, and at that time he saw once more the danger of weakness in government. With the sole exception of the time he had argued before the Continental Congress for exclusive jurisdiction of New Hampshire courts, he was a nationalist in outlook. This point of view and his obvious abilities as a leader caused him to help influence the outcome of the struggle over ratification of the United States Constitution. In John Sullivan the nationalists had found a worthy champion. A man of action, he recognized duty and met it unhesitatingly. The swagger, the pomp, the conceit have vanished; his service to the young nation, his faith in its future, remain.

NOTES

LIST OF ABBREVIATIONS

CHS	Connecticut Historical Society
LC	Library of Congress
MHS	Massachusetts Historical Society
NA	National Archives
NHHS	New Hampshire Historical Society
NHSL	New Hampshire State Library
NYHS	New-York Historical Society
NYPL	New York Public Library
PHS	Historical Society of Pennsylvania

NOTES

I: EMERGENCE OF A PATRIOT

1. The Parish of Summersworth became the Town of Somersworth, April 22, 1754. In 1849 that part of Somersworth near Salmon Falls separated from the town and became Rollinsford. There has been difference of opinion over the whereabouts of John Sullivan's birthplace. Everett S. Stackpole, *History of New Hampshire* (New York, 1916–18), II, 391–400, brings together the evidence for Somersworth. The *New-Hampshire Gazette*, March 10, 1787, contained a letter which stated: "President Sullivan was born in Somersworth in the County of Strafford." The letter was an answer to the charge that Sullivan had been born out of the state in Berwick, Maine.

2. The date of his birth, February 17, 1740, unquestionably is old style. The Durham obituary records, printed in *The New Hampshire Genealogical Record*, I, No. 3 (January, 1904), 102, give February 28 as the date of birth, which would be new style. Sullivan's gravestone gives his date of birth as February 17.

3. Stackpole, *History of New Hampshire*, II, 391–414; Thomas C. Amory, *Life of James Sullivan* (2 vols., Boston, 1859), I, 8–10; Thomas C. Amory, comp., *Materials for a History of the Family of John Sullivan of Berwick, New England, and of the O'Sullivans of Ardea, Ireland* (Cambridge, Mass., 1893), p. 110.

4. Nothing is known about Margery Brown prior to her marriage. Her gravestone gives Cork and 1714 as place and date of birth.

5. Somersworth Town Records, I, 35–36, microfilm in NHSL; John Scales, "Master John Sullivan of Somersworth and Berwick and His Family," NHHS *Proceedings*, IV (1899–1905), 193.

6. Amory, *Materials for a History of the Family of John Sullivan*, p. 149.

7. Boston *Evening Post*, July 25, 1743, cited by Amory, *Materials for a History of the Family of John Sullivan*, p. 35; *ibid.*, p. 10.

8. Scales, "Master John Sullivan of Somersworth and Berwick and His Family," NHHS *Proceedings,* IV (1899–1905), 182; *The New England Historical and Genealogical Register,* LXXIV (July, 1920), 212.

9. Amory, *Materials for a History of the Family of John Sullivan,* pp. 6, 40, 149; Thomas C. Amory, *The Military Services and Public Life of Major-General John Sullivan* (Boston, 1868), p. 9.

10. For full genealogical material see J. Fox Worcester, *The Descendants of Rev. William Worcester* (Rev. ed., Boston, 1914); Winifred L. Holman, *Remick Genealogy, Compiled from Manuscript of Lieutenant Oliver Philbrick Remick for The Maine Historical Society* (Concord, N. H., 1933).

11. William Plumer, "John Sullivan," *New Hampshire State Papers,* XXI, 819. The exact date of their marriage is unknown.

12. Deed of sale, December 19, 1764, New Hampshire Province Deeds, LXXIV, 360, microfilm in NHSL. New Hampshire deeds are in the State Library until the division into counties in 1771. After that time deeds are recorded at county seats.

13. Amory, *Materials for a History of the Family of John Sullivan,* pp. 42–45, 149.

14. *Ibid.,* p. 10. This physical description was given by his grandson who was born after Sullivan's death.

15. Court file 29833, MS in NHHS.

16. Court file 919, MS in NHHS. This was a complaint in Inferior Court, and there is no record of further action.

17. Superior Court Records, 1764–67, pp. 390–92, MS vol. in NHHS.

18. *Ibid.;* Superior Court Records, 1767–70, pp. 58–62, MS vol. in NHHS; Court file 23,000, MS in NHHS; *New Hampshire State Papers,* VII, 109–10.

19. These figures have been determined by examining the records of both the Inferior and Superior Courts (MS vols. in NHHS). There are four volumes of records of the Superior Court, lettered "D" for 1760–63, "E" for 1764–67, "F" for 1767–70, and "G" for 1771–73. There are two volumes of records for the Inferior Court, one volume for 1770–71, and the other for the balance of the year 1771. In addition there are numerous writs and occasional judgments for cases in the Inferior Court. These are indexed by name of person involved so that it was relatively easy to trace actions concerning John Sullivan. These records are in the NHHS until 1771 when

New Hampshire was divided into counties. From that time—1773 for Strafford and Grafton counties—the records are at the individual county seats.

20. *New-Hampshire Gazette,* May 19, 1769.

21. *New Hampshire State Papers,* XIII, 176; *ibid.,* XXIX, 310.

22. Deeds of sale examined in New Hampshire Province Deeds, XC, XCVII, microfilm in NHSL; Exeter Register, CI, CII, CIV; Dover Register, Books 1, 3, 17, 22.

23. *New-Hampshire Gazette,* May 27, 1774.

24. *Ibid.,* November 13, 1772.

25. Everett S. Stackpole and Lucien Thompson, *History of the Town of Durham, New Hampshire* (2 vols., Concord, N. H., 1913), I, 252.

26. Amory, *Materials for a History of the Family of John Sullivan,* p. 151.

27. John Adams to Abigail Adams, June 29, 1774, John Adams, *Familiar Letters,* pp. 2–3.

28. Lawrence S. Mayo, *John Wentworth, Governor of New Hampshire, 1767–1775* (Cambridge, 1921), pp. 73–86; *New Hampshire State Papers,* XVIII, 615–39; NHHS *Collections* IX (1889), 305–63.

29. Sullivan to Selectmen of Newmarket, N. H., March 22, 1774, *Hammond,* I, 45.

30. *Ibid.*

31. *New-Hampshire Gazette,* June 10, 1774.

32. July 18, 1774, Durham Town Records, I, 97, microfilm in NHSL.

33. *New Hampshire State Papers,* VII, 407–8.

34. *New-Hampshire Gazette,* August 10, 1774.

35. John Adams, *Works,* II, 348–49.

36. *Ibid.,* pp. 357–58.

37. Galloway to William Franklin, September 3, 1774, Burnett, *Letters,* I, 6.

38. Adams, *Works,* II, 366–67.

39. *Journals of the Continental Congress,* I, 25.

40. "Address to the People," December 24, 1774, Hammond, I, 53.

41. *Journals of the Continental Congress,* I, 42, 63–73.

42. Sullivan to John Langdon, October 5, 1774, Hammond, I, 48, incorrectly dated as September 5, 1774.

43. *Journals of the Continental Congress,* I, 67.

44. Adams, *Works*, II, 397.

45. *Journals of the Continental Congress*, I, 68–69.

46. *Ibid.*, I, 71–73.

47. *Ibid.*, I, 39–40.

48. *Ibid.*, I, 75–81, 102*n.*

49. *Ibid.*, I, 102; Joseph Hewes to James Iredell, October 31, 1774, Burnett, *Letters*, I, 83.

50. *New-Hampshire Gazette*, November 18, 1774.

51. Durham Town Records, I, 98–99, microfilm in NHSL; Sullivan and John Adams to Boston Committee, November 21, 1774, Stackpole and Thompson, *History of the Town of Durham*, I, 116–17.

52. Sullivan to Folsom, November 24, 1774, Hammond, I, 49.

53. Sullivan's reply to Ebenezer Thompson, *New-Hampshire Spy*, March 17, 1789, quoted in Charles L. Parsons, "The Capture of Fort William and Mary, December 14 and 15, 1774," NHHS *Proceedings*, IV (1899–1905), 37–38; Elwin L. Page, "The King's Powder, 1774," *New England Quarterly*, XVIII (March, 1945), 86.

54. *New-Hampshire Spy*, March 17, 1789, quoted in Parsons, "The Capture of Fort William and Mary," NHHS *Proceedings*, IV (1899–1905), 37–38.

55. Wentworth to Earl of Dartmouth, December 20, 1774, Wentworth, Letterbook, p. 42, in NHHS.

56. Gentleman in Boston to Mr. Rivington, December 20, 1774, Force I, 1054. The writer of the letter referred to "their [the crowd's] Demosthenes" as being the person who persuaded the above vote. Although it cannot be documented, it seems more than likely that Sullivan was "Demosthenes."

57. Sullivan to New Hampshire Senate, February 14, 1785, *New Hampshire State Papers*, XVIII, 749; Sullivan's reply to "Honestus," April 23, 1785, Hammond, III, 420.

58. Wentworth to Earl of Dartmouth, December 20, 1774, Wentworth, Letterbook, p. 42, in NHHS; Sullivan to New Hampshire Senate, February 14, 1785, *New Hampshire State Papers*, XVIII, 749.

59. Wentworth to Earl of Dartmouth, December 28, 1774, Wentworth, Letterbook, p. 47, in NHHS; Wentworth to Thomas Gage, December 29, 1774, *ibid.*, p. 38.

60. Wentworth to Earl of Dartmouth, December 20, 1774, *ibid.*, p. 42; Wentworth to Dartmouth, January 14, 1775, MHS *Proceedings*, XIV (1875–76), 342.

61. Sullivan to New Hampshire Senate, February 14, 1785, *New Hampshire State Papers*, XVIII, 749.

62. "Address to the People," December 24, 1774, Hammond, I, 53.

63. Wentworth to Earl of Dartmouth, December 28, 1775, *New England Historical and Genealogical Register*, XXIII, No. 3 (July, 1869), 277.

64. *New Hampshire State Papers*, VII, 443.

65. *Ibid.*, VII, 442–44.

66. Wentworth to T. W. Waldron, January 27, 1775, MHS *Collections*, 6th ser., IV (1891), 73.

67. *Ibid.;* Wentworth to Waldron, February 8, 1775, *ibid.*, 6th ser., IV (1891), 79–80; Wentworth to Thomas Gage (?), February 13, 1775, Wentworth to Earl of Dartmouth, March 10, 1775, Wentworth, Letterbook, pp. 61, 68, in NHHS.

68. Earl of Dartmouth to Wentworth, February 22, 1775, MHS *Proceedings*, XIV (1875–76), 342; Wentworth to Dartmouth, March 10, 1775, *ibid.*, XIV (1875–76), 342–43; Wentworth to Dartmouth, December 2, 1774, *New Hampshire State Papers*, VII, 419.

69. Letter from informer to Thomas Gage, April 9, 1775, Allen French, *General Gage's Informers* (Ann Arbor, Mich., 1932), pp. 20–21.

70. Scammell to Sullivan, May 3, 1775, Hammond, I, 58–59.

71. *Journals of the Continental Congress*, II, 56.

72. *Ibid.*, II, 65.

73. Adams, *Works*, II, 409.

74. *Ibid.*, II, 410.

75. *Ibid.*, III, 16.

76. *Ibid.*

77. *Journals of the Continental Congress*, II, 84.

78. Adams, *Works*, III, 17–18.

79. *Journals of the Continental Congress*, II, 97–99.

80. June 22, 1775, *ibid.*, II, 103; George W. Nesmith, "Services of General Sullivan," *Granite Monthly*, I, No. 11 (April, 1878), 325–30; Howard P. Moore, *A Life of General John Stark of New Hampshire* (Boston, 1949), p. 209.

II: THE FIRST YEAR OF CONFLICT

1. *Pennsylvania Gazette*, June 28, 1775.

2. Washington to Philip Schuyler, July 10, 1775, Fitzpatrick, III, 332.

3. General Orders, July 22, 1775, *ibid.*, III, 355–56.

4. Washington to R. H. Lee, August 29, 1775; Washington to New York Legislature, August 30, 1775, *ibid.*, III, 453, 458; Sullivan to New Hampshire Committee of Safety, August 29, 1775, Hammond, I, 79.

5. Washington to the brigadier and major generals, September 8, 1775, Fitzpatrick, III, 483; Council of War, September 11, 1775, Force, 4th ser., III, 768.

6. Council of War, October 18, 1775, *ibid.*, III, 1153; Douglas S. Freeman, *George Washington* (6 vols., New York, 1948–54), III, 554–56.

7. Washington to President of Congress, October 24, 1775, Fitzpatrick, IV, 41.

8. Sullivan to Meshech Weare, December 12, 1775, Hammond, I, 142–43.

9. *Ibid.*, I, 143.

10. Sullivan to John Adams, December 21, 1775, *ibid.*, I, 152.

11. *Ibid.*, I, 153.

12. Abigail Adams to John Adams, December 10, 1775, John Adams, *Familiar Letters*, p. 129.

13. Sullivan to Samuel Adams, January 3, 1776, MHS *Proceedings*, XIV (1876), 275; Horatio Gates to Sullivan, December 29, 1775, Hammond, I, 155; Freeman, *George Washington*, III, 586n.

14. Sullivan's General Orders, December 22, 1775, quoted in Allen French, *The First Year of the American Revolution* (Boston, 1934), p. 524.

15. Washington to President of Congress, March 7, 1776, Fitzpatrick, IV, 371–74; Horatio Gates to John Adams, March 8, 1776, MHS *Proceedings*, XIV (1876), 281–82; Joseph Ward to John Adams, March 14, 1776, *ibid.*, XIV (1876), 282–83; French, *First Year of the Revolution*, pp. 658–63.

16. Sullivan to John Adams, March 19, 1776, MHS *Proceedings*, XIV (1876), 284.

17. Sullivan to New Hampshire Committee of Safety, March 14, 1776, Hammond, I, 187.

18. Sullivan to New Hampshire General Assembly, March 24, 1776, *ibid.*, I, 191.

19. Washington to President of Congress, April 26, 1776, Fitzpatrick, IV, 519.

20. Philip Schuyler to Washington, May 24, 1776, Philip Schuyler

Papers, February 25–November 19, 1776, in NYPL; Sullivan to Schuyler, May 25, 27, 1776, Hammond, I, 209–10.

21. Sullivan to Schuyler, May 27, 1776, *ibid.*, I, 210; John Thomas to Washington, May 8, 1776, Force, 4th ser., VI, 453–54; Benjamin Franklin, Samuel Chase, and Charles Carroll to President of Congress, May 10, 1776, *ibid.*, 4th ser., VI, 450.

22. Washington to Schuyler, May 22, 1776, Fitzpatrick, V, 76; Chase and Carroll to John Thomas, May 26, 1776, Sparks, *Correspondence of the American Revolution*, I, 518–20; William Thompson to James Wilson, May 19, 1776, Gratz Collection, Case 4, Box 15, in PHS.

23. Thomas to Wooster, May 21, 1776, MHS *Proceedings*, 2d ser., XVIII (1903–4), 431; Chase and Carroll to Congress, May 27, 1776, Force, 4th ser., VI, 589–90; Sullivan to John Hancock, June 1, 1776, Hammond, I, 212.

24. William Irvine to James Wilson, June 1, 1776, Gratz Collection, Case 4, Box 12, in PHS; Schuyler to Congress, May 31, 1776, Philip Schuyler Papers, February 25–November 19, 1776, in NYPL; note on back of "Continental Forces in Canada," June 12, 1776, Horatio Gates Papers, Box of Army Returns, in NYPL.

25. Force, 4th ser., VI, 628.

26. Sullivan to Hancock, June 1, 1776, Hammond, I, 212.

27. Sullivan to Washington, June 5, 1776, *ibid.*, I, 218.

28. William Thompson to Washington, June 2, 1776, Sparks, *Correspondence of the American Revolution*, I, 207–10; Benedict Arnold to Sullivan, June 5, 1776, *ibid.*, I, 524–25; Arnold to Schuyler, June 6, 1776, *ibid.*, I, 526–27; Sullivan to Washington, June 6, 1776, Hammond, I, 219.

29. Sullivan to William Thompson, June 6, 1776, *ibid.*, I, 222.

30. Sullivan to Washington, June 6, 1776, *ibid.*, I, 220.

31. Sullivan to Washington, June 7, 1776, *ibid.*, I, 226.

32. William Irvine's Account, Irvine Papers, I, 47, in PHS; William Thompson to Sullivan, June 7, 1776, Force, 4th ser., VI, 1038; Thomas Hartley to Jasper Yeates, June 12, 1776, *Pennsylvania Archives*, 5th ser., II, 82–86; Sullivan to Washington, June 12, 1776, Hammond, I, 230; good account in Justin H. Smith, *Our Struggle for the Fourteenth Colony* (2 vols., New York, 1907), II, 402–17.

33. Sullivan to Schuyler, June 12, 1776, Hammond, I, 234.

34. Sullivan to Washington, June 12, 1776, *ibid.*, I, 230.

35. Extract of letter from Crown Point, July 3, 1776, Force, 4th

ser., VI, 1252–53; Arnold to Washington, June 25, 1776, Sparks, *Correspondence of the American Revolution*, I, 237; Sullivan to Schuyler, June 19, 1776, Hammond, I, 251–52; Smith, *Our Struggle for the Fourteenth Colony*, II, 430–35.

36. Sullivan to Schuyler, June 19, 1776, Hammond, I, 253.

37. Arthur St. Clair to James Wilson, June 20, 1776, Gratz Collection, Case 4, Box 14, in PHS.

38. Sullivan to Schuyler, June 26, 1776, George Washington Papers, XXIX, 20, in LC.

39. Sullivan to Hancock, July 2, 1776, Hammond, I, 277.

40. Washington to President of Congress, June 17, 1776, Fitzpatrick, V, 152.

41. Sullivan to Schuyler, July 6, 1776, Hammond, I, 280–81.

42. Josiah Bartlett to John Langdon, July 29, 1776, Burnett, *Letters*, II, 29–30; *Journals of the Continental Congress*, V, 613; Thomas Jefferson to R. H. Lee, July 29, 1776, Burnett, *Letters*, II, 28; President of Congress to Washington, July 31, 1776, *ibid.*, II, 32.

43. Jefferson, Papers, I, 479*n*.

44. Jefferson to R. H. Lee, July 29, 1776, Burnett, *Letters*, II, 28.

45. Enoch Poor to Nathaniel Folsom, August 12, 1776, Dreer Collection, Letters of Generals of the American Revolution, II, 53, in PHS.

46. President of Congress to Washington, July 31, 1776, Burnett, *Letters*, II, 32.

III: LONG ISLAND TO TRENTON
AND PRINCETON

1. Douglas S. Freeman, *George Washington* (6 vols., New York, 1948–54), IV, 148*n.*; Washington to Jonathan Trumbull, August 7, 1776, Fitzpatrick, V, 389.

2. *Journals of the Continental Congress*, V, 641; William Williams to Joseph Trumbull, August 10, 1776, Burnett, *Letters*, II, 46, for details on balloting.

3. General Orders, August 20, 1776, Fitzpatrick, V, 469; Joseph Reed to William Livingston, August 30, 1776, Thomas W. Field, *Battle of Long Island* (Long Island Historical Society Memoirs, II, Brooklyn, 1869), p. 397.

4. Freeman, *George Washington*, IV, 157–58; Henry P. John-

ston, *Campaign of 1776 around New York* (Long Island Historical Society Memoirs, III, Brooklyn, 1878), Part I, pp. 64–84, 143; Samuel Parsons to John Adams, October 8, 1776, *ibid.,* Part II, pp. 34–36.

5. Washington to Putnam, August 25, 1776, Fitzpatrick, V, 488.

6. Matthew L. Davis, *Memoirs of Aaron Burr* (New York, 1837), cited by Johnston, *Campaign of 1776,* Part I, p. 151*n.*; Joseph Reed to William Livingston, August 30, 1776, Field, *Battle of Long Island,* p. 397.

7. Since no records have been found limiting Putnam's command, Douglas Freeman assumes it "was real, and not merely titular." Freeman, *George Washington,* IV, 155*n.* Henry Knox wrote somewhat ambiguously that Putnam commanded on Long Island with a number of other generals. Knox to Lucy Knox, August 26, 1776, Knox Papers, III, 28, in MHS.

8. Sullivan to Hancock, October 25, 1777, Hammond, I, 551.

9. Freeman, *George Washington,* IV, 370.

10. Johnston, *Campaign of 1776,* Part II, p. 27.

11. Sullivan to John Langdon, November 9, 1777, Hammond, I, 575.

12. "Journal of Colonel Samuel Miles," Johnston, *Campaign of 1776,* Part II, pp. 60–63. This is a serious charge, implying laxity on Sullivan's part. It must be remembered that Miles wrote his account after the war when he had been blamed by some for the failure of the American left to be aware of the British flanking move which occurred during the battle.

13. *Ibid.,* Part I, p. 153, pp. 153–54*n.* This may have been the visit mentioned by Miles.

14. Robert Harrison to President of Congress, August 27, 1776, Field, *Battle of Long Island,* pp. 393–94.

15. Johnston, *Campaign of 1776,* Part I, pp. 155–57, for the positions of the various regiments.

16. *Ibid.,* Part II, p. 30.

17. William Stirling to Washington, August 29, 1776, Field, *Battle of Long Island,* pp. 395–97; extract from "President Stiles' Diary," *ibid.,* pp. 485–86; Freeman, *George Washington,* IV, 162.

18. *South Carolina and American General Gazette,* October 2, 1776, quoted in Johnston, *Campaign of 1776,* Part II, p. 59. Johnston wonders whether the word "went" was meant for "sent." One par-

ticipant, John Burnham, places Sullivan at the front in the morning, but his account does not establish the time; Freeman, *George Washington,* IV, 163*n.*

19. Sullivan to Hancock, October 25, 1777, Hammond, I, 551. That he probably was in error about the command has already been pointed out.

20. Max von Eelking, *The German Allied Troops in the North American War of Independence,* 1776–1783, tr. J. G. Rosengarten (Albany, 1893), pp. 30–31.

21. Johnston, *Campaign of 1776,* Part I, pp. 157–58, 194*n.*

22. *South Carolina and American General Gazette,* October 2, 1776, quoted in *ibid.,* Part II, p. 59. The Yellow Hook Road was part of the Gowanus Road.

23. "I went to the Hill near Flat Bush to reconitre [*sic*] the enemy." Sullivan to Hancock, October 25, 1777, Hammond, I, 551. Johnston, *Campaign of 1776,* Part I, p. 174*n.*, interprets this statement to mean that Sullivan went from the main camp and that he was not already at Flatbush Pass.

24. Field, *Battle of Long Island,* pp. 164–65; Johnston, *Campaign of 1776,* Part I, pp. 155–56, lists the troops present.

25. Howe's report of September 3, 1776, Field, *Battle of Long Island,* p. 380.

26. *Ibid.;* extract of a letter from a field officer, September 1, 1776, Willard, *Letters on the American Revolution,* p. 355.

27. Johnston, *Campaign of 1776,* Part I, pp. 176–79, 194n.; "Journal of Colonel Samuel Miles," *ibid.,* Part II, pp. 62–63; Field, *Battle of Long Island,* pp. 158–61; "Affidavit of Lt. Robert Troup," *ibid.,* pp. 419–20; Howe's report of September 3, 1776, *ibid.,* pp. 379–80; Robertson, *Archibald Robertson,* pp. 93–94, for description of flanking move.

28. Sullivan to Hancock, October 25, 1777, Hammond, I, 551; Field, *Battle of Long Island,* pp. 183–84; extract from a "Journal Left by Capt. George Harris," *ibid.,* p. 406.

29. Eelking, *The German Allied Troops in the North American War,* p. 31; Howe's report of September 3, 1776, Field, *Battle of Long Island,* p. 380.

30. Some accounts have chosen to place Sullivan closer to Stirling's sector of the battle on the right. One spectator claims that between 9:00 A.M. and 10:00 A.M. General Samuel Parsons on Sullivan's left was threatened by British at his rear and that Sullivan and

his men went to his assistance. "President Stiles' Diary," Field, *Battle of Long Island,* p. 495. It is unlikely that Sullivan was able to advance to his right toward Parsons, and Parsons's own accounts make no mention of Sullivan's joining him. Parsons to John Adams, August 29, October 8, 1776, Johnston, *Campaign of 1776,* Part II, pp. 33–36. It appears more likely that, rather than moving toward Stirling, Sullivan was isolated somewhere near the center of the field.

31. Benson J. Lossing, *The Pictorial Field Book of the Revolution* (2 vols., New York, 1851–52), II, 603*n.*; Eelking, *The German Allied Troops in the North American War,* pp. 31–32, 35; extract of a letter of a British officer, September 3, 1776, Field, *Battle of Long Island,* pp. 402–3; letter of a Hessian chaplain, September 7, 1776, Pettengill, *Letters from America,* p. 154; Johnston, *Campaign of 1776,* Part I, p. 185*n.*; Lord Percy to the Duke of Northumberland, September 1, 1776, Percy, *Letters,* p. 68.

32. Lossing, *The Pictorial Field Book of the Revolution,* II, 600*n.*, 603–4, 604*n.*

33. Sullivan to Hancock, October 25, 1777, Hammond, I, 551.

34. Eelking, *The German Allied Troops in the North American War,* p. 33.

35. Lewis Morris, Jr., to Lewis Morris, August 28, 1776, New-York Historical Society *Collections,* 1875, p. 440. Benson Lossing is the only person, to the author's knowledge, who has tried to ascertain the place where Sullivan was captured. He wrote: "Sullivan and his men were made prisoners . . . upon the slope between the Flatbush Avenue and the Long Island rail-way, between Bedford and Brooklyn, near 'Baker's Tavern,' at a little east of the junction of these avenues." Lossing, *The Pictorial Field Book of the Revolution,* II, 604*n.* The map on p. 600 places Baker's Tavern east of the Flatbush Road.

36. Letter of Daniel Brodhead, September 5, 1776, Johnston, *Campaign of 1776,* Part II, p. 65.

37. Both Washington and Parsons blamed Miles. Washington to John A. Washington, September 22, 1776, Fitzpatrick, VI, 93; Parsons to John Adams, October 8, 1776, Johnston, *Campaign of 1776,* Part II, p. 36.

38. "Journal of Colonel Samuel Miles," *ibid.,* Part II, pp. 60–63.

39. For criticism of Washington, see Charles F. Adams, *Studies Military and Diplomatic, 1775–1865* (New York, 1911), pp. 54–56; for summary of other historians' conclusions, see Christopher Ward,

The War of the Revolution, ed. John R. Alden (2 vols., New York, 1952), I, 227–30; Freeman, *George Washington,* IV, 368–70, argues that Sullivan was most responsible for the flanking movement's success.

40. Searle, *American Journal,* p. 84.

41. Mackenzie, *Diary,* I, 39.

42. Eelking, *The German Allied Troops in the North American War,* p. 33.

43. *Ibid.,* p. 36; Troyer Anderson, *The Command of the Howe Brothers during the American Revolution* (New York, 1936), pp. 155–56, for the extent of their instructions.

44. Searle, *American Journal,* pp. 81–82.

45. Richard Howe to Lord Germain, September 20, 1776, Stevens, *Facsimiles of Manuscripts in European Archives,* XII, No. 1201; Caesar Rodney to George Read, September 4, 1776, Burnett, *Letters,* II, 68.

46. Washington to President of Congress, August 31, September 11, 1776, Fitzpatrick, V, 507; VI, 44–45; Sullivan to Richard Howe, August 30, 1776, Hammond, I, 299; Howe to Sullivan, August 30, 1776, *ibid.,* I, 299–300.

47. Josiah Bartlett to Nathaniel Folsom, September 2, 1776, Burnett, *Letters,* II, 65.

48. *Journals of the Continental Congress,* V, 723, 728; Caesar Rodney to George Read, September 4, 1776, Burnett, *Letters,* II, 68; Lewis Morris to John Jay, September 8, 1776, *ibid.,* II, 81; Adams, *Works,* III, 73.

49. *Ibid.; Journals of the Continental Congress,* V, 728, 730–31.

50. Burnett, *Letters,* II, 70n.

51. Josiah Bartlett to William Whipple, September 3, 1776, *ibid.,* II, 66–67.

52. *Journals of the Continental Congress,* V, 735, 737; Hancock to Washington, September 8, 1776, Burnett, *Letters,* II, 81–82.

53. Josiah Bartlett to William Whipple, September 14, 1776, *ibid.,* II, 88–89; John Adams to Samuel Adams, September 17, 1776, *ibid.,* II, 91–93; Benjamin Rush's account, *ibid.,* II, 74n.; Committee's report to Congress, September 17, 1776, *Journals of the Continental Congress,* V, 765–66; Anderson, *The Command of the Howe Brothers,* pp. 156–60.

54. Adams, *Works,* III, 80–81.

55. John R. Alden, *General Charles Lee, Traitor or Patriot?* (Baton Rouge, La., 1951), pp. 152–55.

56. Edwin M. Stone, *The Life and Recollections of John Howland* (Providence, 1857), p. 65.

57. Sullivan to Washington, December 13, 1776, Force, 5th ser., III, 1232.

58. Washington to President of Congress, December 20, 1776, Fitzpatrick, VI, 407.

59. Freeman, *George Washington,* IV, 306*n.,* for inception of plan; William S. Stryker, *Battles of Trenton and Princeton* (Boston, 1898), pp. 40–41.

60. Freeman, *George Washington,* IV, 306–8.

61. Washington to President of Congress, December 27, 1776, Fitzpatrick, VI, 442; description based on Freeman, *George Washington,* IV, 314.

62. Order of March, December 25, 1776, Knox Papers, III, 92, in MHS; Stryker, *Battles of Trenton and Princeton,* p. 142.

63. Wilkinson, *Memoirs,* I, 129; Washington to President of Congress, December 27, 1776, Fitzpatrick, VI, 442; Freeman, *George Washington,* IV, 314–15.

64. Tench Tilghman to James Tilghman, December 27, 1776, Stryker, *Battles of Trenton and Princeton,* p. 366; also see *ibid.,* pp. 151–52.

65. Henry Knox to Lucy Knox, December 28, 1776, Stryker, *Battles of Trenton and Princeton,* p. 372.

66. Wilkinson, *Memoirs,* I, 130; Washington to President of Congress, December 27, 1776, Fitzpatrick, VI, 443; Tench Tilghman to James Tilghman, December 27, 1776, Stryker, *Battles of Trenton and Princeton,* p. 366.

67. Wilkinson, *Memoirs,* I, 130.

68. Stryker, *Battles of Trenton and Princeton,* pp. 167–68.

69. *Ibid.,* p. 179.

70. Washington to John Cadwalader, December 27, 1776, Fitzpatrick, VI, 446.

71. Alfred H. Bill, *The Campaign of Princeton, 1776–1777* (Princeton, 1948), pp. 84–88; Washington to President of Congress, January 5, 1777, Fitzpatrick, VI, 467; William B. Reed, *Life and Correspondence of Joseph Reed* (2 vols., Philadelphia, 1847), I, 287–88; Wilkinson, *Memoirs,* I, 134–39; John Haslet to Caesar Rod-

ney, January 2, 1777, Stryker, *Battles of Trenton and Princeton,* pp. 376–77. Freeman points out that this letter supposedly by Haslet is really a portion of Thomas Rodney's diary; Freeman, *George Washington,* IV, 342n.

72. Thomas J. Wertenbaker, "The Battle of Princeton," in *The Princeton Battle Monument* (Princeton, 1922), p. 66, quotes a Captain Hall that British sentries knew there was uncommon activity in the American camp.

73. Stone, *The Life and Recollections of John Howland,* p. 74.

74. Mercer apparently was not in the van as previously assumed by writers. See Wertenbaker, "The Battle of Princeton," in *The Princeton Battle Monument,* pp. 68–73; Wilkinson, *Memoirs,* I, 141–42.

75. *Ibid.,* I, 142; Wertenbaker, "The Battle of Princeton," in *The Princeton Battle Monument,* pp. 76–78.

76. Sullivan to Meshech Weare, February 13, 1777, Hammond, I, 320; Wertenbaker, "The Battle of Princeton," in *The Princeton Battle Monument,* pp. 101–7.

77. Sullivan to Weare, February 13, 1777, Hammond, I, 320; Bill, *The Campaign of Princeton,* pp. 111–12; Wertenbaker, "The Battle of Princeton," in *The Princeton Battle Monument,* pp. 109–10; Stone, *The Life and Recollections of John Howland,* p. 76; Wilkinson, *Memoirs,* I, 144.

78. Washington to President of Congress, January 5, 1777, Fitzpatrick, VI, 470; Washington to Israel Putnam, January 5, 1777, *ibid.,* VI, 471; Freeman, *George Washington,* IV, 358.

IV: NEW JERSEY TO BRANDYWINE

1. Sullivan to Washington, February 9, 1777, Hammond, I, 315.

2. Sullivan was incorrectly informed. On March 25 Congress ordered Gates to repair immediately to Ticonderoga and "take command of the army there." On April 1 Congress ordered St. Clair to serve under Gates. Ill will arose because Schuyler had been replaced. On May 15 the Board of War returned Schuyler to the northern command and gave Gates choice of serving under Schuyler or of resuming his earlier position as Adjutant-General. Gates soon was to return to the northern command after Ticonderoga fell. *Journals of the Continental Congress,* VII, 202, 217, 364. See also Randolph

G. Adams, "Horatio Gates," in *Dictionary of American Biography*, VII, 185.

3. Sullivan to Washington, March 9, 1777, Hammond, I, 327.

4. Washington to Sullivan, March 15, 1777, Fitzpatrick, VII, 290–91.

5. Peter Livius to Sullivan, June 2, 1777, Hammond, I, 357.

6. Edward Bancroft wrote to Silas Deane on February 13, 1777: "Some members of the Administration have lately made here some secret and suspicious inquiries about General Sullivan. They are such as might lead one to suspect that they wish to obtain some service from him. But in this case conjecture is not enough." Silas Deane, *The Deane Papers*, I, 489, for identification of Bancroft. Carl Van Doren, *Secret History of the American Revolution* (New York, 1941), pp. 43–44.

7. *Ibid.*, pp. 44–45; Schuyler to Washington, June 15, 1777, Washington Papers, XLIX, 38, in LC; Schuyler to Washington, June 16, 1777, Sparks, *Correspondence of the American Revolution*, I, 384; Washington to Schuyler, June 20, 1777, Fitzpatrick, VIII, 274; Sullivan to Washington, June 21, 1777, quoted in Van Doren, *Secret History of the American Revolution*, p. 47.

8. Sullivan to Hancock, July 1, 1777, Hammond, I, 403; Edmund C. Burnett, *The Continental Congress* (New York, 1941), p. 243.

9. *Journals of the Continental Congress*, VIII, 528, 531, 537; James Lovell to William Whipple, July 7, 1777, Burnett, *Letters*, II, 403; John Adams to Nathanael Greene, July 7, 1777, *ibid.*, pp. 404–5; Eliphalet Dyer to Joseph Trumbull, July 7, 1777, *ibid.*, pp. 405–7.

10. Sullivan to Washington, August 7, 1777, Hammond, I, 424.

11. William Plumer, "John Sullivan," *New Hampshire State Papers*, XXI, 825; Charles L. Whittemore, M.D., in a letter of July 1, 1955, to the author offers this opinion on Sullivan's illness: "He makes no mention of pain which is a very characteristic part of a peptic ulcer, but his reference to 'a violent bilious disorder' and 'this being the fourth time I have bled' would lead one to believe that he probably suffered from an ulcer. . . . As . . . he died in 1795, I would certainly say that he had no malignancy, at least in the beginning. His being highly nervous and extremely sensitive and his recurrence of complaints after drinking would again seem to point to an ulcer."

12. Sullivan to Samuel Loudon, August 6, 1777, quoted in Van Doren, *Secret History of the American Revolution*, p. 48.

13. Arthur St. Clair to Sullivan, August 30, 1777, Hammond, I, 446.

14. British intelligence report, July 27, 1777, Clinton Papers, in Clements Library, Ann Arbor, Mich. The author is indebted to Colonel John Bakeless for calling his attention to this item.

15. Sullivan to Hancock, August 31, 1777, *Pennsylvania Journal and the Weekly Advertiser,* September 10, 1777.

16. Sullivan to Washington, August 24, 1777, Hammond, I, 440; Major Joseph Vaughan's "Testimony," *ibid.,* I, 524–25; "Statement of Major Edward Sherburne," *ibid.,* I, 499–500; *Pennsylvania Gazette,* August 27, 1777, quoted in *New Jersey Archives,* 2d ser., I, 459–60.

17. Sullivan to Washington, August 24, 1777, Hammond, I, 441.

18. Washington to Sullivan, August 22, 1777, Fitzpatrick, IX, 115–16.

19. Washington to President of Congress, September 3, 1777, *ibid.,* IX, 172.

20. Washington to William Smallwood, September 9, 1777, *ibid.,* IX, 198.

21. Sullivan to Washington, October 24, 1777, Hammond, III, 639.

22. Sullivan to Hancock, October 6, 1777, *ibid.,* I, 475; Sullivan to Washington, September 11, 1777, correct version in Douglas S. Freeman, *George Washington* (6 vols., New York, 1948–54), IV, 476.

23. "Certificate of Major Eustace," *The Collector: a Magazine for Autograph and Historical Collectors,* LIX, No. 11 (December, 1946), 259–60; Sparks, *The Writings of George Washington,* V, 459.

24. Sullivan to Hancock, October 6, 1777, Hammond, I, 475–76; Freeman, *George Washington,* IV, 476.

25. Sullivan to Hancock, October 6, 1777, Hammond, I, 476.

26. Freeman, *George Washington,* IV, 476, gives correct transcription. It is assumed that "the one" and Major Spear are the same. Colonel Hazen's information must have been one of the reports sent by Sullivan to Washington earlier.

27. Sullivan to Hancock, October 6, 1777, Hammond, I, 476; Freeman, *George Washington,* IV, 477.

28. Quoted in Freeman, *ibid.,* IV, 478.

29. Sullivan to Washington, Hammond, I, 453.

30. Dayton, "Papers," p. 184. Some have accused Sullivan of not

believing a report of Squire Thomas Cheyney, a local farmer, that the British were crossing the forks. Supposedly Cheyney rode up to Sullivan in the afternoon with the information, was received discourteously, and insisted on being led to Washington. There is absolutely no evidence, in the light of present knowledge, that Cheyney saw Sullivan. Freeman minimizes the episode, believing Washington must have received Bland's information at about the same time Cheyney arrived on the scene; Freeman, *George Washington*, IV, 478, 478*n*.

31. Lafayette, *Memoirs, Correspondence and Manuscripts*, I, 23; Sullivan to Hancock, September 27, 1777, Hammond, I, 466, places the figure between 3,000 and 4,000.

32. Sullivan to Hancock, September 27, 1777, Hammond, I, 463. Sullivan in his account said Hazen had been at Jones's Ford. He confused that ford and Wistar's.

33. Sullivan's own account is followed here, as given in Sullivan to Hancock, September 27, 1777, Hammond, I, 463, and Sullivan to Messrs. Powars [*sic*] and Willis, n.d., *ibid.*, I, 472–73.

34. Montresor, "Journals," p. 449; Baurmeister, *Letters*, pp. 12, 14–15.

35. Montresor, "Journals," p. 449.

36. Sullivan to Hancock, September 27, 1777, Hammond, I, 463–64. Montresor placed the attack at 3:30 P.M.

37. Elmer, "Journal," p. 105; Freeman, *George Washington*, IV, 481; Sullivan to Hancock, September 27, 1777, Hammond, I, 464.

38. Sullivan to Hancock, September 27, 1777, Hammond, I, 464.

39. "The Actions at Brandywine and Paoli, Described by a British Officer," *The Pennsylvania Magazine of History and Biography*, XXIX (1905), 368.

40. Sullivan to Hancock, September 27, 1777, Hammond, I, 465.

41. Freeman, *George Washington*, IV, 481*n.*; "Statement of Colonel Charles Cotesworth Pinckney," September 24, 1777, Hammond, I, 557; Sullivan to John Langdon, November 5, 1777, Hammond, I, 570.

42. Although most accounts say the flanking march had the larger of the two enemy forces, Montresor says otherwise, placing the larger force under Knyphausen at Chad's Ford. Montresor, "Journals," p. 450.

43. Baurmeister, *Letters*, pp. 16–17; Freeman, *George Washington*, IV, 484.

44. *Ibid.;* Thomas Sullivan, "Journal," pp. 415–16.

45. Thomas Burke to Governor Richard Caswell, September 17, 1777, Burnett, *Letters,* II, 496; complete version of this important letter in *North Carolina State Records,* XI, 620–23.

46. Washington to Sullivan, October 24, 1777, Fitzpatrick, IX, 425–26; James Lovell to William Whipple, September 17, 1777, Burnett, *Letters,* II, 495–96, wrote: "Genl. Washington and some good military men, especially the highest officers, do not charge the want (i.e., lack of intelligence) to Sullivan."

47. Frederick D. Stone, *The Battle of Brandywine* (Philadelphia, 1895), p. 14.

48. Freeman, *George Washington,* IV, 485–87. In Sullivan's note to Washington relaying the information, the words "This morning from" originally read "last night from." Sullivan scratched out the latter phrase and replaced it with the former. This may have been a crude attempt to fix the time more accurately. The original of this note is in George Washington Papers, LVI, 21, in LC.

49. Thomas Burke to Governor Richard Caswell, September 17, 1777, *North Carolina State Records,* XI, 622.

50. Sullivan to Messrs. Powars [*sic*] and Willis, n.d., Hammond, I, 472–73.

51. Thomas Burke to Governor Richard Caswell, September 17, 1777, *North Carolina State Records,* XI, 622.

52. "Gen. Thomas Conway's Statement," September 20, 1777, Hammond, I, 556. An account of Sullivan's actions that differs considerably from this one is Christopher Ward, *The Delaware Continentals, 1776–1783* (Wilmington, Del., 1941), pp. 509–12. Ward accepts Burke's charges.

53. John Marshall, *The Life of George Washington, Commander in Chief of the American Forces . . . and First President of the United States* (2 vols., rev. ed., Philadelphia, 1850), I, 158–59.

V: GERMANTOWN TO VALLEY FORGE

1. *Journals of the Continental Congress,* VIII, 742.

2. James Lovell to William Whipple, September 17, 1777, Burnett, *Letters,* II, 496; Sullivan to Alexander McDougall, January 27, 1781, Hammond, III, 271–72.

3. *Journals of the Continental Congress,* VIII, 727*n.*

4. Washington to President of Congress, September 15, 1777,

Fitzpatrick, IX, 228–29; James Lovell to William Whipple, September 17, 1777, Burnett, *Letters,* II, 496; *Journals of the Continental Congress,* VIII, 749–50.

5. Washington to Sullivan, September 20, 1777, Fitzpatrick, IX, 242.

6. Adam Stephen to Sullivan, September 20, 1777, Hammond, I, 456; Major William Willcocks to Sullivan, September 25, 1777, *ibid.,* I, 457.

7. Matthias Ogden to Sullivan, n.d., *ibid.,* I, 459–60.

8. Sullivan to Hancock, September 27, 1777, *ibid.,* I, 460.

9. *Ibid.,* I, 462.

10. Sullivan to John Adams, September 28, 1777, *ibid.,* I, 471.

11. Washington to William Heath, October 8, 1777, Fitzpatrick, IX, 331*n.*; Sullivan to Meshech Weare, October 25, 1777, Hammond, I, 543; letter of William Smallwood, October 9, 1777, *The Pennsylvania Magazine of History and Biography,* I (1877), 401.

12. Alfred C. Lambdin, "Battle of Germantown," *The Pennsylvania Magazine of History and Biography,* I (1877), 370–75; Douglas S. Freeman, *George Washington* (6 vols., New York, 1948–54), IV, 502–3.

13. Howe to Germain, October 10, 1777, Henry B. Dawson, *Battles of the United States* (2 vols., New York, 1858), I, 330.

14. Freeman, *George Washington,* IV, 505, offers this supposition and it seems plausible.

15. Wilkinson, *Memoirs,* I, 362*n.*

16. Lambdin, "Battle of Germantown," pp. 371–72, 372*n.*

17. This was essentially the plan, although Washington's general orders of October 3, 1777 (Fitzpatrick, IX, 307–8), and his report to Congress of October 5, 1777 (*ibid.,* IX, 308–9), differ as to Sullivan's route. Where there is a discrepancy, it seems advisable to follow the report. Sullivan's account is in closer agreement with Washington's report than with the general orders; Sullivan to Weare, October 25, 1777, Hammond, I, 542–43; Thomas Paine to Benjamin Franklin, May 16, 1778, *The Pennsylvania Magazine of History and Biography,* II (1878), 288.

18. Sullivan to Weare, October 25, 1777, Hammond, I, 544; general orders, October 3, 1777, Fitzpatrick, IX, 307; Washington to President of Congress, October 5, 1777, *ibid.,* IX, 309; Lambdin, "Battle of Germantown," p. 377*n.*

19. An anonymous letter, October 5, 1777, in Clinton, *Public*

Papers, II, 368, says Conway opened the attack at 5:50 A.M. Another source says Sullivan began the attack at 5:00 A.M.; see unknown correspondent to Alexander McDougall, n.d., McDougall Papers, Box 3, in NYHS.

20. Sullivan to Weare, October 25, 1777, Hammond, I, 544–45. This is the source usually employed for the events on the right. Sullivan stated he sent Wayne east of the road since Greene had not yet come up, and the regiments to the west since Armstrong had not come up. Usually this has been interpreted to mean that Greene and Armstrong were to have cooperated with Sullivan, but study of Washington's plan, as given in the general orders, October 3, 1777, Fitzpatrick, IX, 307–8, indicates no such intention. Distances were too great. Sullivan simply meant that he was obliged to make these dispositions since Greene and Armstrong had not as yet opened the attack in the quarters to which they had been directed. For elaboration, see Lambdin, "Battle of Germantown," pp. 378–79*n*. The footnotes in the Lambdin article are the work of Frederick D. Stone who makes as clear as possible a number of crucial and complicated factors.

21. Anthony Wayne to Polly Wayne, October 6, 1777, Charles J. Stillé, *Major-General Wayne and the Pennsylvania Line in the Continental Army* (Philadelphia, 1893), p. 95.

22. Sullivan to Weare, October 25, 1777, Hammond, I, 545; Freeman, *George Washington,* IV, 508–9; Lambdin, "Battle of Germantown," pp. 380–81*n*.

23. Letter of Timothy Pickering, August 23, 1826, in Samuel Hazard, *The Register of Pennsylvania,* I, No. 4 (January 26, 1828); Lambdin, "Battle of Germantown," pp. 380–81*n*. For validity of Pickering as a source, see Freeman, *George Washington,* IV, 505*n*.

24. "Journal of Captain Frederick von Munchhausen," *The Pennsylvania Magazine of History and Biography,* XVI (1892), 198; letter of British officer, October 10, 1777, *ibid.,* XI (1887), 112.

25. Sullivan to Weare, October 25, 1777, Hammond, I, 546; Wayne to Polly Wayne, October 6, 1777, Stillé, *Major-General Wayne,* p. 95.

26. Howe to Clinton, October 8, 1777, cited in Freeman, *George Washington,* IV, 511.

27. Sullivan to Weare, October 25, 1777, Hammond, I, 546; Sullivan to John Langdon, November 9, 1777, *ibid.,* I, 576.

28. Sullivan to Weare, October 25, 1777, Hammond, I, 547; Lambdin, "Battle of Germantown," p. 389*n*.

29. Sullivan to Weare, October 25, 1777, Hammond, I, 547.

30. Walter Stewart to Horatio Gates, October 12, 1777, *The Pennsylvania Magazine of History and Biography*, I (1877), 400; letter of William Smallwood, October 9, 1777, *ibid.*, I (1877), 402; Adam Stephen to Washington, October 7, 1777, Sparks, *Writings of George Washington*, V, 468.

31. George W. Greene, *The Life of Nathanael Greene* (3 vols., New York, 1867–71), I, 476.

32. Lambdin, "Battle of Germantown," p. 379*n*.

33. Washington to President of Congress, October 7, 1777, Fitzpatrick, IX, 320. This is disputed by Freeman who claims Howe's report gives no such indication; Freeman, *George Washington*, IV, 517*n*.

34. Louis du Portail to Washington, December 3, 1777, *The Pennsylvania Magazine of History and Biography*, XXI (1897), 67.

35. "Statement of Battle of Germantown," n.d., Hammond, I, 567; Washington to President of Congress, October 5, 1777, Fitzpatrick, IX, 311.

36. "Findings of the Court of Inquiry," Hammond, I, 531–32; general orders, October 16, 1777, Fitzpatrick, IX, 380.

37. Sullivan to Hancock, October 17, 1777, Hammond, I, 539.

38. *Journals of the Continental Congress*, IX, 822–23.

39. Thomas Burke to Sullivan, October 12, 1777, Hammond, I, 535–36.

40. Washington to Sullivan, October 24, 1777, Fitzpatrick, IX, 425–26.

41. Rush, "Historical Notes," p. 147.

42. "Gen. Thomas Conway's Statement," September 20, 1777, Hammond, I, 555–56.

43. Sullivan to John Adams, November 10, 1777, *ibid.*, I, 577.

44. Recent students have concluded, insofar as the vagueness of the evidence allows, that no cabal existed. They will only say that there was a faction, both within and without Congress, that was dissatisfied with the Commander, but that it had no intention of removing him from command. See Edmund C. Burnett, *The Continental Congress* (New York, 1941), p. 279; Bernhard Knollenberg, *Washington and the Revolution: a Reappraisal* (New York, 1940), pp. 66–67; Kenneth Rossman, *Thomas Mifflin and the Politics of the American Revolution* (Chapel Hill, N. C., 1952), pp. 116–39. Freeman, *George Washington*, IV, 606–11, draws no definite conclusion, but he indicates that Washington always considered there was

a cabal lined up against him, and that he spared no efforts to scotch its rise.

45. "Protest of General Officers to Congress," December 31, 1777, Hammond, I, 606–8; Sullivan to Washington, December 30, 1777, January 2, 1778, *ibid.*, I, 605–6; II, 1.

46. Sullivan to Henry Laurens, January 20, 1778, *ibid.*, II, 16.

47. Sullivan to Washington, December 26, 1777, *ibid.*, I, 603.

48. Sullivan to Washington, February, 1778, *ibid.*, II, 17–18.

49. *Ibid.*, II, 21; Washington to Sullivan, February 14, 1778, Fitzpatrick, X, 460.

50. Sullivan to Washington, March 2, 1778, Hammond, II, 27.

51. *Ibid.*, II, 28.

52. Washington to Sullivan, March 6, 1778, Fitzpatrick, XI, 32.

53. Washington to Sullivan, March 10, 1778, *ibid.*, XI, 57–58.

54. *Journals of the Continental Congress*, X, 47, 94, 188; Freeman, *George Washington*, IV, 613; Washington to Committee from Congress, March 6, 1778, Fitzpatrick, XI, 31.

VI: PREPARATION FOR CONFLICT

1. Sullivan to Nicholas Cook, March 26, 1778, Hammond, II, 30–31.

2. Mackenzie, *Diary*, I, 268.

3. Providence *Gazette*, April 18, 1778; Resolution of Rhode Island Council of War, Hammond, II, 34.

4. Sullivan to Thomas Burke, April 18, 1778, *ibid.*, II, 35.

5. Robert Pigot to Sullivan, April 24, 1778, *ibid.*, II, 37–38.

6. Sullivan to Pigot, April 27, 1778, *ibid.*, II, 40.

7. Sullivan to Washington, May 1, 1778, *ibid.*, II, 44–45.

8. Sullivan to Henry Laurens, May 3, 1778, *ibid.*, II, 46–47.

9. Sullivan to Jeremiah Wadsworth, May 9, 1778, Jeremiah Wadsworth Papers, Box 126, in CHS.

10. Court of Inquiry Records, March 1–4, 1779, George Washington Papers, XCIX, 40–44, in LC.

11. Henry Laurens to Washington, July 11, 1778, Burnett, *Letters*, III, 324–25.

12. Washington to Sullivan, July 17, 1778, Fitzpatrick, XII, 184–85.

13. Sullivan to William Heath, July 18, 1778, Hammond, II, 92; Sullivan to Meshech Weare, July 22, 1778, *ibid.*, II, 97. Official

British figures gave 5,789 as the size of the force as of August 15, 1778; Sparks, *Writings of George Washington*, V, 543.

14. Sullivan to Jeremiah Powell, July 24, 1778, Hammond, II, 107.

15. Washington to Sullivan, July 22, 1778, Fitzpatrick, XII, 202.

16. Washington to President of Congress, July 22, 1778, *ibid.*, XII, 211.

17. Lafayette to Sullivan, July 22, 1778, Hammond, II, 102.

18. Greene to Sullivan, July 23, 1778, *ibid.*, II, 103–4.

19. *Ibid.*, II, 104.

20. See Sullivan's letters to Jonathan Trumbull, Jeremiah Powell, and Meshech Weare, July 22–24, 1778, *ibid.*, II, 102 ff.

21. Sullivan to Heath, July 24, 1778, *ibid.*, II, 106.

22. See letters between Sullivan and Heath, July 25, 1778, *ibid.*, II, 115–19.

23. Sullivan to D'Estaing, July 25, 1778, *ibid.*, III, 640–44.

24. *Ibid.*, II, 114.

25. Sullivan to Jeremiah Wadsworth, August 4, 1778, Jeremiah Wadsworth Papers, Box 126, in CHS.

26. Sullivan to Jeremiah Powell, July 25, 1778, Hammond, II, 115.

27. Heath to Sullivan, July 29, 1778, *ibid.*, II, 144.

28. Washington to Thomas Tillotson, July 26, 1778, Fitzpatrick, XII, 235.

29. Sullivan to Heath, July 29, 1778, Hammond, II, 142.

30. Sullivan to Heath, July 26, 1778, *ibid.*, II, 126; Sullivan to Heath, July 29, 1778, *ibid.*, II, 143.

31. Sullivan to Silas Talbot, July 27, 1778, Rhode Island Historical Society *Collections*, XXV, No. 4 (1932), 115; Sullivan to John Glover, August 1, 1778, William P. Upham, *A Memoir of General Glover of Marblehead* (Salem, Mass., 1863), p. 34.

32. Sullivan to Washington, July 26, 1778, Hammond, II, 126–27.

33. Washington to Sullivan, July 27, 1778, Fitzpatrick, XII, 237–38.

34. Sullivan to Heath, July 29, 1778, Hammond, II, 143.

35. George Bancroft, *History of the United States of America* (6 vols., Centenary ed., Boston, 1876), VI, 150, calls this postponing of action a "whim" on Sullivan's part—an unfair charge.

36. Weare to Sullivan, July 28, 1778, Hammond, II, 131–32. William Whipple observed, "if we send any more soldiers I believe they must be females we may spare a considerable number of that

sort, & have enough left for Breeders." Whipple to Josiah Bartlett, August 2, 1778, Emmet Collection, No. 1543, in NYPL.

37. Massachusetts Council to Sullivan, July 28, 1778, Hammond, II, 132–33; Trumbull to Sullivan, July 25, 27, 29, 1778, *ibid.*, II, 121, 130–31, 148–49; George W. Greene, *The Life of Nathanael Greene* (3 vols., New York, 1867–71), II, 108; Washington to Sullivan, July 28, 1778, Fitzpatrick, XII, 243–44.

38. Sullivan to Jeremiah Powell, July 28, 1778, Hammond, II, 134.

39. John Laurens to Washington, August 4, 1778, Papers of the Continental Congress, No. 152, VI, folio 226, in NA; D'Estaing to Sullivan, July 30, 31, 1778, Hammond, II, 151, 154.

40. D'Estaing to Sullivan, July 30, 1778, *ibid.*, II, 151–52; John Laurens to Henry Laurens, August 4, 1778, Laurens, *Army Correspondence*, pp. 214–15; John Laurens to Washington, August 4, 1778, Papers of the Continental Congress, No. 152, VI, folios 228–29, in NA.

41. D'Estaing to Sullivan, July 30, 1778, Hammond, II, 152.

42. D'Estaing to Washington, August 3, 1778, Sparks, *Correspondence of the American Revolution*, II, 172.

43. John Laurens to Washington, August 4, 1778, Papers of the Continental Congress, No. 152, VI, folios 229–30, in NA.

44. *Ibid.;* John Laurens to Henry Laurens, August 4, 1778, Laurens, *Army Correspondence*, pp. 214–15; Mackenzie, *Diary*, II, 320, 322. There is a discrepancy as to when the French landed on Conanicut. Mackenzie says the French landed on July 30 whereas Laurens says the first party went ashore on the 31st.

45. Sullivan to Henry Laurens, August 1, 1778, Hammond, II, 166–67.

46. Washington to Sullivan, July 31, 1778, Fitzpatrick, XII, 250–51.

47. D'Estaing to Sullivan, August 4, 1778, Hammond, II, 173; see also John Laurens to Henry Laurens, August 22, 1778, Laurens, *Army Correspondence*, pp. 217–18.

48. Louis R. Gottschalk, *Lafayette Joins the American Army* (Chicago, 1937), pp. 247–48.

49. John Laurens to Henry Laurens, August 22, 1778, Laurens, *Army Correspondence*, p. 218.

50. John Laurens to Washington, August 4, 1778, Papers of the Continental Congress, No. 152, VI, folios, 237–39, in NA.

51. Sullivan to Henry Laurens, August 6, 1778, Hammond, II, 182; Gibbs, "Major Gibbs Diary," p. 734; Sullivan to Heath, August 6, 1778, Hammond, II, 182.

52. D'Estaing to Sullivan, August 7, 1778, Hammond, II, 184.

53. *Ibid.*

54. "A Diary of the Revolution," p. 105; John Laurens to Henry Laurens, August 22, 1778, Laurens, *Army Correspondence*, p. 219. A detailed "Plan of Battle" is in the United States Military Academy Library, West Point, N. Y.

55. Mackenzie, *Diary*, II, 336; Pigot to Clinton, August 31, 1778, Henry B. Dawson, *Battles of the United States* (2 vols., New York, 1858), I, 442; Sullivan to Heath, August 11, 1778, Hammond, II, 198.

56. Sullivan to William Greene, August 12, 1778, *ibid.*, II, 199. D'Estaing placed Sullivan's numbers at 2,000, an underestimation, when he crossed from Tiverton; D'Estaing to Secrétaire d'Etat de la Marine, November 5, 1778, Henri Doniol, *Histoire de la participation de la France à l'establissement des Etats-Unis d'Amérique* (6 vols., Paris, 1884–92), III¹, 451. An aide to Lafayette said Sullivan had 2,000 to 3,000; *ibid.*, III¹, 375.

57. Sullivan to Henry Laurens, August 10, 1778, Hammond, II, 191.

58. D'Estaing to Congress, August 26, 1778, Sparks, *Writings of George Washington*, VI, 30n.

59. Almy, "Mrs. Almy's Journal," p. 27; D'Estaing to Congress, August 26, 1778, George Washington Papers, LXXXII, 67–76, in LC.

60. John J. Meng, *D'Estaing's American Expedition, 1778–1779* (Franco-American Pamphlet Series, No. 8; New York, 1936), p. 5.

61. D'Estaing to Congress, August 26, 1778, Sparks, *Writings of George Washington*, VI, 31n. Sparks gives just a portion of this important letter.

VII: CONFLICT AND CONTROVERSY

1. Sullivan to Washington, August 10, 1778, Hammond, II, 192.

2. Sullivan to Henry Laurens, August 10, 1778, *ibid.*, II, 191.

3. *Ibid.*, II, 192.

4. Rhode Island Historical Society *Proceedings*, 1877–78, p. 90.

5. Gibbs, "Major Gibbs Diary," pp. 734–35; Heath to Sullivan, August 11, 1778, Hammond, II, 197.

6. Sullivan to William Greene, August 13, 1778, *ibid.*, II, 203.

7. *Ibid.*

8. *Ibid.;* Sullivan to Washington, August 13, 1778, *ibid.*, II, 207.

9. Sullivan to William Greene, August 13, 1778, *ibid.*, II, 203–4.

10. Sullivan to Henry Laurens, August 14, 1778, *ibid.*, II, 213; Gibbs, "Major Gibbs Diary," pp. 734–35.

11. William Greene to Sullivan, August 14, 1778, Hammond, II, 209; Greene to Jeremiah Powell, August 15, 1778, Rhode Island Historical Society *Collections*, VI (1867), 203–4.

12. William P. Upham, *A Memoir of General Glover of Marblehead* (Salem, Mass., 1863), pp. 48–49.

13. "Diary of Manasseh Cutler," quoted in Edwin M. Stone, *Our French Allies . . . in the Great War of the American Revolution* (Providence, 1884), pp. xvi–xvii.

14. Sullivan to Heath, August 11, 1778, Hammond, II, 197.

15. Sullivan to William Greene, August 15, 1778, *ibid.*, II, 214–15.

16. *Ibid.*, II, 220.

17. Nathanael Greene to wife, August 16, 1778, George W. Greene, *The Life of Nathanael Greene* (3 vols., New York, 1867–71), II, 116.

18. Sullivan to Washington, August 17, 1778, Papers of the Continental Congress, No. 160, folios 153–54, in NA.

19. Sullivan to Henry Laurens, August 19, 1778, Hammond, II, 237.

20. An American deserter informed the British of this fact on August 24, 1778; Mackenzie, *Diary*, II, 371.

21. Sullivan to William Greene, August 19, 1778, Hammond, II, 232–33.

22. Gibbs, "Major Gibbs Diary," p. 735.

23. Massachusetts Council to Sullivan, August 18, 19, 1778, Hammond, II, 230, 236; William Greene to Sullivan, August 17, 1778, *ibid.*, II, 228; Samuel G. Arnold, *History of the State of Rhode Island and Providence Plantations* (2 vols., New York, 1859–60), II, 424.

24. Comte de Cambis to Sullivan, August 20, 1778, Hammond, II, 237–38.

25. Sullivan to Washington, August 21, 1778, Papers of the Continental Congress, No. 160, folios 162–64, in NA; see Lafayette to Washington, August 25, 1778, Sparks, *Correspondence of the*

American Revolution, II, 184; John Laurens to Washington, August 23, 1778, *ibid.,* II, 180.

26. John Laurens to Henry Laurens, August 22, 1778, Laurens, *Army Correspondence,* p. 221; Sullivan's letter to D'Estaing has not been located, but it is referred to in Sullivan to Washington, August 23, 1778, Hammond, II, 264.

27. Sullivan and officers to D'Estaing, August 22, 1778, *ibid.,* II, 243–46; Lafayette to Washington, August 25, 1778, Sparks, *Correspondence of the American Revolution,* II, 184.

28. Sullivan's questions of August 23, 1778, are in Papers of the Continental Congress, No. 152, VI, folio 309, in NA; the officers' opinions are in Hammond, II, 248–63.

29. Orders of August 24, 1778, Hammond, III, 645.

30. Lafayette to Washington, August 25, 1778, Sparks, *Correspondence of the American Revolution,* II, 185; Joshua Longstreet to unknown, December 3, 1778, as cited in Louis R. Gottschalk, *Lafayette Joins the American Army* (Chicago, 1937), p. 258.

31. "Glover's Orderly Book," quoted in Douglas S. Freeman, *George Washington* (6 vols., New York, 1948–54), V, 71*n.*

32. George W. Cullum, *Historical Sketch of the Fortification Defenses of Narraganset Bay* (Washington, D. C., 1884), pp. 13–15. Mackenzie said the ground on the left was favorable for an attack; Mackenzie, *Diary,* II, 359–60.

33. Sullivan to Henry Laurens, August 16, 1778, Hammond, II, 220; Sullivan to New Hampshire Committee of Safety, August 26, 1778, *ibid.,* II, 267–69.

34. Gibbs, "Major Gibbs Diary," p. 736; Nathanael Greene to Heath, August 27, 1778, Greene, *The Life of Nathanael Greene,* II, 125; Washington to Sullivan, August 22, 1778, Fitzpatrick, XII, 350–51; Sullivan to Washington, August 29, 1778, Hammond, II, 275; Sullivan to President of Congress, August 31, 1778, *ibid.,* II, 281–82. In these last two references Sullivan gives different dates, August 26 and August 28, for the meeting of the Council which decided to move the army. Probably a tentative decision was made early but not reaffirmed until the 28th.

35. Sullivan to President of Congress, August 31, 1778, *ibid.,* II, 282.

36. Nathanael Greene to Washington, August 31, 1778, Greene, *The Life of Nathanael Greene,* II, 130.

37. Pigot to Clinton, August 31, 1778, Henry B. Dawson, *Battles of the United States* (2 vols., New York, 1858), I, 443.

38. Sullivan to President of Congress, August 31, 1778, Hammond, II, 282; Nathanael Greene to John Brown, September 6, 1778, *ibid.*, II, 316–17; Nathanael Greene to Washington, August 31, 1778, Greene, *The Life of Nathanael Greene*, II, 130.

39. Sullivan to Washington, August 29, 1778, Hammond, II, 275–76; *New-Hampshire Gazette*, September 8, 1778, quoted in Moore, *Diary of the American Revolution*, II, 88–89; Trumbull, *Autobiography, Reminiscences and Letters*, pp. 52–53.

40. Sullivan to President of Congress, August 31, 1778, Hammond, II, 283.

41. *Ibid.*, II, 283–84.

42. *Ibid.*, II, 283; Nathanael Greene to Washington, August 31, 1778, Greene, *The Life of Nathanael Greene*, II, 130.

43. Thomas C. Amory, "The Siege of Newport," *The Rhode Island Historical Magazine*, V (1884–85), 127.

44. Sullivan to President of Congress, August 31, 1778, Hammond, II, 283; Nathanael Greene to Washington, August 31, 1778, Greene, *The Life of Nathanael Greene*, II, 131. Mackenzie said the Americans were forced from both Quaker Hill and the swamp in front of Turkey Hill, a hill on the western side of Butts Hill; Mackenzie, *Diary*, II, 383.

45. Pigot to Clinton, August 31, 1778, Dawson, *Battles of the United States*, I, 443, gives no indication of a retreat.

46. Sullivan to Washington, August 29, 1778, Hammond, II, 275; Sullivan to President of Congress, August 31, 1778, *ibid.*, II, 284–85; Sullivan to Washington, August 31, 1778, *ibid.*, II, 287; Pigot's return for August 29, 1778, *Rhode Island Historical Tracts*, VI (1878), 93*n*.

47. Washington to Sullivan, August 28, 1778, *Fitzpatrick*, XII, 368–69.

48. Sullivan to President of Congress, August 31, 1778, Hammond, II, 285; Lafayette to Washington, September 1, 1778, Sparks, *Correspondence of the American Revolution*, II, 199; D'Estaing to Sullivan, August 29, 1778, George Washington Papers, LXXXII, 141–42, in LC.

49. Sullivan to President of Congress, August 31, 1778, Hammond, II, 285; Sullivan to Washington, August 31, 1778, *ibid.*, II,

287; Pigot to Clinton, August 31, 1778, Dawson, *Battles of the United States,* I, 144.

50. Sullivan to President of Congress, August 31, 1778, Hammond, II, 285; Sullivan to Washington, August 31, 1778, *ibid.,* II, 287.

51. Sullivan to President of Congress, August 31, 1778, *ibid.,* II, 286.

52. Washington to Lafayette, September 1, 1778, Fitzpatrick, XII, 383.

53. *Journals of the Continental Congress,* XII, 894.

54. D'Estaing to Sullivan, August 30, 1778, Hammond, II, 278; D'Estaing to Greene, October 1, 1778, Greene, *The Life of Nathanael Greene,* II, 148–49.

55. D'Estaing to Secrétaire d'Etat de la Marine, November 5, 1778, Henri Doniol, *Histoire de la participation de la France à l'establissement des Etats Unis d'Amérique* (6 vols., Paris, 1884–92), III¹, 449–50.

56. William Stewart to William Goddard, September 10, 1778, Military Papers, V, 35, in Rhode Island Historical Society.

57. Greene to John Brown, September 6, 1778, Hammond, II, 317.

58. Lafayette to Washington, September 1, 1778, Sparks, *Correspondence of the American Revolution,* II, 198.

59. Joseph Reed to Greene, November 5, 1778, Charles Lee, *The Lee Papers,* III, 245.

60. Reed to unknown addressee, September 4, 1778, Gratz Collection, Case 4, Box 14, in PHS.

61. Some years later Rhode Island's Governor Arthur Fenner commented that no station of importance in the United States could be so easily defended against a mere land army as Rhode Island proper. Sullivan's experience caused Fenner to offer this opinion. Fenner to James McHenry, June 4, 1789, Letters from the Governor, MS vol. in Rhode Island Archives, Providence.

62. Washington to John Augustine Washington, September 23, 1778, Fitzpatrick, XII, 488.

63. Greene to Sullivan, October 24, 1778, Hammond, II, 404.

64. Greene to Washington, September 19, 1778, Greene, *The Life of Nathanael Greene,* II, 146.

65. Sullivan to Washington, November 4, 1778, Hammond, II,

422. In a letter to Alexander McDougall Sullivan said that Gates was a man of restless ambition, and that in this respect he resembled Caesar, but that he lacked Caesar's bravery. He then complained that he thought Gates would be after his post, but that he would never gain it even if Congress so resolved. Sullivan to McDougall, November 27, 1778, Alexander McDougall Papers, Box 3, in NYHS.

66. Sullivan to Jeremiah Powell, October 17, 1778, Hammond, II, 392–93; Massachusetts Council to Sullivan, October 21, 1778, *ibid.,* II, 398–99.

67. Sullivan to Henry Laurens, October 26, 1778, *ibid.,* II, 408.

68. *Journals of the Continental Congress,* XII, 1177.

69. Court of Inquiry Papers, March 1–4, 1779, George Washington Papers, XCIX, 40–44, in LC; Solomon Southwick to Peter Colt, October 31, 1778, Jeremiah Wadsworth Papers, Box 127, in CHS; Colt to Sullivan, November 6, 1778, Hammond, II, 423; Colt to George Clinton, November 9, 1778, Clinton, *Public Papers,* IV, 257–59; Sullivan to Colt, November 10, 1778, Hammond, II, 426; Colt to Sullivan, November 14, 1778, Jeremiah Wadsworth Papers, Box 127, in CHS.

70. Sullivan to Washington, November 20, 23, 27, 29, 1778, Hammond, II, 438–40, 443–44, 446–47, 448–49; Washington to Sullivan, November 18, 1778, Fitzpatrick, XIII, 277–78.

71. Wadsworth to Washington, November 25, 1778, Jeremiah Wadsworth Papers, Box 127, in CHS.

72. Washington to Sullivan, November 26, 1778, Fitzpatrick, XIII, 337.

73. Sullivan to Wadsworth, December 1, 1778, Jeremiah Wadsworth Papers, Box 127, in CHS.

74. Wadsworth to Colt, December 4, 1778, *ibid.*

75. Wadsworth to Sullivan, December 18, 1778, *ibid.;* Sullivan to Wadsworth, January 10, 1779, *ibid.*

76. Sullivan to Jonathan Trumbull, February 17, 1779, Hammond, II, 514–15; Trumbull to Sullivan, February 18, 1779, *ibid.,* II, 516.

77. Washington to Wadsworth, March 3, 1779, Fitzpatrick, XIV, 183–84.

78. Court of Inquiry Papers, March 1–4, 1779, George Washington Papers, XCIX, 40–44, in LC.

79. Colt to Wadsworth, December 27, 1778, Jeremiah Wadsworth Papers, Box 127, in CHS.

80. Wadsworth to Washington, March 15, 1779, George Washington Papers, C, 87, in LC.

81. Greene to Wadsworth, March 25, 1779, in envelope of Nathanael Greene MS letters, in CHS.

82. Gates to Sullivan, March 16, 1779, Hammond, II, 534; Washington to Sullivan, March 6, 1779, Fitzpatrick, XIV, 201.

83. Washington to Gates, March 6, 1779, *ibid.*, XIV, 198–201. Gates received the letter on March 15, and the next day refused the assignment; *ibid.*, XIV, 200*n*.

84. Sullivan to Gates, March 17, 1779, Hammond, II, 536.

85. Sullivan to Gates, March 23, 1779, *ibid.*, II, 542.

86. Jeremiah Hill to Sullivan, March 25, 1779, *ibid.*, II, 552.

87. Providence *Gazette,* April 3, 1779, quoted in *ibid.*, II, 557.

VIII: PLANNING FOR THE INDIAN CAMPAIGN

1. Washington to Sullivan, March 6, 1779, Fitzpatrick, XIV, 201.

2. Washington to President of Congress, November 11, 1778, *ibid.*, XIII, 223–44.

3. Washington to President of Congress, December 13, 1778, *ibid.*, XIII, 390–91.

4. Washington to Committee of Conference, January 13, 1779, *ibid.*, XIV, 6.

5. For letters seeking intelligence, see *ibid.*, XIV, 45–46, 58–62, 74–76, 94–98, 114–18.

6. *Journals of the Continental Congress,* XIII, 252; Washington to George Clinton, March 4, 1779, Fitzpatrick, XIV, 189.

7. Washington to John Armstrong, May 18, 1779, *ibid.*, XV, 99.

8. Washington to John Jay, April 14, 1779, *ibid.*, XIV, 384–85.

9. Greene to Washington, April 26, 1779, Sparks, *Correspondence of the American Revolution,* II, 280.

10. Alexander Flick argues that Washington wished to secure the vast and rich lands to the west for the young nation. Flick, *Sullivan-Clinton Campaign,* p. 10.

11. Washington to Schuyler, March 21, 1779, Fitzpatrick, XIV, 268–70.

12. Flick, *Sullivan-Clinton Campaign,* pp. 10, 12.

13. See Washington's questions to Schuyler, February 11, 1779, Fitzpatrick, XIV, 94–98; also his questions of March, answered by General Hand, and Colonels John Cox, William Patterson, and

Charles Stewart, in Flick, "New Sources on the Sullivan-Clinton Campaign," pp. 195–207; also a second questionnaire, *ibid.*, pp. 208–10.

14. Sullivan to Washington, April 15, 1779, Hammond, III, 2.

15. *Ibid.*, III, 3.

16. *Ibid.*, III, 1–3; see Schuyler to Washington, March 1, 1779, George Washington Papers, XCIX, 31–38, in LC, a letter which Sullivan certainly saw. Schuyler estimated the enemy strength at 2,050, and advised that 3,000 men attack by way of Albany, and 500 by way of Wyoming. Efforts should be concentrated against the Senecas.

17. Sullivan to Washington, April 15, 1779, Hammond, III, 4.

18. Sullivan to Washington, April 16, 1779, *ibid.*, III, 6.

19. Washington to President of Congress, August 15, 1779, Fitzpatrick, XVI, 99.

20. Sullivan to John Jay, July 21, 1779, Hammond, III, 80.

21. Washington to Sullivan, April 29, 1779, Fitzpatrick, XIV, 462–63.

22. Wadsworth to Nathanael Greene, April 23, 1779 (photostat in Connecticut State Library, Hartford).

23. Greene to Wadsworth, April 30, 1779, in envelope of Nathanael Greene MS letters, in CHS.

24. Flick, *Sullivan-Clinton Campaign*, p. 13.

25. Washington to Daniel Brodhead, April 21, 1779, Fitzpatrick, XIV, 421–22. Brodhead, however, did undertake an expedition.

26. Washington to Sullivan, May 4, 1779, *ibid.*, XIV, 492–93.

27. Sullivan to Washington, May 8, 1779, Hammond, III, 14–16; Sullivan to Jay, July 21, 1779, *ibid.*, III, 81; Sullivan to Hand, May 8, 1779, *ibid.*, III, 16.

28. Sullivan to Joseph Reed, May 11, 1779, *ibid.*, III, 19; Sullivan to Washington, May 12, 1779, *ibid.*, III, 20; Robert Hooper to Nathanael Greene, May 15, 18, 1779; Hooper to Sullivan, May 18, 1779, Nathanael Greene Papers, VII, No. 101, V, Nos. 11 and 15, in American Philosophical Society.

29. Sullivan to Jay, July 21, 1779, Hammond, III, 82, in which reference is made to Claiborne letter of May 19 to Sullivan; Claiborne to Hand, May 19, 1779, *The Pennsylvania Magazine of History and Biography*, LII (1928), 174–75.

30. Board of War to Sullivan, May 20, 1779, Hammond, III,

28–29; Board of War to Reed, May 19, 1779, *Pennsylvania Archives*, VII (1853), 418.

31. Reed to Sullivan, May 21, 1779, Hammond, III, 28–29.

32. Hand to Sullivan, May 20, 1779, *ibid.*, III, 26–27.

33. Sullivan to Hand, May 22, 1779, Charles F. Jenkinson Collection, in PHS.

34. Hamilton to Nathanael Greene, May 22, 1779, Nathanael Greene Papers, V, No. 59, in American Philosophical Society.

35. Sullivan to Washington, May 31, 1779, Hammond, III, 47–48.

36. Washington to Sullivan, May 31, 1779, Fitzpatrick, XV, 190–91.

37. Sullivan to Washington, June 2, 1779, Papers of the Continental Congress, No. 169, V, folios 540–41, in NA; Washington to Sullivan, June 4, 1779, Fitzpatrick, XV, 226–27.

38. Armstrong to Gates, May 22, 1779, Burnett, *Letters*, IV, 226–27.

39. Sullivan to Hand, June 10, 1779, Hammond, III, 59–60.

40. This letter presumably is lost, but reference is made to it in James Clinton to George Clinton, June 15, 1779, Wright, *The Sullivan Expedition of 1779*, in *Studies in History*, No. 6, p. 34.

41. Sullivan to Washington, June 12, 1779, Hammond, III, 60.

42. "Journal of Lt. Col. Henry Dearborn," Cook, *Journals of the Military Expedition*, p. 63. Although this valuable compilation was issued over the name of Frederick Cook, Secretary of State, the actual compiler was George S. Conover. Quite obviously some of the diarists copied others' accounts, but there is no reason why the authenticity of the journals should be questioned.

43. *Ibid.*, p. 63.

44. "Journal of Dr. Jabez Campfield," *ibid.*, pp. 52–53.

45. Maxwell to Elias Boudinot, July 2, 1779, Gratz Collection, Case 4, Box 13, in PHS.

46. Sullivan to Washington, June 25, 1779, Papers of the Continental Congress, No. 169, VI, folios 70–71, in NA.

47. Sullivan to Stewart, June 26, 1779, Jeremiah Wadsworth Papers, Box 128, in CHS.

48. Greene to Hooper, June 26, 1779, Nathanael Greene Papers, VI, No. 95, in American Philosophical Society.

49. Stewart to Sullivan, July 6, 1779, Stewart Papers, in Houghton Library, Harvard University.

50. Sullivan to Stewart, July 11, 1779, Stewart Papers, in Houghton Library, Harvard University.

51. Sullivan to James Clinton, June 27, 1779, in PHS; Sullivan to Washington, July 10, 1779, Hammond, III, 76; "Journal of Major James Norris," Cook, *Journals of the Military Expedition*, p. 225.

52. Sullivan to Washington, June 29, 1779, Hammond, III, 65–66.

53. Washington to Sullivan, July 1, 1779, Fitzpatrick, XV, 349.

54. Washington to Sullivan, July 5, 1779, *ibid.*, XV, 370–72.

55. Sullivan to Washington, July 10, 1779, Hammond, III, 75–77. The printed version has deletions because of tears in the original letter in the Library of Congress. A complete copy is in the Jeremiah Wadsworth Papers, Box 128, in CHS.

56. Greene to Hooper, July 10, 1779, Nathanael Greene Papers, X, No. 15, in American Philosophical Society.

57. Samuel Kirkland to wife, July 5, 1779, Oscar J. Harvey, *A History of Wilkes-Barre . . . Pennsylvania* (6 vols., Wilkes-Barre, Pa., 1909–30), II, 1191.

58. *Ibid.*

59. *Ibid.*

60. Barber, "Orderly Book," p. 21.

61. Reed to Washington, July 11, 1779, *Pennsylvania Archives*, VII (1853), 556.

62. Sullivan to Jay, July 21, 1779, Hammond, III, 80–84.

63. Washington to Jay, August 15, 1779, Fitzpatrick, XVI, 104.

64. Timothy Pickering to Congress, August 4, 1779, Papers of the Continental Congress, No. 93, folio 283, in NA.

65. "Journal of Serg't Major George Grant," Cook, *Journals of the Military Expedition*, p. 108.

66. Barber, "Orderly Book," pp. 39–44.

67. Sullivan to Henry Laurens, July 26, 1779, Gratz Collection, Case 4, Box 15, in PHS.

68. William Maclay to Reed, July 26, 1779, *Pennsylvania Archives*, VII (1853), pp. 586–87.

69. Sullivan to Pickering, July 26, 1779, Hammond, III, 86.

70. Barber, "Orderly Book," p. 47.

71. *Ibid.*, p. 52.

72. John Cook to Sullivan, July 29, 1779, Wright, *The Sullivan Expedition of 1779*, in *Studies in History*, No. 5, p. 36; extract of a letter to Sullivan from Minisink, July 28, 1779, *ibid.*, pp. 34–35; "Journal of Major James Norris," Cook, *Journals of the Military*

Expedition, p. 227; John McDonnell (sometimes called McDonald) to John Butler, August 5, 1779, Flick, "New Sources on the Sullivan-Clinton Campaign," pp. 276–77; William Maclay to Pennsylvania Council, July 30, 1779, *Pennsylvania Archives,* VII (1853), 597–98.

73. Sullivan to John Cook, July 30, 1779, Hammond, III, 89.

74. Sullivan to Colonel Samuel Hunter, July 30, 1779, *ibid.*

75. Statement of Colonel Matthew Smith, n.d., *Pennsylvania Archives,* VII (1853), 595.

76. Reed to Board of War, August 12, 1779, *ibid.,* VII (1853), 640. George Clinton also was critical. He argued that Sullivan's delay at Wyoming had left the frontiers open to the attacks; Clinton to Dr. Ker (Kerr), July 30, 1779, Wright, *The Sullivan Expedition of 1779,* in *Studies in History,* No. 5, p. 23.

77. Sullivan to Washington, July 30, 1779, Hammond, III, 88.

78. Sullivan to James Clinton, July 30, 1779, *ibid.,* III, 90.

79. Greene to Charles Pettit, July 29, 1779, Nathanael Greene Papers, XI, No. 4, in American Philosophical Society.

IX: THE MARCH AGAINST THE SIX NATIONS

1. It is difficult to ascertain the time of departure. Units apparently were leaving camp throughout the day, but the main body does not seem to have moved until noon, or an hour later. See "Journal of Lt. William Barton," "Journal of Lt. Col. Henry Dearborn," "Journal of Thomas Grant," and "Journal of Rev. William Rogers," in Cook, *Journals of the Military Expedition,* pp. 5, 68, 137, 255. Two diarists say there were only 120 boats, but Proctor claimed there were 214. Elias Dayton placed the number at 130; letter of Elias Dayton, July 27, 1779, Dreer Collection, II, 87, in PHS. Proctor's number probably is too high.

2. "Journal of Rev. William Rogers," Cook, *Journals of the Military Expedition,* p. 255; "Journal of Lt. William Barton," *ibid.,* p. 5.

3. Letter of Elias Dayton, July 27, 1779, Dreer Collection, II, 87, in PHS.

4. Washington to Sullivan, July 29, 1779, Fitzpatrick, XVI, 2; Daniel Brodhead to Joseph Irvine, July 17, 1779, *Pennsylvania Archives,* XII (1856), 138.

5. Washington to Sullivan, August 1, 1779, Fitzpatrick, XVI,

29–31. The Butlers had good information as to the American activities, and reported frequently to Lieutenant Colonel Mason Bolton at Niagara and General Sir Frederick Haldimand at Quebec. See their letters in Flick, "New Sources on the Sullivan-Clinton Campaign," pp. 217–18, 220–24, 265–73.

6. Sullivan to Jay, September 30, 1779, Hammond, III, 134–35.

7. For interesting account that Samuel Wallis of Northumberland County, secretly pro-British, supplied the Pennsylvania Council with false maps of the Indian Country, which in turn were used by Washington, see Carl Van Doren, *Secret History of the American Revolution* (New York, 1941), pp. 217–20. Washington had requested maps from Pennsylvania; Washington to Reed, February 27, 1779, Fitzpatrick, XIV, 159–60. Wallis also claimed that he could send along a person with Sullivan's expedition who would make occasional reports. Van Doren notes that no maps which might have been prepared by Wallis have come to light and that no reports have been uncovered. A spy may have accompanied Sullivan's army. Before the army left Wyoming, Sullivan ordered an inquiry into one report that a certain John Brown with the army was a British spy. No further reference is known to exist; Barber, "Orderly Book," pp. 51–52. Captain Benjamin Lodge accompanied the army as surveyor, and his maps later were of much value. The maps are in the Simeon DeWitt Collection of Robert Erskine's maps and surveys in the New-York Historical Society. (Robert Erskine was geographer to the army.) Copies are in the end pockets of Cook, *Journals of the Military Expedition.*

8. Stewart to Sullivan, June 3, 1779, *The Pennsylvania Magazine of History and Biography*, XXXIII (1909), 358–60.

9. Barber, "Orderly Book," p. 58.

10. "Journal of Dr. Jabez Campfield," in Cook, *Journals of the Military Expedition*, p. 53.

11. Barber, "Orderly Book," p. 59.

12. "Journal of Lt. Col. Adam Hubley," in Cook, *Journals of the Military Expedition*, pp. 149–50. Sheshequin was on the east side of the river across from the present town of Ulster.

13. "Journal of Lt. Col. Henry Dearborn," in *ibid.*, p. 69.

14. "Journal of Lt. Col. Adam Hubley," in *ibid.*, pp. 150–51.

15. Sullivan to President of Congress, August 15, 1779, Hammond, III, 95.

16. *Ibid.* Some writers refer to the Chemung River as the Tioga River.

17. *Ibid.*, p. 96; "Journal of Lt. John Jenkins," in Cook, *Journals of the Military Expedition*, p. 170.

18. Barber, "Orderly Book," pp. 65–66.

19. Sullivan to President of Congress, August 15, 1779, Hammond, III, 96–98; Sullivan to Washington, August 15, 1779, *ibid.*, III, 98–100; "Journal of Lt. Col. Henry Dearborn," in Cook, *Journals of the Military Expedition*, pp. 69–70.

20. "Journal of Major James Norris," in *ibid.*, p. 229.

21. Sullivan to Washington, August 15, 1779, Hammond, III, 99–100.

22. Major Marshall to brother, August 15, 1779, Wright, *The Sullivan Expedition of 1779*, in *Studies in History*, No. 6, p. 46.

23. *Ibid.*, p. 47.

24. Barber's "Orderly Book," pp. 67–68.

25. Sullivan to Washington, August 20, 1779, extract in Wright, *The Sullivan Expedition of 1779*, in *Studies in History*, No. 6, p. 49.

26. A "Return of the troops on the Western Expedition" is in the Papers of the Continental Congress, No. 152, VII, folio 739, in NA. Rank and file for Maxwell's brigade, as of July 10, was 1,137; for Poor's brigade, as of July 10, was 1,101; for Hand's brigade, as of July 17, was 732; and for Clinton's brigade, as of July 9, was 1,475. Total rank and file was 4,445; total rank and file present and fit for duty was 3,799. Adding 404 sergeants, and 266 battalion officers, besides the staff, drums, and fifes, brought the total fit for duty to 4,469.

27. "Journal of Lt. William McKendry," in Cook, *Journals of the Military Expedition*, p. 203; Washington to Sullivan, September 3, 1779, Fitzpatrick, XVI, 222.

28. Sullivan to Shreve, August 24, 1779, Hammond, III, 102.

29. Hand to Jasper Yeates, August 26, 1779, Gore, *Revolutionary Diary*, pp. 32–33.

30. "Journal of Rev. William Rogers," in Cook, *Journals of the Military Expedition*, p. 264.

31. Brodhead proceeded into what is now western New York and returned to Fort Pitt. See Flick, *Sullivan-Clinton Campaign*, p. 14. Wright, *The Sullivan Expedition of 1779*, in *Studies in History*, No. 6, pp. 11–24, has convenient compilation of important docu-

ments on Brodhead's expedition. Van Schaick's raid the previous April on the Onondaga villages, and Brodhead's expedition have been considered part of the Sullivan-Clinton campaign, but as General Sullivan had no personal connection with either venture they are not described here.

32. "Journal of Major James Norris," in Cook, *Journals of the Military Expedition*, p. 231.

33. Butler to Bolton, August 26, 1779, Flick, *Sullivan-Clinton Campaign*, p. 131.

34. "Journal of Lt. Erkuries Beatty," in Cook, *Journals of the Military Expedition*, p. 26.

35. Sullivan to Washington, August 30, 1779, Hammond, III, 107.

36. James Clinton to George Clinton, August 30, 1779, Flick, *Sullivan-Clinton Campaign*, pp. 132–33.

37. Sullivan to Washington, August 30, 1779, Hammond, III, 107–8.

38. *Ibid.*, III, 108–9, for description of the terrain.

39. *Ibid.*, III, 109.

40. "Journal of Lt. Erkuries Beatty," in Cook, *Journals of the Military Expedition*, p. 27.

41. James Clinton to George Clinton, August 30, 1779, Flick, *Sullivan-Clinton Campaign*, pp. 132–33; Sullivan to Washington, August 30, 1779, Hammond, III, 110.

42. "Journal of Lt. Col. Adam Hubley," in Cook, *Journals of the Military Expedition*, p. 156; "Journal of Lt. Col. Henry Dearborn," in *ibid.*, p. 72, places the time later.

43. "Diary of Lt. Robert Parker," in Flick, *Sullivan-Clinton Campaign*, p. 197.

44. "Journal of Lt. Col. Henry Dearborn," in Cook, *Journals of the Military Expedition*, p. 72, gives good description of the fighting in Poor's sector. Other descriptions are in James Clinton to wife, August 30, 1779, in PHS; and in Philip Van Cortlandt, Autobiography, MS vol. in NYPL.

45. Sullivan to Washington, August 30, 1779, Hammond, III, 110. John Butler to Mason Bolton, August 31, 1779, Flick, *Sullivan-Clinton Campaign*, pp. 135–38, indicates that Butler did not anticipate the flanking move, but that he had a hard time persuading the Indians to change their position to meet the threat.

46. Sullivan to Jay, September 30, 1779, Hammond, III, 126.

47. Howard Swiggett, *War Out of Niagara, Walter Butler and the Tory Rangers* (New York, 1933), p. 198.

48. Sullivan to Washington, August 30, 1779, Hammond, III, 111; Butler to Bolton, August 31, 1779, Flick, *Sullivan-Clinton Campaign*, p. 137.

49. Swiggett, *War Out of Niagara*, pp. 198–99.

50. Butler to Bolton, August 31, 1779, Flick, *Sullivan-Clinton Campaign*, p. 138.

51. Sullivan to Washington, August 30, 1779, Hammond, III, 111.

52. Sullivan to Jay, September 30, 1779, *ibid.*, p. 124; his address to army asking the men to accept half-rations, *ibid.*, pp. 112–13.

53. "Journal of Dr. Jabez Campfield," in Cook, *Journals of the Military Expedition*, p. 56; Sullivan to Jay, September 30, 1779, Hammond, III, 124. The town was named after Catherine Montour, a sister of Queen Esther, and granddaughter of Madame Montour. Catherine married Thomas Hudson (or Telenemut), a Seneca chief.

54. "Journal of Major Jeremiah Fogg," in Cook, *Journals of the Military Expedition*, p. 96; "Journal of Lt. Erkuries Beatty," in *ibid.*, p. 28.

55. Gore, *Revolutionary Diary*, p. 25.

56. Sullivan to Jay, September 30, 1779, Hammond, III, 127; Adam Hubley to Joseph Reed, October 1, 1779, *Pennsylvania Archives*, VII (1853), 722; "Journal of Lt. Col. Henry Dearborn," in Cook, *Journals of the Military Expedition*, pp. 73–74.

57. "Journal of Lt. Col. Henry Dearborn," in *ibid.*, p. 74.

58. "Journal of Major Jeremiah Fogg," in *ibid.*, p. 97.

59. In *ibid.*, p. 98; "Journal of Lt. Col. Adam Hubley," in *ibid.*, p. 160.

60. John Butler to Mason Bolton, September 8, 1779, Flick, *Sullivan-Clinton Campaign*, pp. 145–46.

61. "Journal of Major John Burrowes," in Cook, *Journals of the Military Expedition*, p. 47.

62. "Journal of Lt. Col. Adam Hubley," in *ibid.*, p. 161.

63. Sullivan to Jay, September 30, 1779, Hammond, III, 129.

64. *Ibid.*, III, 129–30; "Journal of Lt. Erkuries Beatty," in Cook, *Journals of the Military Expedition*, pp. 31–32. This encounter is known as the Groveland Ambuscade in which all of Boyd's party except those who made their way to camp were killed. Boyd and one other were captured, were forced to suffer unspeakable tor-

tures, and were decapitated. In many ways the best account is in General John Clark's long footnote to "Journal of Lt. John Hardenbergh," in *ibid.*, p. 131*n*. Butler's account is in his letter to Mason Bolton, September 14, 1779, Flick, *Sullivan-Clinton Campaign*, pp. 148–49. It has been assumed that Butler allowed the Indians to torture Boyd because he would not divulge information, but his letter calls Boyd an "intelligent Person" who did give some information. Swiggett, *War Out of Niagara*, pp. 254–56, doubts that Butler allowed the Indians to torture the two men, although Swiggett admits Butler did not give them protection.

65. "Journal of Lt. Col. Henry Dearborn," in Cook, *Journals of the Military Expedition*, p. 75.

66. Sullivan to Jay, September 30, 1779, Hammond, III, 130–31. Arthur C. Parker, "The Indian Interpretation of the Sullivan-Clinton Campaign," *Rochester Historical Society Publication Fund Series*, VIII (1929), 55–56, presents a religious interpretation of the torturing of Boyd and Parker, offering the opinion their ordeal may have been a sacrifice to the Sun God.

67. Sullivan to Henry Laurens, July 26, 1779, Gratz Collection, Case 4, Box 15, in PHS.

68. *Ibid.*

69. Sullivan to Jay, September 30, 1779, Hammond, III, 132. Washington wrote Sullivan that he wished the Indians to be pushed so far from their settlements that they would fall back upon the British, and that the settlements should be so thoroughly destroyed that the Indians could not return to them that season; Washington to Sullivan, September 15, 1779, Fitzpatrick, XVI, 293. There is no mention of Niagara.

70. "Journal of Major John Burrowes," in Cook, *Journals of the Military Expedition*, p. 48.

71. "Notes of Captain John Weidman during General Sullivan's Campaign from June 19, 1779 to December 9, 1780," entry for September 15, 1779, pp. 38–39 (typed copy in PHS).

72. "Journal of Lt. Col. Henry Dearborn," in Cook, *Journals of the Military Expedition*, p. 76. Sullivan in his report, written on the 30th, said the Indians met him at Canadasaga, which the army reached on the 19th; Sullivan to Jay, September 30, 1779, Hammond, III, 132. The diary accounts agree that the meeting took place on the 18th. Sullivan may have been mistaken.

73. Sullivan's address to the Oneida Indians, n.d., Hammond, III, 116–19.

74. "Journal of Lt. Col. Henry Dearborn," in Cook, *Journals of the Military Expedition*, p. 76; "Journal of Lt. Col. Adam Hubley," in *ibid.*, p. 164.

75. Sullivan to Gansevoort, September 20, 1779, Hammond, III, 122–23. Sullivan was in error as to the unfriendliness of the Mohawks. Schuyler interceded in their behalf, and Sullivan's orders to Gansevoort were superseded by Washington. See Schuyler to Gansevoort, October 7, 1779, in Cook, *Journals of the Military Expedition*, p. 372n; Gansevoort to Sullivan, October 8, 1779, in *ibid.*, pp. 372–73; Washington to Schuyler, October 12, 1779, Fitzpatrick, XVI, 460–61.

76. "Journal of Lt. Col. Adam Hubley," in Cook, *Journals of the Military Expedition*, p. 164; "Journal of Lt. Col. Henry Dearborn," in *ibid.*, p. 76.

77. "Journal of Major Jeremiah Fogg," in *ibid.*, p. 100; "Journal of Lt. Erkuries Beatty," in *ibid.*, pp. 33–34.

78. "Journal of Lt. William Barton," in *ibid.*, p. 13.

79. "Journal of Lt. Erkuries Beatty," in *ibid.*, p. 34.

80. "Journal of Major Jeremiah Fogg," in *ibid.*, p. 100; "Journal of Lt. Col. Adam Hubley," in *ibid.*, p. 166; Sullivan to Jay, September 30, 1779, Hammond, III, 133–35.

81. *Ibid.*, III, 136.

82. "Journal of Major John Burrowes," in Cook, *Journals of the Military Expedition*, pp. 50–51; "Journal of Lt. Erkuries Beatty," in *ibid.*, p. 36, says he left Wyoming on the 9th, which is unlikely.

83. Wright, *The Sullivan Expedition of 1779*, in *Studies in History*, No. 7, pp. 24–28.

84. *Journals of the Continental Congress*, XV, 1170.

85. Fitzpatrick, XVI, 478–79.

86. "Journal of Major Jeremiah Fogg," in Cook, *Journals of the Military Expedition*, p. 101.

87. Hand to Joseph Reed, September 25, 1779, *Pennsylvania Archives*, VII (1853), 715.

88. Petition of Inhabitants of Tryon County, September 30, 1779, Clinton, *Public Papers*, V, 304–5; Reed to Pennsylvania General Assembly, November 13, 1779, *Pennsylvania Archives*, 4th ser., III (1900), 740.

89. William Gordon, *The History of the Rise, Progress, and Establishment of the Independence of the United States of America* (3 vols., New York, 1789), III, 22.

90. Hazard to Belknap, December 15, 1779, Belknap, *The Belknap Papers*, I, 23.

91. R. W. G. Vail argues that the power of the confederacy was broken. Gore, *Revolutionary Diary*, p. 8.

92. Parker, "Indian Interpretation of the Sullivan-Clinton Campaign," p. 57. He does not believe the power of the Indians was broken. Solon J. and Elizabeth H. Buck, *The Planting of Civilization in Western Pennsylvania* (Pittsburgh, 1939), p. 194; Randolph C. Downes, "Indian War on the Upper Ohio," *The Western Pennsylvania Historical Magazine*, XVII (1934), 94, 100. It is interesting to note that the Indians called Washington "Anadakariask," which means "Town Destroyer." They realized only too well that Washington had been the real leader of the campaign that had destroyed their homes. See Louise W. Murray, ed., *Notes from Craft Collection in Tioga Point Museum on the Sullivan Expedition* (Athens, Pa., 1929), p. 7.

93. Hand to Jasper Yeates, October 21, 1779, Hand Papers, in NYPL; Madison to Jefferson, June 2, 1780, Burnett, *Letters*, V, 181.

94. *Journals of the Continental Congress*, XIV, 1009–10; XV, 1163–64.

95. Sullivan to Washington, November 6, 1779, Hammond, III, 158.

96. Sullivan to President of Congress, November 9, 1779, *ibid.*, III, 161–62; *Journals of the Continental Congress*, XV, 1263–64.

97. *Ibid.*, XV, 1333.

98. November 30, 1779, *ibid.*, XV, 1334. William Plumer contended that Sullivan had exaggerated his account of the raid on the land of the Six Nations, thereby incurring the ridicule of officers in Washington's army. Plumer therefore argued that this reception helped determine Sullivan to resign. Plumer wrote: "The account he gave Congress of his expedition was greatly exaggerated, and exposed him to the censure and ridicule of the officers of the army. . . . After his return he was mortified by the cold reception he met from the officers of the army, and being disgusted and dissatisfied with the service . . . he tendered his resignation." William Plumer, "John Sullivan," *New Hampshire State Papers*, XXI, 823. Plumer's account probably is overemphasized.

99. Sullivan to Nathanael Greene, November 30, 1779, Hammond, III, 167.

100. Sullivan to Washington, December 1, 1779, *ibid.*, 169.

101. Washington to Sullivan, December 15, 1779, Fitzpatrick, XVII, 265–67.

102. *Journals of the Continental Congress*, XV, 1344.

103. Sullivan's pay from January 1, 1777 to November 30, 1779 totaled $4,257 22/90; Hammond, III, 164–65.

X: RETURN TO CONGRESS

1. Address of the New Hampshire Council and Assembly, February 19, 1780, Hammond, III, 182.

2. *Ibid.*, III, 183.

3. Sullivan to Speaker of House, November 3, 1784, *ibid.*, III, 382.

4. *New-Hampshire Gazette*, May 13, 1780.

5. *New Hampshire State Papers*, VIII, 887; Sullivan to Weare, February 5, 1781, Hammond, III, 283; Sullivan to Speaker of House, November 3, 1784, *ibid.*, III, 382.

6. Massachusetts also had claims in the area, but her role in the controversy was a minor one. For background on this conflict, see Matt B. Jones, *Vermont in the Making* (Cambridge, Mass., 1939), pp. 20–75; Jeremy Belknap, *The History of New Hampshire* (3 vols., Boston, 1791–92), II, 440–49; *Journals of the Continental Congress*, XV, 1095–99; Vermont Historical Society *Collections*, II (1871), 16–33.

7. "Journal of the New Hampshire Committee of Safety," New Hampshire *Laws*, IV, 781; Committee of Safety to Jedidiah Jewitt, August 19, 1780, *New Hampshire State Papers*, X, 526–27; *Journals of the Continental Congress*, XVIII, 816–17.

8. Sullivan to Speaker of House, November 3, 1784, Hammond, III, 382.

9. *Journals of the Continental Congress*, XVII, 482, 499; XVIII, 820.

10. Thomas Chittenden to Congress, July 25, 1780, Slade, *Vermont State Papers*, p. 122.

11. Moses Hazen to Sullivan, September 13, 1780, Hammond, III, 185–87; Sullivan to Weare, September 16, 1780, *ibid.*, III, 187–88; Joseph Marsh, Peter Olcott, and Bezaleel Woodward to Presi-

274 Notes: return to congress

dent of Congress, July 20, 1780, and Bezaleel Woodward to Samuel Livermore, July 25, 1780, *New Hampshire State Papers*, X, 363–66.

12. Sullivan to Weare, February 5, 1781, Hammond, III, 283–84.

13. Sullivan to Weare, September 16, 1780, *ibid.*, III, 188.

14. *Ibid.*, III, 188–89.

15. Scott to George Clinton, September 26, 1780, Burnett, *Letters*, V, 390–91.

16. James Duane to Clinton, October 7, 1780, *ibid.*, V, 410.

17. Sullivan to Weare, November 15, 1780, Hammond, III, 204.

18. Jacob Bayley to Weare, November 22, 1780, *New Hampshire State Papers*, X, 380.

19. Statement of Jonathan Chase and Abel Curtiss, January 12, 1781, *ibid.*, XIII, 765–66.

20. Sullivan to Weare, December 11, 1780, February 5, 1781, Hammond, III, 240–41, 282–87.

21. Sullivan to John Wendell, January 21, 1781, *ibid.*, III, 268; Instructions of General Assembly, January 13, 1781, *New Hampshire State Papers*, X, 385–86; New York Delegates to George Clinton, March 11, 1781, Burnett, *Letters*, VI, 24.

22. Sullivan to Weare, March 6, 1781, Hammond, III, 289–91.

23. Weare to Sullivan, March 19, April 2, 1781, *ibid.*, III, 299, 303–4; *New Hampshire State Papers*, X, 388–96.

24. Weare to Sullivan and Livermore, June 20, 1781, *New Hampshire State Papers*, X, 401–2.

25. Sullivan to Weare, July 10, 1781, Hammond, III, 334–35.

26. *Journals of the Continental Congress*, XXI, 830–31, 831*n.*, 836–39, 841–42.

27. Sullivan to Weare, August 7, 1781, Hammond, III, 341–42; Livermore to Weare, August 14, 1781, Burnett, *Letters*, VI, 184.

28. Sullivan to Weare, October 2, 1780, Hammond, III, 191.

29. *Ibid.*, III, 192.

30. Edmund C. Burnett, *The Continental Congress* (New York, 1941), p. 484.

31. Sullivan to Weare, November 15, 1780, Hammond, III, 201.

32. *Ibid.*, III, 204.

33. *Journals of the Continental Congress*, XVIII, 1028.

34. Sullivan to Washington, November 12, 1780, Hammond, III, 198.

35. Fortunately Sullivan kept notes on their deliberations; Burnett, *Letters*, V, 464–72.

36. *Ibid.,* V, 468.

37. *Ibid.,* V, 469–72.

38. *Journals of the Continental Congress,* XVIII, 1157–64.

39. *Ibid.,* XIX, 102–3, 105.

40. *Ibid.,* XIX, 111–12.

41. Sullivan to Washington, January 29, 1781, Hammond, III, 277.

42. There was much discussion on finance on the floor, but in the meantime Congress was planning for a department of finance. Sullivan's committee "appears to have melted away or lost its leadership." Burnett, *Letters,* V, 464*n.*

43. *Journals of the Continental Congress,* XX, 487.

44. *Ibid.,* XX, 545–47.

XI: WOOED BY FRIEND AND FOE

1. Sullivan to Weare, November 15, 1780, Hammond, III, 200–4; Burnett, *Letters,* V, 446*n.*

2. After telling Vergennes that he had read Sullivan's intercepted letter, Luzerne continued: "Des cette épogue il me parut nécessaire d'ouvrir ma bourse à ce Délégué, dont l'Ennemi connaissait les besoins par sa propre confession, et sous l'apparence d'un prêt, je lui remis 68 guinées 4 septièmes." Luzerne to Vergennes, May 13, 1781, Thomas C. Amory, *General Sullivan Not a Pensioner of Luzerne* (Boston, 1875), pp. 20–21. Amory argues with vehemence and denies all accusations that Sullivan was on Luzerne's payroll. He asserts that one must assume Sullivan intended to repay as soon as possible, and he claims that there is "every reason to presume" that Sullivan eventually repaid the loan. *Ibid.,* p. 29.

3. Vergennes to Luzerne, July 27, 1781, *The Magazine of American History with Notes and Queries,* XI (January, 1884), 160.

4. Robert Harrison wrote that both Sullivan and Daniel Carroll of Maryland had "contributed immeasurably, by their independent conduct, to destroy the EASTERN ALLIANCE." This eastern alliance, so-called, had been under the influence of Arthur Lee and Samuel Adams and soon became an anti-Gallican clique. Robert Harrison to Alexander Hamilton, October 27, 1780, Hamilton, *Works,* ed. John C. Hamilton, I, 192.

5. *Journals of the Continental Congress,* XVIII, 910, 1130; Sullivan to Washington, November 26, 1780, Hammond, III, 223.

6. For background see Paul C. Phillips, *The West in the Diplomacy of the American Revolution* (University of Illinois Studies in the Social Studies, II, Nos. 2 and 3; Urbana, 1913), pp. 150–80; Irving Brant, *James Madison, the Nationalist, 1780–1787* (his *James Madison*, II, Indianapolis, 1948), pp. 70–88; *Journals of the Continental Congress*, XVIII, 900–2, 908.

7. *Journals of the Continental Congress*, XVIII, 1070–71; XIX, 151–54; Madison to Joseph Jones, November 25, 1780, Burnett, *Letters*, V, 457; Brant, *James Madison*, II, 85.

8. Sullivan to Washington, March 6, 1781, Hammond, III, 293; see Jennings B. Sanders, *Evolution of Executive Departments of the Continental Congress, 1784–1789* (Chapel Hill, N. C., 1935), p. 96n.

9. Sullivan to Washington, March 6, 1781, Hammond, III, 292–93; Sanders, *Evolution of Executive Departments*, pp. 109–10.

10. Ezekiel Cornell to Governor Greene, February 19, 1781, Burnett, *Letters*, V, 573n.

11. Sullivan to Washington, March 6, 1781, Hammond, III, 293.

12. William V. Wells, *The Life and Public Services of Samuel Adams* (3 vols., Boston, 1865), III, 129–31; Luzerne to Vergennes, March 25, 1781, quoted in Sparks, *Writings of George Washington*, VII, 400n.

13. Thomas Rodney, "Diary," March 10, 1781, Burnett, *Letters*, VI, 19.

14. Sullivan to Weare, November 15, 1780, Hammond, III, 200–4; Weare to Sullivan, March 17, 1781, *ibid.*, III, 298–99; Burnett, *Letters*, VI, 84n.

15. Thomas C. Amory, *The Military Services and Public Life of Major-General John Sullivan* (Boston, 1868), p. 288; Kenneth Scott, "Major General Sullivan and Colonel Stephen Holland," *New England Quarterly*, XVIII (September, 1945), 308–9.

16. Sullivan to John Langdon, September 10, 1782, Hammond, III, 344.

17. Scott, "Major General Sullivan and Colonel Stephen Holland," p. 313. Both drafts of Holland's letters are in the Clinton Papers, in Clements Library, Ann Arbor, Mich., and are quoted in Scott's article, pp. 310–13.

18. Holland to Sullivan, draft of letter, n.d., *ibid.*, pp. 312–13.

19. Sullivan to Weare, May 8, 1781, Hammond, III, 316.

20. Luzerne to Vergennes, May 13, 1781, quoted in Scott, "Major General Sullivan and Colonel Stephen Holland," p. 316.

21. *Ibid.*

22. *Ibid.,* pp. 316–17.

23. Holland to Sullivan, June 9, 1781, *ibid.,* p. 318.

24. *Ibid.,* p. 319.

25. Hammond, III, 314.

26. Scott, "Major General Sullivan and Colonel Stephen Holland," pp. 303–24, brings together all the source material for this episode. Scott implies that Sullivan was looking after his own interest. Carl Van Doren, *Secret History of the American Revolution* (New York, 1941), pp. 400–4, argues that Sullivan never wavered. Thomas C. Amory, *Daniel Sullivan's Visits . . . to General John Sullivan in Philadelphia* (Cambridge, Mass., 1884), pp. 22–23, argues that Sullivan's character and career to that point were completely incompatible with any attempt at double-dealing with the American cause.

27. Sullivan to Hancock, September 27, 1777, Hammond, I, 462. Sullivan never did identify the person he so described.

28. Sullivan to McDougall, January 27, March 16, 1781, *ibid.,* III, 271–75, 296–98; McDougall to Sullivan, May 22, 1781, *ibid.,* pp. 320–21.

29. Luzerne to Congress, May 26, 1781, *Journals of the Continental Congress,* XX, 561.

30. *Ibid.,* XX, 562; Brant, *James Madison,* II, 136–37; Luzerne to Vergennes, June 8, 1781, Archives des Affaires Etrangères, Correspondence politique, Etats-Unis, XVII, transcripts in LC.

31. *Journals of the Continental Congress,* XX, 562–69; Sullivan and Livermore to Weare, May 29, 1781, Hammond, III, 325–27.

32. Luzerne to Vergennes, June 8, 1781, Archives des Affaires Etrangères, Correspondence politique, Etats-Unis, XVII, in LC; *Journals of the Continental Congress,* XX, 616.

33. *Ibid.,* XX, 606.

34. *Ibid.,* XX, 605–6; Brant, *James Madison,* II, 138.

35. *Journals of the Continental Congress,* XX, 606.

36. *Ibid.,* XX, 607–15; the instructions on p. 617.

37. *Ibid.,* XX, 626.

38. *Ibid.,* XX, 619.

39. Luzerne to Vergennes, June 14, 1781, Henri Doniol, *Histoire de la participation de la France à l'establissement des Etats Unis d'Amérique* (6 vols., Paris, 1884–92), IV², 621–23; *Journals of the Continental Congress,* XX, 648. Final instructions for the five minis-

ters were entered on the *Journals* under June 15 after a vote on the final form; *ibid.*, XX, 651–54.

40. Edward S. Corwin, *French Policy and the American Alliance of 1778* (Princeton, 1916), pp. 299–300.

41. Sullivan's Reply to "Honestus," April 23, 1785, Hammond, III, 423.

42. Luzerne to Vergennes, May 13, 1781, Amory, *General Sullivan Not a Pensioner of Luzerne*, p. 26.

43. Luzerne to Vergennes, June 11, 1781, Archives Affaires Etrangères, Correspondence politique, Etats-Unis, XVII, in LC; Brant, *James Madison*, II, 138–40; Corwin, *French Policy and the American Alliance*, pp. 303–10.

44. Sullivan to Washington, May 28, 1781, Hammond, III, 322.

45. Luzerne to Vergennes, January 3, 1781, Archives Affaires Etrangères, Correspondence politique, Etats-Unis, XV, Part 1, in LC.

46. *Journals of the Continental Congress*, XXI, 819, 827; James Varnum to Sullivan, August 10, 1781, Peck Manuscripts, VI, 46, in Rhode Island Historical Society.

47. Luzerne to Vergennes, August 11, 1781, Archives Affaires Etrangères, Correspondence politique, Etats-Unis, XIX, in LC; Sanders, *Evolution of Executive Departments*, pp. 109–11; Arthur Lee to Samuel Adams, August 13, 1781, Burnett, *Letters*, VI, 176n.; *Journals of the Continental Congress*, XXI, 851–52.

XII: NEW HAMPSHIRE LAWYER

1. Luzerne to Vergennes, August 11, 1781, Archives Affaires Etrangères, Correspondence politique, Etats-Unis, XIX, transcripts in LC.

2. *New Hampshire Gazette*, November 17, 1781.

3. Address of the Convention and the Proposed Constitution of 1781 are in *New Hampshire State Papers*, IX, 845–77.

4. William Plumer, "John Pickering," *ibid.*, XXII, 840–41.

5. Samuel Philbrick to Josiah Bartlett, June 17, 1778, James F. Colby, *Manual of the Constitution of the State of New Hampshire* (Concord, N. H., 1912), pp. 78–79; Josiah Bartlett to John Langdon, July 13, 1778, Bancroft Transcript of Letters between Langdon, Whipple, Lovell, and Bartlett, MS vol., pp. 371–73, in NYPL; Weare to Bartlett, July 3, 1778, Emmet Collection, No. 1973, in NYPL.

6. Sullivan to Weare, December 12, 1775, Hammond, I, 142–43.

7. Durham Town Records, II, 201–2, in NHHS.

8. *Ibid.*, II, 206, in NHHS.

9. Colby, *Manual of the Constitution of . . . New Hampshire,* p. 86.

10. *New Hampshire State Papers,* IX, 884–88.

11. See letters of "A Member of the Convention," *New-Hampshire Gazette,* August 30, October 4, 1783; "A Citizen of New Hampshire," *ibid.,* September 13, 1783; and "A Watchman," *ibid.,* October 25, 1783. For discussion on maneuvers to gain ratification, see Forrest McDonald, *We the People: the Economic Origins of the Constitution* (Chicago, 1958), pp. 239–40.

12. *New Hampshire State Papers,* VIII, 945; Sullivan's Reply to "Cincinnatus," July 21, 1783, Hammond, III, 355; Sullivan's Reply to "Honestus," April 23, 1785, *ibid.,* III, 424–26.

13. The Superior Court records are intact in the court houses for the five counties: Exeter for Rockingham County, Dover for Strafford County, Nashua for Hillsborough County, Keene for Cheshire County, and Woodsville for Grafton County.

14. Letter of "Spectator Indepens," *New-Hampshire Gazette,* November 17, 1781.

15. Report of the Council and Assembly of Vermont, October 16–19, 1781, *New Hampshire State Papers,* X, 422–26; Thomas Chittenden to Elisha Payne, December 14, 1781, *ibid.,* X, 450–51; Payne to Weare, December 21, 1781, *ibid.,* X, 453–54.

16. *Ibid.,* VIII, 926, 928, 930; Sullivan to Jeremy Belknap, November 2, 1790, Hammond, III, 627.

17. *Ibid.; New Hampshire State Papers,* X, 485.

18. Thomas C. Amory, *The Military Services and Public Life of Major-General John Sullivan* (Boston, 1868), pp. 193–97; William Plumer, Jr., *Life of William Plumer* (Boston, 1856), pp. 67–71; Jeremy Belknap, *The History of New Hampshire* (3 vols., Boston, 1791–92), II, 457–58; Superior Court Records, 1772–84, pp. 232, 236–37, MS vol. in Keene Courthouse.

19. State v. Carlton, Superior Court Records, 1785–95, pp. 32–33, MS vol. in Keene Courthouse.

20. Government and People v. Sarah Bartlett, Superior Court Records, 1774–95, p. 19, MS vol. in Woodsville Courthouse.

21. Letter of "Cincinnatus," *New-Hampshire Gazette,* July 12, 1783.

22. Sullivan's Reply to "Cincinnatus," July 21, 1783, Hammond, III, 355–56.

23. *Ibid.*, III, 360.

24. New Hampshire *Laws*, V, 195–96.

25. Report of Committee, January 13, 1784, *Journals of the Continental Congress*, XXVI, 18–19.

26. November 6, 1781, Journal of the House of Representatives, 1781–85, MS vol., p. 481, in NHHS.

27. *Ibid.*, p. 477.

28. Abiel Foster to Weare, January 8, 1784, Burnett, *Letters,* VII, 409.

29. Hammond, III, 367.

30. *Journals of the Continental Congress*, XXVI, 175. Six states voted "aye," two states voted "no," and two states were divided.

31. Hammond, III, 362–64; *Journals of the Continental Congress*, XXVI, 14–15.

XIII: THE STATE POLITICIAN

1. Jeremy Belknap, *The History of New Hampshire* (3 vols., Boston, 1791–92), II, 158–80, 258–82; *New Hampshire State Papers*, XXIX, 313–34.

2. *Ibid.*, pp. 345–50.

3. *New Hampshire Gazette*, April 8, 1785.

4. Plumer, "John Sullivan," *New Hampshire State Papers*, XXI, 825; Thomas C. Amory, *The Military Services and Public Life of Major-General John Sullivan* (Boston, 1868), pp. 251–53.

5. *New Hampshire State Papers*, XXII, 770–71.

6. J. Hugo Tatsch, *Freemasonry in the Thirteen Colonies* (New York, 1929), pp. 199–200.

7. Plumer, "John Sullivan," *New Hampshire State Papers*, XXI, 825.

8. Belknap to Ebenezer Hazard, December 21, 1783, Belknap, *Belknap Papers*, I, 288.

9. Probate Records, IV, 268–70, in Dover Courthouse.

10. Amory, *The Military Services and Public Life of Major-General John Sullivan*, p. 251.

11. Sullivan to Jefferson, April 16, 1787, Hammond, III, 521; see also Sullivan to Jefferson, March 12, 1784, *ibid.*, III, 372–74;

Sullivan to Jefferson, June 22, 1784, *ibid.*, III, 379–81; Jefferson to Sullivan, January 7, 1786, *ibid.*, III, 445–46.

12. Jefferson to W. S. Smith, September 28, 1787, Jefferson, *Papers*, XII, 193; see also Abigail Adams Smith to Jefferson, July 11, 1787, *ibid.*, XI, 580; see also *ibid.*, XI, 580*n.*; W. S. Smith to Jefferson, August 3, 1787, *ibid.*, XI, 674–75; see also *ibid.*, XI, 675*n.*; Sullivan to Jefferson, April 26, 27, 30, 1787, Hammond, III, 523–25; see also Dumas Malone, *Jefferson and the Rights of Man* (his *Jefferson and His Time*, II, Boston, 1951), pp. 99–101.

13. Jefferson to Sullivan, October 5, 1787, Jefferson, *Papers*, XII, 208–9.

14. Plumer to Jesse Johnson, December 23, 1784, William Plumer Papers, 1781–1804, pp. 57–60, MS vol. in LC.

15. Sullivan to Wendell, February 7, 1785, Hammond, III, 397.

16. *New-Hampshire Gazette*, March 4, 1785.

17. Sullivan to Wendell, February 18, 1785, Hammond, III, 398.

18. Letters of "Honestus," *New-Hampshire Gazette*, April 1, 15, 1785.

19. April 8, 22, 1785, Hammond, III, 415–27.

20. *New Hampshire State Papers*, XX, 344, 351.

21. Sullivan to Wendell, March 14, 1785, Hammond, III, 411–12.

22. *New Hampshire State Papers*, XX, 253.

23. Sullivan to Freemen of New Hampshire, January 27, 1785, Hammond, III, 386.

24. *Ibid.*, III, 393.

25. Sullivan to the "Gentlemen of Family, Fortune and Education," February 24, 1785, *ibid.*, III, 399–407; Sullivan's Appeal for Military Instruction, February 27, 1785, *ibid.*, III, 407.

26. *New Hampshire State Papers*, XX, 338, 356.

27. Thomas Sheafe to David Sargent, May 25, 1784, Thomas Sheafe Letterbook, in NYPL; *New-Hampshire Gazette*, February 18, April 1, May 13, 1785.

28. Wheelock to M. L'Estevon, April 1, 1784, MS No. 784251.1, in Baker Library, Dartmouth College.

29. Letter of "Episcopus," *New-Hampshire Mercury*, May 24, 1785.

30. *New Hampshire State Papers*, XX, 388; Hammond, III, 431–37.

31. *New Hampshire State Papers*, XX, 420, 434–35; New Hampshire *Laws*, V, 98–100.

32. *Ibid.*, V, 78–81; *New Hampshire State Papers*, XX, 495–96, 502–4, 526; Sullivan to Jefferson, March 4, 1786, Hammond, III, 448–49.

33. *New Hampshire State Papers*, XX, 518–19.

34. *Ibid.*, XX, 562–63; Thomas C. Amory, *Life of James Sullivan* (2 vols., Boston, 1859), I, 253.

35. Sullivan's Farewell Address, March 3, 1786, Hammond, III, 447.

36. Belknap to Hazard, March 9, 1786, Belknap, *Belknap Papers*, I, 433; see also Lawrence S. Mayo, *John Langdon of New Hampshire* (Concord, N. H., 1937), p. 194*n*.

37. *New Hampshire State Papers*, XX, 614.

38. Examination of town records on microfilm in NHSL enabled a partial tabulation of the voting by towns.

39. William Plumer to Samuel Plumer, Jr., postscript dated June 17, 1786, to letter dated June 6, 1786, Colonial Society of Massachusetts *Publications*, XI (1910), 385.

40. Hammond, III, 454–56.

41. Ebenezer Sullivan to John Sullivan, October 30, 1785, *ibid.*, III, 437–38; *New-Hampshire Gazette*, October 21, November 18, 1785; *New-Hampshire Mercury*, October 25, 1785.

42. Monsieur Gillet de la Vallee and Company, established by Sullivan's assistance near him at Packersfalls, offered for sale such items as buttons, garters, and fine cloths. *New-Hampshire Gazette*, December 30, 1785.

43. Belknap to Hazard, March 9, 1786, Belknap, *Belknap Papers*, I, 431.

44. By August, 1786, £90,252/16.5 was outstanding in taxes since 1775; New Hampshire's Treasurer's Accounts, 1775–91, MS vol. in NHHS. See also *New-Hampshire Mercury*, January 21, 1785; Plumer to William Coleman, May 31, 1786, Colonial Society of Massachusetts *Publications*, XI (1910), 384; Thomas Sheafe to Messrs. Lane, Son & Frazer, June 23, August 5, 1786, Thomas Sheafe Letterbook, in NYPL.

45. *New Hampshire State Papers*, VIII, 913; New Hampshire *Laws*, IV, 420–21.

46. *Ibid.*, V, 56; Belknap, *History of New Hampshire*, II, 461–62.

47. *New-Hampshire Mercury*, May 24, 1786.

48. *Ibid.*, September 13, 1786.

49. *New-Hampshire Gazette*, February 18, April 1, 1785.

50. *Ibid.,* September 9, 1785.

51. These statistics were gathered from *New Hampshire State Papers,* town histories, and town records on microfilm in NHSL. Quite obviously other towns must have petitioned also, but their records have been lost.

52. See letters in Hammond, III, 468–72; also see James White to Sullivan, August 11, 1786, Burnett, *Letters,* VIII, 420; James Monroe to Sullivan, August 16, 1786, *ibid.,* VIII, 430.

53. *New Hampshire State Papers,* XX, 587.

54. Belknap to Sally Belknap, September 5, 1786, Belknap Papers, in NHHS.

55. Plumer to John Hale, September 18, 1786, Colonial Society of Massachusetts *Publications,* XI (1910), 388.

56. *New Hampshire State Papers,* XX, 676, 689–91, 695–96.

57. Hammond, III, 475–79.

58. Plumer to Hale, September 20, 1786, Colonial Society of Massachusetts *Publications,* XI (1910), 391.

59. *Ibid.; New-Hampshire Mercury,* September 27, 1786, as quoted in New Hampshire Historical Society *Collections,* III (1832), 117–22.

60. Plumer to Hale, September 20, 1786, Colonial Society of Massachusetts *Publications,* XI (1910), 392. One further source of friction should be mentioned. On September 15 the House and Senate voted to pass an act in compliance with the treaty between Great Britain and the United States ending the War for Independence. The law prohibited further confiscations of absentee estates and allowed loyalists who had not borne arms to return to live in the state. The representatives from Londonderry, a Scotch-Irish district, had voted against the measure and circulated reports that the act obliged the state to repurchase confiscated estates and return them to the absentees. They said that a heavy tax would be assessed to pay for the repurchase. These were alarming and far from accurate rumors which unfortunately added to the tension. One rioter later said that he had been misled: "My error arose from the gross misrepresentations of many persons—whose intentions I now firmly believe to be as vile, as their hearts were wicked." *Essex Journal,* January 17, 1787. See also *New Hampshire State Papers,* XX, 677, 697–99; Plumer to Hale, September 18, 1786, Colonial Society of Massachusetts *Publications,* XI (1910), 389–90.

61. Plumer to Hale, September 21, 1786, *ibid.,* XI, 393–94.

62. Plumer to Hale, September 26, 1786, *ibid.,* XI, 394–95.

63. *New Hampshire State Papers,* XX, 683, 711–12.

64. Belknap, *History of New Hampshire,* II, 477.

XIV: BATTLE FOR THE CONSTITUTION

1. Humphreys to Washington, September 24, 1786, George Washington Papers, CCXXXVI, 86, in LC.

2. Belknap to Hazard, October 25, 1786, Belknap, *Belknap Papers,* I, 446.

3. Plumer to Hale, October 22, 1786, Colonial Society of Massachusetts *Publications,* XI (1910), 402.

4. *New-Hampshire Mercury,* November 29, 1786.

5. *Ibid.*

6. Samuel Hobart to Belknap, December 18, 1786, Belknap, *Belknap Papers,* III, 321.

7. Hammond, III, 493.

8. *Ibid.,* III, 483–84.

9. *New Hampshire State Papers,* XX, 732, 776; *Essex Journal,* January 17, 1787.

10. *New Hampshire State Papers,* XX, 772.

11. Thomas C. Amory, *The Military Services and Public Life of Major-General John Sullivan* (Boston, 1868), pp. 211–12; *New-Hampshire Spy,* January 16, 1787.

12. Eleazar Wheelock to Sullivan, December 12, 1786, Hammond, III, 495; Jedediah [*sic*] Huntington to Sullivan, January 6, 1787, *ibid.,* III, 497–98.

13. Sullivan to James Bowdoin, February 9, 1787, *ibid.,* III, 506–7; Sullivan to Bowdoin, February 12, 1787, in envelope on Shays's Rebellion, in MHS; Sullivan to Bowdoin, February 13, 1787, Hammond, III, 508; Sullivan's Proclamation of February 27, 1787, *ibid.,* III, 509–12.

14. Sullivan's Petition to Congress, March 10, 1785, *ibid.,* III, 408–10; Sullivan to President of Congress, December 24, 1785, *ibid.,* III, 442–45.

15. *Journals of the Continental Congress,* XXXI, 608.

16. *New Hampshire State Papers,* XX, 734, 778.

17. Sullivan to Joseph Whipple, March 29, 1787, Hammond, III, 514–16; John T. Gilman to Sullivan, April 9, 1787, *ibid.,* III, 517–19.

18. *New-Hampshire Mercury*, February 21, 1787.

19. *New-Hampshire Spy*, March 6, 1787.

20. *New Hampshire State Papers*, XXI, 9–11.

21. Hammond, III, 556–58; Joshua Wentworth to Sullivan, August 29, 1786, *New Hampshire State Papers*, XVIII, 772–73; *ibid.*, XX, 672, 688.

22. *Ibid.*, XX, 744–45, 797–98; Charles Thomson to Sullivan, March 31, 1787, Hammond, III, 516–17; Burnett, *Letters*, VIII, 566*n*.

23. Henry Knox to Sullivan, May 21, 1787, Hammond, III, 527; New Hampshire *Laws*, V, 264–65.

24. Nicholas Gilman to Sullivan, September 18, 1787, Hammond, III, 543–44; Thomson to Sullivan, September 28, 1787, *New Hampshire State Papers*, XXI, 836–37.

25. Sullivan to Nicholas Gilman, November 20, 1787, in PHS.

26. Letter of "A Republican," *New-Hampshire Spy*, October 13, 1787.

27. Libbey to Belknap, October 24, 1787, Belknap, *Belknap Papers*, III, 341.

28. Langdon to Washington, November 6, 1787, George Washington Papers, CCXXXIX, 54, in LC; Plumer to Daniel Tilton, December 10, 1787, William Plumer, Jr., *Life of William Plumer* (Boston, 1856), p. 98.

29. Hammond, III, 556–68; Madison to Washington, December 7, 20, 1787, George Washington Papers, CCXXXIX, 83, 93, in LC; Knox to Washington, December 11, 1787, *ibid.*, CCXXXIX, 85.

30. *New Hampshire State Papers*, XXI, 148–49, 158–61; Forrest McDonald, *We the People: the Economic Origins of the Constitution* (Chicago, 1958), pp. 236–38.

31. Letter of "Probus," *Freeman's Oracle*, December 22, 1787.

32. Knox to Sullivan, January 19, 1788, Hammond, III, 560.

33. "Journal of the Convention," *New Hampshire State Papers*, X, 12.

34. *Ibid.*, X, 12–15.

35. *New-Hampshire Spy*, February 23, 1788.

36. *Ibid.*

37. *Ibid.*

38. *Ibid.*, Jeremiah Libbey to Belknap, February 22, 1788, Belknap, *Belknap Papers*, III, 389–90.

39. Sullivan to Belknap, February 26, 1788, Hammond, III, 567–68.

40. Libbey to Belknap, February 19, 1788, Belknap, *Belknap Papers*, III, 388.

41. Libbey to Belknap, February 22, 1788, *ibid.*, III, 389–90.

42. Langdon to Washington, February 28, 1788, George Washington Papers, CCXL, 41, in LC.

43. Libbey to Belknap, February 26, 1788, Belknap, *Belknap Papers*, III, 396; *American Herald*, March 3, 1788; *Freeman's Oracle*, March 14, 1788; "Journal of the Convention," *New Hampshire State Papers*, X, 15. Atherton's speech against slavery was probably written out long after the event. It first appeared in the *New Hampshire Statesman*, July 7, 1827; see Joseph B. Walker, *A History of the New Hampshire Convention for the Investigation, Discussion, and Decision of the Federal Constitution* (Boston, 1888), pp. 4–5. Sullivan's speech is the only one for which there is any contemporary record.

44. Sullivan to Belknap, February 26, 1788, Hammond, III, 566–67.

45. Sullivan to Gilman, February 28, 1788, in PHS.

46. Sullivan to Belknap, February 26, 1788, Hammond, III, 566–67; Knox to Washington, March 10, 1788, George Washington Papers, CCXL, 47, in LC.

47. *Connecticut Courant*, March 3, 1788; also issue of February 25, 1788.

48. Benjamin Lincoln to Washington, February 24, 1788, George Washington Papers, CCXL, 40, in LC; Dr. Philip Thomas to Horatio Gates, March 21, 1788, Horatio Gates Papers, in NYHS.

49. Hammond, III, 568–69.

50. Sullivan to Belknap, February 26, 1788, *ibid.*, III, 566.

51. McDonald, *We The People*, p. 247; *New-Hampshire Mercury*, February 27, 1788; Sullivan to Pickering and Hodsdon, March 5, 1788, Hammond, III, 571–72; Inferior Court of Common Pleas, Dover Case Books No. 4, No. 5, *passim*, for suits to recover debts.

52. *New Hampshire State Papers*, XXI, 263.

53. *Ibid.*, XXI, 289.

54. *Ibid.*, XXI, 299, 305.

55. Lamb to Peabody, May 18, 1788, Miscellaneous Manuscripts, "Lamb," in NYPL.

56. Tobias Lear to Washington, June 2, 1788, George Washington Papers, CCXLI, 4, in LC.

57. "Journal of Convention," *New Hampshire State Papers,* X, 16.

58. Atherton to Lamb, June 11, 1788, John Lamb Papers, Box 5, No. 16, in NYHS.

59. "Journal of Convention," *New Hampshire State Papers,* X, 16–18.

60. *Ibid.,* X, 18.

61. *Ibid.,* X, 2–7.

62. Sullivan to Hancock, June 21, 1788, Hammond, III, 588; Sullivan to Knox, June 21, 1788, *ibid.*

63. Knox to Sullivan, June 29, 1788, *ibid.,* III, 590.

64. Atherton to Lamb, June 23, 1788, John Lamb Papers, Box 5, No. 25, in NYHS.

65. Lear to Washington, June 22, 1788, George Washington Papers, CCXLI, 24, in LC.

66. *New-Hampshire Spy,* June 24, 1788; Libbey to Belknap, June 23, 1788, Belknap, *Belknap Papers,* III, 412.

67. William Plumer, "John Pickering," Manuscript Biographical Sketches, IV, 317–21, in NHHS.

68. See map opposite Table of Contents in Orin G. Libby, *The Geographical Distribution of the Vote of the Thirteen States on the Federal Constitution, 1787–1788* (Bulletin of the University of Wisconsin, Economics, Political Science and History Series, Vol. I, No. 1, Madison, Wis., 1894).

69. As early as 1784 the *Massachusetts Spy,* printed in Worcester and later for ratification, advertised that its issues would be delivered along the river in New Hampshire; *Massachusetts Spy,* January 8, 1784. The *Connecticut Courant,* printed in Hartford and also for ratification, undoubtedly circulated in the area. That paper carried a letter by Oliver Ellsworth addressed to the people of New Hampshire urging ratification; "A Landholder to Citizens of New Hampshire," *Connecticut Courant,* March 10, 1788. The *Recorder* was a federalist paper. For the fact that interior towns did not have ready access to newspapers, see *New-Hampshire Spy,* February 16, 1787.

70. *Recorder,* April 8, 1788, quoting from the *Connecticut Courant.*

71. In Rockingham County, of those towns which had a vote in

the convention either separately or joined with other towns, 25 voted "Yes." Of those towns at least 7 had been for paper and 6 against. In that same county 16 had voted "No." Of those, at least 5 favored paper, and 4 did not. No trend is apparent for Rockingham. In Strafford County 13 towns favored the Constitution, 10 towns plus the Locations did not. Where the statistics are available for the towns that were against ratification, 5 favored paper and 2 did not. This seems to indicate a closer connection between paper money advocates and those against ratification. In Hillsborough 7 towns voted for the Constitution. Of those, at least 1 town was for paper and 4 were against. Of the 23 towns which were against the Constitution, 3 had been for paper and at least 5 had not. In Cheshire 12 towns voted for the Constitution. Of those 12 at least 2 had been for paper and 3 against. Against the Constitution were 16 towns, although they had only 11 votes in the convention. Of those, 7 had been for paper, and no town has left a record as being against it. Thus there was a parallel between the demand for paper in Hillsborough and Cheshire and the votes against ratification, although Hillsborough had not been a strong paper money area. Grafton County, however, defies the pattern. It is difficult to break down Grafton's vote because one delegate usually represented so many towns. But Grafton had been overwhelmingly for paper money and for ratification. Here, as already discussed, personal influence and the geographic factor were far more important. The votes have been gathered from town records, both published and those on microfilm in NHSL. For another analysis on the vote see McDonald, *We the People,* pp. 242–43.

72. *Freeman's Oracle,* July 4, 1788; McDonald, *We the People,* pp. 235–41, for his description of the contest in New Hampshire.

XV: DECLINING YEARS

1. *New Hampshire State Papers,* XXI, 587, 589, 593.

2. Sullivan ran behind in Cheshire only after the money riots. These observations on voting pattern have been reached after studying the voting returns in town records, both published and on microfilm in NHSL.

3. *New Hampshire State Papers,* XXI, 594–95, 597–98.

4. Sullivan to Wheelock, September 16, 1789, in PHS; Whee-

lock to Sullivan, September 1, 1789, Hammond, III, 603–4. Harvard also had awarded Sullivan a degree, a Master of Arts, in 1780; Harvard University *Quinquennial Catalogue, 1636–1930* (Cambridge, 1930).

5. Sullivan to Knox, September 16, 1789, Hammond, III, 604–5.

6. Washington to the District Judges of the United States, September 30, 1789, Fitzpatrick, XXX, 425.

7. Sullivan to Washington, October 27, 1789, Hammond, III, 607–8.

8. *New-Hampshire Gazette,* November 5, 1789.

9. Records of United States District Court, I, 1–3, in U. S. Post Office Building, Concord, N. H.

10. *New Hampshire State Papers,* XXI, 634, 671–72, 695–96.

11. *Ibid.,* XXII, 47–48.

12. Amory claims that Sullivan met with an accident during the Indian campaign and that that had led to a spinal disease which eventually incapacitated him; Thomas C. Amory, *The Military Services and Public Life of Major-General John Sullivan* (Boston, 1868), p. 234. That a spinal disease developed from the accident is unlikely and cannot be documented. Plumer said that Sullivan used his supposed ill health as a pretext for resigning from the army; William Plumer, "John Sullivan," *New Hampshire State Papers,* XXI, 823.

13. Records of United States Circuit Court, pp. 1–18, in U. S. Post Office Building, Concord, N. H.; Records of United States District Court, I, 4–6.

14. Inferior Court Records, February, 1790, Dover Courthouse; Superior Court Records, 1774–89, MS vol. in Dover Courthouse.

15. Sullivan's Petition to General Court, December 24, 1789, Documents Series of 1901, XLVIII, 103, MS vol. in NHHS.

16. Sullivan to Ebenezer Thompson, June 16, 1790, Charles L. Parsons, "The Capture of Fort William and Mary, December 14 and 15, 1774," NHHS *Proceedings,* IV (1899–1905), 39; New Hampshire *Laws,* V, 522; *New Hampshire State Papers,* XXII, 79–80; Superior Court Records, 1790–95, MS vol. in Dover Courthouse.

17. Deeds of sale, Dover Register, Books 12–16, *passim.*

18. Inventory and Supplementary Inventory of Sullivan's Estate, Probate Records, IV, 268–70, in Dover Courthouse.

19. Probate Records, XXVII, 291–92, in Dover Courthouse.

Sullivan died intestate. The claims against the estate mounted to over $3,000 which were later proportioned at $1,721.76. As late as 1821, $207.63 of the proportion of claims remained unpaid.

20. Amory, *The Military Services and Public Life of Major-General John Sullivan,* p. 245.

21. Plumer, "John Sullivan," *New Hampshire State Papers,* XXI, 825–26.

22. Louise W. Murray, ed., *Notes from Craft Collection in Tioga Point Museum on the Sullivan Expedition* (Athens, Pa., 1929), pp. 18–19.

BIBLIOGRAPHY

BIBLIOGRAPHY

This study has emerged mainly from an examination of the primary sources which are listed in this bibliography. The secondary sources relied upon are given full bibliographical identification in the notes to the text. Any student of the American Revolution would indeed be ungracious if he did not single out Douglas S. Freeman's magnificent biographical study of *George Washington* (6 volumes, New York, 1948–54). The minute detail and accuracy of Freeman's craftsmanship merit high praise, and for those parts of the Revolution in which Sullivan participated, I found numerous valuable bibliographical leads. Another source of bibliographical leads for this period is John R. Alden, *The American Revolution, 1775–1783* (New York, 1954).

Fortunately the student of John Sullivan's career has access to his published correspondence in *The Letters and Papers of Major General John Sullivan*, edited by Otis G. Hammond (3 volumes, New Hampshire Historical Society Collections, XIII–XV, Concord, 1930–39). Hammond succeeded in bringing together most of the Sullivan materials extant. The bulk of the letters deals with the war years and serves as a major source for the war during the time Sullivan was in the army.

MANUSCRIPT LETTERS

Scattered unprinted Sullivan items, principally letters to him, were found in the following collections:

American Philosophical Society
   Nathanael Greene Papers
Connecticut Historical Society
   Jeremiah Wadsworth Papers

Houghton Library (Harvard University)
  Charles Stewart Papers
Library of Congress
  George Washington Papers
Massachusetts Historical Society
  Sullivan Papers
  Letters on Shays's Rebellion
National Archives
  Papers of the Continental Congress
New Hampshire Historical Society
  Documents Series of 1901
    A collection of miscellaneous documents deposited by the Sec-
    retary of State. Volumes 34–55 cover the years 1781–1795.
    Some of Sullivan's petitions to the legislature are in this col-
    lection.
Pennsylvania Historical Society
  Conarroe Collection
  Dreer Collection
  Etting Collection
  Gratz Collection
  William Irvine Papers
  Charles F. Jenkinson Collection
  Miscellaneous Manuscripts
  Anthony Wayne Papers
Rhode Island Archives (Capitol Building, Providence)
  Letters from the Governors
Rhode Island Historical Society
  Peck Manuscripts

OTHER MANUSCRIPT MATERIALS

Other manuscripts and unpublished materials used were from the
following repositories, with exact location given in the notes:

American Philosophical Society
  Benjamin Franklin Papers. Calendared. Occasional item of value.
  Nathanael Greene Papers. Calendared. Some items of value for
    the Indian Campaign.
Baker Library (Dartmouth College)
  Josiah Bartlett Papers. Two volumes, mainly letters to Bartlett.
  Jonathan Freeman Papers. Scattered holdings.

Miscellaneous Documents. Manuscripts are catalogued chronologically, and some scattered items were of interest.

Concord, New Hampshire (U. S. Postoffice Building)

Records of the United States District Court, Volume I.

Records of the United States Circuit Court, one volume.

Connecticut Historical Society

Nathanael Greene Papers. One envelope of letters, mainly connected with Jeremiah Wadsworth on supply problems in Rhode Island.

Jeremiah Wadsworth Papers. Extensive collection, of value for supply problems in Rhode Island.

Connecticut State Library

Jeremiah Wadsworth Papers. Photostatic copies of letters in the Wadsworth Athenaeum which are not readily accessible.

Library of Congress

Archives des Affaires Etrangères, correspondence politique, Etats-Unis.

William Plumer Papers. One volume of letters for 1781–1804.

George Washington Papers. Calendared. A number of letters to Washington were of value, particularly on the Indian Campaign and on the struggle in New Hampshire for ratification of the United States Constitution.

Dover, New Hampshire (Strafford County seat)

Cases in Inferior Court of Common Pleas, 1773–1795, 10 volumes.

Superior Court Records, 1774–1795, 2 volumes.

Deeds examined where Sullivan was either grantor or grantee. Deeds are indexed.

Probate Records, IV, V. Contain material on Sullivan's estate.

Exeter, New Hampshire (Rockingham County seat)

Superior Court Records, 1782–1788, 2 volumes.

Deeds examined where Sullivan was either grantor or grantee. Deeds are indexed.

Keene, New Hampshire (Cheshire County seat)

Superior Court Records, 1772–1791, 2 volumes.

Massachusetts Historical Society

Henry Knox Papers. Of practically no value for Sullivan. The interesting items have been published.

Sullivan's Brigade Book—Camp on Winter Hill, July, 1775 to March, 1776.

Meshech Weare Papers. Occasional item of value.

Nashua, New Hampshire (Hillsborough County seat)
Superior Court Records, 1772–1793, 2 volumes.
New Hampshire Historical Society
Josiah Bartlett Papers. One folder and a box of letters, some of which pertain to Josiah. The rest pertain to other members of the family.
Jeremy Belknap Papers. One box, mainly personal items.
Court Records. Superior Court Records, 1760–1773, 4 volumes. After 1771 (1773 for Strafford and Grafton Counties) all court records are found at the various county seats.
Inferior Court Records, 1770–1771, 2 volumes.
Court Proceedings. Catalogued and filed in folders.
Jonathan Freeman Papers. One box, mainly too late for the period.
John Langdon Papers. One volume of correspondence between John and Woodbury Langdon, and Nathaniel Peabody. Two boxes of letters and receipts, of little value for Sullivan.
Journal of the House of Representatives, 1781–1785, one volume. Parts of this were not published in New Hampshire State Papers.
Memoranda of Samuel Livermore, Esq., collected by Arthur Livermore, his grandson. This volume contains transcripts of Livermore's letters, some of which do not appear in Edmund C. Burnett, *Letters of Members of the Continental Congress* (8 vols., Washington, D. C., 1921–36).
Minutes of John Wentworth's reply to Questions proposed by Government. Concerned with period November 1773–November 1774.
Miscellaneous Documents. Boxes of materials on the post-war years, arranged chronologically. Documents Series of 1901, volumes 34–55, already mentioned, contain legislative petitions, committee reports, receipts, orders on the state treasurer, and occasional letters.
William Plumer. Five volumes of manuscript biographical sketches written by Plumer on his contemporaries. (Some have appeared in print in *New Hampshire State Papers*, XXI, XXII.) These sketches are indexed in New Hampshire Historical Society, *Proceedings*, I.
Tax Records. Tax Book, 1775–1781, 1 volume. Account Book, 1775–1791, 1 volume.
Town Records. Numerous volumes of original town records.

Jean Joseph Toscan Papers. Three boxes of material which offer some sidelights on New Hampshire. Toscan was French Consul in Portsmouth.

Meshech Weare Papers. Twelve volumes of value for New Hampshire history during the Revolution and post-war years. The Sullivan items are in print.

John Wentworth Papers. Transcripts of the Letterbooks in Nova Scotia, 1767–1778. They were of some value.

New Hampshire State Library

William Plumer Papers. An extensive collection containing a few items for the period, but mainly concerned with the years after Sullivan's death.

Town Records. Microfilm holdings of all New Hampshire town records extant.

New-York Historical Society

Horatio Gates Papers. Extensive collection. Some items of value.

John Lamb Papers. Extensive collection containing many items of value for study of the ratification of the United States Constitution in New Hampshire.

Joseph Reed Papers. Of little value for Sullivan.

New York Public Library

George Bancroft Transcripts. Letters between John Langdon, William Whipple, James Lovell, and Josiah Bartlett (1774–1789).

Emmet Collection. Calendared. A few items of value.

Edward Hand Papers. Offer some sidelights on the Indian Campaign.

Hudson Collection. Contains correspondence of Portsmouth, Boston, and New York merchants, and is interesting as sidelight material.

Philip Schuyler Papers. Of value for the retreat from Canada.

Thomas Sheafe Papers. Letterbook and miscellaneous accounts, 1784–1797, offering interesting sidelight material on mercantile conditions in New Hampshire.

Philip Van Cortlandt Autobiography.

Newport Historical Society

Henry Sherburne Military Book, 1778.

Pennsylvania Historical Society

John Langdon Papers. One volume, of considerable value for history of New Hampshire.

Anthony Wayne Papers. Extensive collection, and of some value.
John Weidman. Notes of Captain John Weidman during General
　Sullivan's Campaign from June 19, 1779 to December 9, 1780.
　Typed copy.
Rhode Island Historical Society
　Military Papers, Volume V.
　Sullivan's Orderly Book for 1778.
Sterling Memorial Library (Yale University)
　Knollenberg Collection. Photostatic copies of revolutionary cor-
　respondence.
Woodsville, New Hampshire (Grafton County seat)
　Superior Court Records, 1774–1795, 1 volume.

PRIMARY PRINTED SOURCES

Newspapers on the whole were disappointing for the military years.
Only occasionally were items located that did not appear elsewhere.
New Hampshire papers referred to Sullivan on a number of occasions and were valuable in piecing together the materials on the
paper money troubles in New Hampshire and on the struggle for
the ratification of the United States Constitution. The Connecticut
and Massachusetts papers were examined for information on the
ratification struggle. The Providence and Philadelphia papers were
given cursory examination for military items. The New Hampshire
papers were given full examination for Sullivan's activities and for
background material. For location of newspapers see Clarence L.
Brigham, *History and Bibliography of American Newspapers, 1690–
1820* (2 vols., Worcester, Mass., 1947).

American Herald (Boston)
Connecticut Courant (Hartford)
Essex Journal (Newburyport, Massachusetts)
Freeman's Oracle (Exeter, New Hampshire)
Independent Chronicle (Boston)
Massachusetts Centinel (Boston)
Massachusetts Spy (Worcester)
New-Hampshire Gazette (Portsmouth)
New-Hampshire Mercury (Portsmouth)
New-Hampshire Recorder (Keene)
New-Hampshire Spy (Portsmouth)
Pennsylvania Gazette (Philadelphia)

Pennsylvania Journal and the Weekly Advertiser (Philadelphia)
Providence Gazette
Salem (Mass.) Gazette
Salem (Mass.) Mercury

Listed below are the printed primary sources: public records, correspondence, diaries, journals, and memoirs. Numerous letters were scattered in the publications of the various states or state historical societies, or in various state historical magazines. These letters have not been listed in the bibliography, but complete reference is given in the notes.

Adams, John. Familiar Letters of John Adams and his wife, Abigail Adams, during the Revolution, ed. C. F. Adams. New York, 1876.
—— The Works of John Adams, Second President of the United States: with a Life of the Author, ed. C. F. Adams. 10 vols. Boston, 1856.
Adams, Samuel. The Writings of Samuel Adams, ed. Harry A. Cushing. 4 vols. New York, 1904–8.
Address of the Convention for Framing A Constitution of Government for the People of New-Hampshire, An. Portsmouth, 1783. (A copy is in the New Hampshire Historical Society.)
Almy, Mrs. "Mrs. Almy's Journal," Newport Historical Magazine, I, No. 1 (July, 1880), 17–36.
Barber, Francis. "Orderly Book of Lieutenant Colonel Francis Barber," in Louise W. Murray, ed., Notes from Craft Collection in Tioga Point Museum on the Sullivan Expedition of 1779 and its Centennial Celebration of 1879. Athens, Pa., 1929.
Baurmeister, Carl. Letters from Major Baurmeister to Colonel von Jungkenn Written during the Philadelphia Campaign, 1777–1778, ed. Bernhard A. Uhlendorf and Edna Vosper. Philadelphia, 1937.
Beebe, Lewis. "Journal of Dr. Lewis Beebe," The Pennsylvania Magazine of History and Biography, LIX, No. 4 (1935), 321–61.
Belknap, Jeremy. The Belknap Papers, Parts I, II, III. Massachusetts Historical Society Collections, 5th series, II, III; 6th series, IV. Boston, 1877, 1891.
—— "Journal of My Tour to the Camp, and Other Observations I Made There (1775)," Massachusetts Historical Society Proceedings, 1st series, IV (1858–60), 77–86.
Burnett, Edmund C., ed. Letters of Members of the Continental Congress. 8 vols. Washington, D. C., 1921–36.

Clark, Joseph. "Diary of Joseph Clark," New Jersey Historical Society *Proceedings*, VII, No. 3 (1854), 93–110.

Clinton, George. Public Papers of George Clinton, First Governor of New York. 10 vols. Albany, 1899–1914.

Cook, Frederick, ed. Journals of the Military Expedition of Major General John Sullivan against the Six Nations of Indians in 1779 with records of Centennial Celebrations. Auburn, N. Y., 1877. (An invaluable collection of soldiers' journals.)

Dayton, Elias. "Papers of General Elias Dayton," New Jersey Historical Society *Proceedings*, IX, No. 4 (1863–64), 175–94.

Deane, Silas. The Deane Papers. 5 vols. New-York Historical Society Collections, 1886–90. New York, 1887–91.

Dearborn, Henry. Revolutionary War Journals of Henry Dearborn, 1775–1783, ed. Lloyd A. Brown and Howard H. Peckham. Chicago, 1939.

"Diary of the Revolution, A," *The Historical Magazine and Notes and Queries Concerning the Antiquities, History and Biography of America*, IV (1860), 69–72, 105–7, 134–37.

Elliot, Jonathan, ed. The Debates in the Several State Conventions on the Adoption of the Federal Constitution. . . . 5 vols. Philadelphia, 1907.

Elmer, Ebenezer. "Journal of Ebenezer Elmer," *The Pennsylvania Magazine of History and Biography*, XXXV, No. 1 (1911), 103–7.

Evelyn, W. Glanville. Memoir and Letters of Captain W. Glanville Evelyn, of the 4th Regiment . . . 1774–1776, ed. G. D. Scull. Oxford, 1879.

Farnsworth, Amos. "Amos Farnsworth's Diary," Massachusetts Historical Society *Proceedings*, 2d series, XII (1897–99), 78–102.

Fitzpatrick, John C., *see* Washington, George.

Flick, Alexander C., ed. "New Sources on the Sullivan-Clinton Campaign in 1779," *Quarterly Journal of New York Historical Association*, X, Nos. 3 and 4 (July and October, 1929). (Invaluable collection of materials.)

—— The Sullivan-Clinton Campaign in 1779 . . . . Albany, 1929. (A collection of primary sources on the campaign.)

Force, Peter, comp. American Archives. 9 vols. Washington, D. C., 1837–53.

Ford, Worthington C., *et al.*, eds. Journals of the Continental Congress. 34 vols. Washington, D. C., 1904–36.

Gage, Thomas. The Correspondence of General Thomas Gage with the Secretaries of State, and with the War Office and the Treasury, 1763–1775, ed. Clarence E. Carter. 2 vols. New Haven, 1931–33.

Gerard, Conrad Alexandre. Despatches and Instructions of Conrad Alexandre Gerard, 1778–1780; Correspondence of the First French Minister to the United States with the Comte de Vergennes . . . ed. John J. Meng. Baltimore, 1939.

Gibbs, Major. "Major Gibbs Diary," *Pennsylvania Archives*, VI (1853), 734–36.

Gordon, William. "Letters of the Reverend William Gordon, Historian of the American Revolution, 1770–1790," Massachusetts Historical Society *Proceedings*, LXIII (1929–30), 303–613.

Gore, Obadiah. The Revolutionary Diary of Lieut. Obadiah Gore, Jr., ed. Robert W. G. Vail. New York, 1929.

Hamilton, Alexander. The Works of Alexander Hamilton; Comprising His Correspondence, and His Political and Official Writings, ed. John C. Hamilton. 7 vols. New York, 1850–51.

—— The Works of Alexander Hamilton, ed. Henry C. Lodge. 9 vols. New York, 1885–86.

Hammond, Otis G., *see* Sullivan, John. Letters and Papers.

Heath, William. The Heath Papers, Parts II, III. Massachusetts Historical Society *Collections*, 7th series, IV, V. Boston, 1904–5.

—— Memoirs of Major-General William Heath by Himself, ed. William Abbatt. New York, 1901.

Historical Manuscript Commission. Report on American Manuscripts in the Royal Institution of Great Britain. 4 vols. London, 1904–09. (Contains a letter from Sullivan to Lord Howe, September 19, 1776.)

Huntington, Ebenezer. Letters Written by Ebenezer Huntington during the American Revolution. New York, 1915.

Huntington, Joshua and Jedediah. Huntington Papers: Correspondence of the Brothers Joshua and Jedediah Huntington during the Period of the American Revolution. Connecticut Historical Society Collections, XX. Hartford, 1923.

Jay, John. The Correspondence and Public Papers of John Jay, ed. Henry P. Johnston. 4 vols. New York, 1890–93.

Jefferson, Thomas. The Papers of Thomas Jefferson, ed. Julian P. Boyd. Vols. I–XV. Princeton, 1950 to date.

Jordan, John W., ed. "Bethlehem (Pennsylvania) during the Revolution. Extracts from the Diaries in the Moravian Archives at Bethlehem . . . ," *The Pennsylvania Magazine of History and Biography*, XII, No. 4 (1888), 385–406.

Journals of the Continental Congress, *see* Ford.

Kemble, Stephen. The Kemble Papers. 2 vols. New-York Historical Society Collections, 1883–84. New York, 1884–85.

Kirkwood, Robert. The Journal and Order Book of Captain Robert Kirkwood, of the Delaware Regiment of the Continental Line. Historical Society of Delaware Papers, No. LVI. Wilmington, 1910.

Lacey, John. "Memoirs of Brigadier General John Lacey, of Pennsylvania," *The Pennsylvania Magazine of History and Biography*, XXV, Nos. 1–4 (1901), 1–13, 191–207, 341–54, 498–515.

Lafayette, Marquis de. Memoirs, Correspondence and Manuscripts of General Lafayette. Only 1 vol. published. New York, 1837.

Laurens, John. The Army Correspondence of Colonel John Laurens in the Years 1777–8 . . . with a Memoir by Wm. Gilmore Simms. New York, 1867.

Lee, Andrew. "Extract from the Diary of Captain Andrew Lee," *The Pennsylvania Magazine of History and Biography*, III, No. 2 (1879), 169–73.

Lee, Charles. The Lee Papers. 4 vols. New-York Historical Society Collections, 1871–74. New York, 1872–75.

Mackenzie, Frederick. Diary of Frederick Mackenzie, Giving a Daily Narrative of his Military Service as an Officer of the Regiment of Royal Welch Fusiliers during the Years 1775–1781 in Massachusetts, Rhode Island, and New York. 2 vols. Cambridge, Mass., 1930. (An important British account.)

McMichael, James. "Diary of Lieutenant James McMichael of the Pennsylvania Line, 1776–1778," *The Pennsylvania Magazine of History and Biography*, XVI, No. 2 (1892), 129–59.

Madison, James. The Writings of James Madison, Comprising His Public Papers and His Private Correspondence, ed. Gaillard Hunt. 9 vols. New York, 1900–10.

Montresor, John. "Journals of Captain John Montresor," in New-York Historical Society Collections, 1881. New York, 1882. Pp. 115–520.

Moore, Frank, ed. Diary of the American Revolution from Newspapers and Original Documents. 2 vols. New York, 1860.

Morris, Lewis. "Letters to General Lewis Morris," New-York Historical Society Collections, 1875. New York, 1876. Pp. 433–512.

Morton, Robert. "The Diary of Robert Morton," *The Pennsylvania Magazine of History and Biography*, I, No. 1 (1877), 1–39.

New Hampshire. Laws. Laws of New Hampshire, A. S. Batchellor, H. Metcalf, and E. Bean, eds. 8 vols. Bristol, N. H., 1904–20.

—— Legislature. Provincial and State Papers. 40 vols. Concord and Manchester, N. H., 1867–1943. (An invaluable collection of primary materials.)

New Hampshire State Papers, *see* New Hampshire. Legislature, Provincial and State Papers.

Percy, Hugh. Letters of Hugh Earl Percy from Boston and New York, 1774–1776, ed. Charles K. Bolton. Boston, 1902.

Pettengill, Ray W., tr. Letters from America, 1776–1779; Being the Letters of Brunswick, Hessian, and Waldeck Officers with the British Armies during the Revolution. Boston, 1914.

Plumer, William. "Letters of William Plumer, 1786–1787," Colonial Society of Massachusetts Publications, XI, 383–403. Boston, 1910.

Reed, Joseph. "General Joseph Reed's Narrative of the Movements of the American Army in the Neighborhood of Trenton in the Winter of 1776–1777," *The Pennsylvania Magazine of History and Biography*, VIII, No. 4 (1884), 391–402.

Rhode Island. "Revolutionary Correspondence from 1775 to 1782," Rhode Island Historical Society Collections, VI (1867), 107–304.

Richards, Samuel. Diary of Samuel Richards, Captain of Connecticut Line . . . 1775–1781. Philadelphia, 1909.

Robertson, Archibald. Archibald Robertson, Lieutenant-General Royal Engineers, His Diaries and Sketches in America, 1762–1780, ed. Harry M. Lydenberg. New York, 1930.

Rodney, Caesar. Letters to and from Caesar Rodney, 1756–1784, ed. George H. Ryden. Philadelphia, 1933.

Rodney, Thomas. Diary of Captain Thomas Rodney, 1776–1777. Historical Society of Delaware Papers, Vol. VIII. Wilmington, 1888.

Rush, Benjamin. Letters of Benjamin Rush, ed. Lyman H. Butterfield. 2 vols. Princeton, 1951.

—— "Historical Notes of Dr. Benjamin Rush, 1777," *The Pennsylvania Magazine of History and Biography*, XXVII, No. 2 (1903), 129–50.

Serle, Ambrose. The American Journal of Ambrose Serle, Secretary to Lord Howe, 1776–1779, ed. Edward H. Tatum, Jr. San Marino, Calif., 1940.

Slade, William, Jr., comp. Vermont State Papers, Being a Collection of Records and Documents Connected with the Assumption and Establishment of Government by the People of Vermont. Middlebury, Vt., 1823.

Sparks, Jared, ed. Correspondence of the American Revolution: Being Letters of Eminent Men to George Washington. 4 vols. Boston, 1853.

—— see also Washington, George.

Stevens, Benjamin F., comp. Facsimiles of Manuscripts in European Archives Relating to America, 1773–1783. 26 vols. London, 1889–95.

Sullivan, John. The Letters and Papers of Major General John Sullivan, ed. Otis G. Hammond. 3 vols. New Hampshire Historical Society Collections, XIII–XV. Concord, 1930–39. (The major source for John Sullivan.)

Sullivan, Thomas. "Extracts from the Journal of Sergeant Thomas Sullivan of H.M. 49th Regt. of Foot," The Pennsylvania Magazine of History and Biography, XXXII, No. 1 (1908), 54–57.

Tallmadge, Benjamin. Memoir of Colonel Benjamin Tallmadge, ed. Henry P. Johnston. New York, 1904.

Townsend, Joseph. "Some Account of the British Army under . . . General Howe, and of the Battle of Brandywine," Historical Society of Pennsylvania Proceedings, I, No. 7 (September, 1846).

Trumbull, John T. Autobiography, Reminiscences and Letters of John Trumbull, from 1756 to 1841. New York, 1841.

Trumbull, Jonathan. The Trumbull Papers, Part IV, Massachusetts Historical Society Collections, 7th series, III. Boston, 1902.

Waldo, Albigence. "Valley Forge, 1777–1778: Diary of Surgeon Albigence Waldo," The Pennsylvania Magazine of History and Biography, XXI, No. 3 (1897), 299–323.

Warren, James. Warren-Adams Letters, Being Chiefly a Correspondence among John Adams, Samuel Adams, and James Warren. 2 vols. Massachusetts Historical Society Collections, LXXIII. Boston, 1925.

Washington, George. The Writings of George Washington from the Original Manuscript Sources, 1745–1799, ed. John C. Fitzpatrick. 39 vols. Washington, D. C., 1931–44.

—— The Writings of George Washington; Being His Correspond-
ence, Addresses, Messages, and Other Papers, Official and Private,
Selected and Published from the Original Manuscripts, ed. Jared
Sparks. 12 vols. Boston, 1834–38.

Webb, Samuel B. Correspondence and Journals of Samuel Blachley
Webb, ed. Worthington C. Ford. 3 vols. 1893–94.

Wharton, Francis, ed. The Revolutionary Diplomatic Correspondence of the United States. 6 vols. Washington, D. C., 1889.

Wilkinson, James. Memoirs of My Own Times. 3 vols. Philadelphia,
1816. (Although a dubious source, the book provided some fac-
tual details which appear reliable.)

Willard, Margaret W., ed. Letters on the American Revolution,
1774–1776. Boston, 1925.

Wright, Albert H., comp. The Sullivan Expedition of 1779; Contemporary Newspaper Comment and Letters. Studies in History
Nos. 5, 6, 7, and 8. Ithaca, N. Y., 1943.

Young, William. "Journal of Sergeant William Young," *The Pennsylvania Magazine of History and Biography*, VIII, No. 3 (1884),
255–78.

INDEX